D0345007

THE AMERICAN ALCOHOLIC

THE
AMERICAN
ALCOHOLIC

The Nature-Nurture Controversy in
Alcoholic Research and Therapy

Third Printing

By

WILLIAM MADSEN

Professor of Anthropology
University of California
Santa Barbara, California

CHARLES C THOMAS · PUBLISHER
Springfield · Illinois · U.S.A.

Published and Distributed Throughout the World by
CHARLES C THOMAS • PUBLISHER
BANNERSTONE HOUSE
301-327 East Lawrence Avenue, Springfield, Illinois, U.S.A.

© *1974, by* CHARLES C THOMAS • PUBLISHER
ISBN 0-398-02926-1
Library of Congress Catalog Card Number: 73-8975

First Printing, 1974
Second Printing, 1977
Third Printing, 1980

With THOMAS BOOKS *careful attention is given to all details of
manufacturing and design. It is the Publisher's desire to present books
that are satisfactory as to their physical qualities and artistic possibilities
and appropriate for their particular use.* THOMAS BOOKS *will be
true to those laws of quality that assure a good name and good will.*

Printed in the United States of America

C-1

Library of Congress Cataloging in Publication Data

Madsen, William.
    The American alcoholic.

    Includes bibliographical references.
    1. Alcoholism. 2. Alcoholism—Treatment.
I. Title.   [DNLM: 1. Alcoholism. WM274 M183a
1973]
HV5035.M34   362.2'92   73-8975
ISBN 0-398-02926-1

Respectfully dedicated to the
memory of
E. M. Jellinek and Bill Wilson
who made this study possible.

INTRODUCTION

T HE NEWSSTANDS PROVIDE the lay reader with a revealing insight into the fantasyland of alcoholic research and therapy. *Time* magazine reports on the scientific findings of the Alcoholism Research Unit in Baltimore which stated that alcoholics can be trained to drink socially (1). Thus, alcoholism appears as a bad habit subject to correction through education. At the same time, however, the *San Francisco Chronicle* reports that Dr. Stanley Gilow of the Mount Sinai School of Medicine in New York has concluded that alcoholics have genetically determined constitutions which will forever make social drinking impossible for them (2). This may confuse the layman, but he can comfort himself in the fact that there is equal confusion within the ranks of the *alcohologists*. A large part of this confusion is the product of the complicated and mysterious nature of the *disease* of alcoholism. Highly qualified researchers, such as those mentioned above, have for years been unable to determine whether alcoholism is a physical or mental problem. The outstanding specialists in the disease, however, such as Ruth Fox (3), E. M. Jellinek (4) and Marty Mann (5) have all realized that alcoholism embraces cultural, psychological and physical factors. This reasoned view is today under attack by a flood of monocausal theories. In part, this deluge of *expert* opinions is the product of unqualified and inexperienced individuals leaping into the field of alcoholism in pursuit of the massive funding that is suddenly available. Mono-causal explanations are also a function of the frantic search for an ultimate answer that will bring logic and order into the field of alcoholism, and fame and fortune to its author. A number of alcohologists, therefore, show a shortcoming that Sherlock Holmes attributed to detectives when he said, "The temptation to form premature theories upon insufficient data is the bane of our profession" (6: p. 23).

I am keenly aware of the temptation to force one's data into

an obliging theory in the hope that it will thus become meaningful, relevant and useful. However, I also realize that no existing
theory can accommodate the collected data on alcoholism. I have
long looked in vain for such a theory to explain data on the
affliction that I have collected in several settings.

I have observed alcoholics in varied environments and conditions ranging from those in mental hospitals in which I have
served as a consultant to individuals living in various communities
that I have studied. My first professional exposure to drinking
and *problem drinking* was a by-product of a study of religious
acculturation in Mexico during the years 1952 and 1953 made
possible by a Wenner-Gren Fellowship. Drinking patterns were
highly significant to the Indian population with which I worked
(7, 8). I also had the opportunity to witness and participate
in numerous drinking sessions with Mestizos and thereby note
the profound differences between Indian and Mestizo drinking
patterns (9). From 1957 through 1962, funded by the Hogg
Foundation for Mental Health, I directed a research project on
Mexican-American acculturation and mental health in south
Texas. This is another area in which drinking patterns are a
significant part of the total culture (10, 11, 12) and problem
drinking was clearly recognized (13).

In both of these areas I had accepted the psychological model
which interprets alcoholism as a purely psychological response
to stress. During the years 1962 and 1963 my perception was
broadened while I was a Fellow at the Center for Advanced
Study in the Behavioral Sciences. In part this was the product
of enough leisure to read in the literature on alcoholism. More
specifically, it resulted from a friendship formed with Dr. E. M.
Jellinek following an invitation to lead a seminar at the Institute
for the Study of Human Problems on the Stanford University
campus. The following year I joined that Institute myself as a
Research Associate and directed my own project investigating
the sociocultural aspects of alcoholism and alcoholic rehabilitation. My focus was on conducting an ethnographic investigation
of Alcoholics Anonymous (14).

This study was possible only because of the help given me
by many people. Dr. Nevitt Sanford, director of the Institute,

made every facility available to me including an off-campus building and a full-time secretary.[1] Dr. Jellinek shared his vast knowledge of alcoholism with me and introduced me to Mr. Bill Wilson, the late co-founder of Alcoholics Anonymous. Bill Wilson, in turn, invited me to visit him and his lovely wife at their home in New York. He liked my project and urged its support, thus assuring me the most marvelous cooperation conceivable from every A.A. group that I contacted in California. Above all, I am indebted to the innumerable members of A.A. who gave freely of their time and energy. Several, after brief training from me, spent hours collecting data from others. A few of these still note down facts and ideas that they think would interest me and so I still receive large amounts of information from them. Some have moved out of the state and write me of the variations in the basic A.A. culture in other parts of the U.S. and abroad. My own activities during the project utilized most of the standard anthropological research procedures. Primarily, I relied upon *participant observation.* I attended A.A. meetings and ran a continuing seminar of members to discuss points which seemed vague and confusing to me and to discern the range of inter-pretation found in utilizing the A.A. program. Further, extensive use was made of questionnaires, biographies and taped inter-views. I also ate and played with A.A.'s, visited their homes and families, attended a few A.A. conventions with them and accompanied them on *12th Step calls.* Playing the Good Samaritan, in the hope of keeping them from serious harm, I accompanied those who slipped back into alcoholic drinking. On several occasions, I attended funerals of those who never made it back to the safety of A.A. I also came to appreciate the total nature of their affliction and to realize that they were not playing *games* (15), but were engaged in a life-or-death struggle in a society that is largely indifferent or openly hostile.

These exposures to alcoholics, I think, have made me more sensitive and perceptive of their feelings, frustrations and desires.

---

[1] The center also allowed me the assistance of Dr. Frank Schmidt (Trinity University, San Antonio, Texas) for his knowledge of psychology and Dr. William Carter (University of Texas) for aid in devising statistical procedures during the first summer of my research.

I have also become aware of the total inadequacy of many of the simplistic theories which bloom in the field of alcoholism. I can no longer hold that the alcoholic is simply a naughty child who can be straightened out by a spanking in the form of incarceration in a jail or punishment by any of the multitude of conditioning therapies (electric and insulin shock, emetics, etc.). Nor can I visualize the alcoholic as simply fulfilling a destructive constitutional destiny which can be corrected with vitamins and improved nutrition. The psychiatric interpretation of an inadequate psyche is probably largely true, but psychiatry has failed to *cure* the alcoholic so it cannot be the whole answer.

It is odd in a scientific age, when men walk on the moon and explode atoms, that the most successful therapy for alcoholism is a system of folk medicine known as Alcoholics Anonymous. As Milton Maxwell says, "it is probable that more contemporary alcoholics have found sobriety through the fellowship of Alcoholics Anonymous than through all other agencies combined" (16: p. 211).

Anthropologists have always taken a perverse delight when primitive or folk approaches excel over civilization, progress and science. They also realize in such cases that scientific failure is usually produced by the overspecialization of the various sciences which prevents each from recognizing all the factors of body, mind and culture involved in any human problem. A.A. grew up within the problem and its creators were thereby more sensitive to its many facets than were the scientific specialists looking at it from the outside. Further, the A.A.'s had the motivation of survival which is always stronger than that of scientific curiosity. Somehow, in its creation, A.A. did construct a pragmatic and workable model of sobriety that works for hundreds of thousands of alcoholics. Science would do well to look at that model calmly and objectively and try to learn from it in the same way that pharmacology has leaped ahead by examining the value of primitive medicines. Many of our alcohologists, however, have emotional blocks that prevent them from learning from anyone outside the union of professionalism. Some years ago I suggested to an eminent scholar and a contemporary giant in alcoholic studies that perhaps psychiatric approaches to alcoholism could be improved by studying the techniques of A.A. and borrowing from them. His reply rather startled me. He said, "There is nothing we could learn from them. I admit they're successful, but they're not scientific."

A.A.'s are not perhaps "scientific," but I believe their success rests upon a very sound definition of alcoholism: that it is a physical, psychological and cultural disability and must be simultaneously approached on each of these levels. It is my belief that some day a biological keystone to the structure of alcoholism will be found, but until that time the alcoholic must be approached as a person with a psychophysical affliction. Today, however, specialists in mind and body have grown so apart that a dialogue putting man together again is going to be most difficult. Eysenck recognizes this and regrets it when he remarks on ". . . the futile battle between 'environmentalists' and 'hereditarians' with its undesirable political overtones . . ." (17: p. 340).

The question then is: who is qualified to reassemble man and describe him as a totality? At one time the answer would have been the anthropologist. Alfred Kroeber in both the 1923 (18) and 1948 (19) editions of his *Anthropology* emphasized that the goal of that discipline was to see man as a whole and total being. In the later edition of that book he states, "Could it be that the specific subject of anthropology is the interrelation of what is biological in man and what is social and historical in him? The answer is yes. Or, more broadly, anthropology does at least concern itself with both organic and social factors in man, whereas nearly all other sciences and studies deal with one or the other " (19: p. 2). Since Kroeber, however, anthropologists have come increasingly under the influence of the behaviorists from whom they have learned much about the mind while losing their perspective of man as a whole. As Walter Goldschmidt says, "The excess of current anthropological doctrine led us to the assumption that man is a perfectly plastic thing and that cultures can take any form. This, to say the least, is a questionable position, but it is a position that is all too rarely questioned" (20: Preface, viii).

Anthropologists like Leslie White (21, 22) claim, as Freedman notes, ". . . that biology may be ignored since culture evolves by its own set of rules" (23: p. 152) . At the level of abstraction with which White is dealing, he is perfectly justified. One can deal with cultural themes as one can with the history of musical styles, without reference to their biological creators. However, for the culturologists and psychological behaviorists to assume that mind and behavior are totally a product of the psycho-cultural environment implies that the biology of all humans is constant and interchangeable. It is comfortable for any specialist to assume that all factors in a field that he does not comprehend are constant although common sense and science indicate the variability and relativity of all things. Very few theories or generalizations apply to the totality of any aspect of existence. The Golden Rule, for example, was not intended for masochists.

It is time that we examine our simplistic either-or, mind-body generalizations and produce a more realistic view of human behavior as the product of the total being. This will not be easy to do, for we have created a formula for problem resolution in our culture which quickly structures and opposes a thesis and an antithesis. Thus, our sports are based on two persons or teams each fighting for an absolute victory. We find a tie totally frustrating. The same pattern applies to our political parties and our wars. The roots of this structure go deeply into our historical past. It was probably first clearly enunciated in Zoroastrianism with the opposition of Mazda (God) and Ahriman (Satan). It is clearly stated that these two gentlemen will never compromise and the schedule calls for the total victory of one and the total defeat of the other. Likewise, today we see the thesis of biological determinism in mortal combat with its antithesis, psychocultural determinism, and each is resolved to destroy the other. This ideological battle is hindering objective research and is in large part probably responsible for the confusion and inadequacy in the field of psychotherapy. The false mind-body dichotomy is an old one and Plato recognized its shortcoming two thousand years ago. Dixon cites him on the subject, "This is the greatest error in the treatment of illness, that there are physicians for the body and physicians for the soul, and yet the two are indivisible" (24: p. 43). Fortunately, a holistic approach involving both mind and body is beginning to emerge from the ideological battlefield. Delgado, I think, points in the right direction when he writes, "Let us accept that the structure of mental qualities and their behavioral manifestations depend on genetic, neurophysiological and cultural factors which can be investigated, known and modified by intelligent planning" (25: p. 252). A number of writers from various disciplines are indeed today beginning to explore and describe the relationship between mental and physical states. As but a sample of these one may cite the anthropologist Eliot Chapple (26), the ethologist Irenaus Eibl-Eibesfeldt (27) and the sociologists Alan Mazur and Leon S. Robertson (28).

Like humanity as a whole, the alcoholic is going to have to be seen in his[2] totality if he is to be understood. At the moment, having been dismantled by the specialists, he lies in parts like Humpty Dumpty on the laboratory floor while each scientist points at a different part of his being shouting, "the trouble lies here." Putting the alcoholic together again will be a difficult task as no one today is fully competent in the multiple fields ranging from cultural analysis through biochemistry that will be involved in any valid description of the alcoholic. As Mazur and Robertson state,

> Even a cursory review of drugs and behavior illustrates the necessity for viewing behavior as the result of interactions of biological, social and chemical phenomena. At the same time, one is frustrated by the complexity of these interactions and the difficulty of designing research which will reveal the particular combinations which result in particular behaviors (28: p. 155).

However, if a dialogue can be begun between the biological determinists and the psychocultural determinists in the field of alcoholism, we may find that our accumulated knowledge has brought us near to the final answer. Such a dialogue should be guided and moderated by the reasonability of those already aware of the principles of multicausality.

I am writing this manuscript in the hope that it may contribute in some small way to an interchange of opinions which

---

[2] In respect to Women's Lib, will all female readers please replace he with she. Alcoholism lacks any chauvinistic sexual overtones and recruits from both sexes.

will one day produce the synthesis necessary to an understanding of alcoholism. I realize that I lack the competence to cover the full range of subjects that will be reviewed in the following pages. For example, I am probably no better equipped to review the literature on the biochemistry of emotions than a plumber is to perform brain surgery. In this area I have had to rely mostly on secondary sources. However, someone must begin the discussions and my inadequacies may stimulate a dialogue between others better qualified to investigate such questions in relation to alcoholism.

WILLIAM MADSEN

Santa Barbara, California

ACKNOWLEDGMENTS

I wish to thank those on my immediate scene who have contributed so greatly to the final writing of this manuscript. I hasten to add that they are in no way responsible for its failings. First and foremost, it would never have been completed had it not been for the abilities and patience of Ellen Cunningham, my secretary, research assistant and morale booster when the going was slow. Numerous scholars have shared their material and their ideas with me. In this regard, I especially wish to thank Dr. Mark B. Sobell, Dr. Irving Geller, Dr. Robert D. Myers, Dr. Jack H. Mendelson and Dr. Denes de Torok. My discussions of the physiological aspects of alcoholism would have been even more inadequate were it not for the conversations I have had with Lowell Sparks, M.D., of the Sansum Clinic in Santa Barbara, Gloria Pierce, M.D., of the University of California at Santa Barbara, and V. W. Westermeyer, M.D., of Santa Barbara. Further, I am most indebted for many of my insights into alcoholism to Mrs. Mildred Pinheiro who until her recent retirement was the Executive Director of the Santa Barbara Council on Alcoholism.

I also wish to thank those who were kind enough to read this book in manuscript form: Mrs. Marty Mann (National Council on Alcoholism), Dr. Mark Keller (Center of Alcohol Studies, Rutgers University), Mrs. Leona Kent (Alcoholic Rehabilitation Clinic of San Joaquin County, California), Dr. Margaret Clark (Langley Porter Clinic, San Francisco), Dr. Mattison Mines (Dept. of Anthropology, University of California at Santa Barbara), Mrs. Mildred Pinhiero and Mr. John Cunningham. Several members of A.A. also were kind enough to read the volume and give me their reactions. Of these, I am most grateful to Bill V. whose keen perception and objectivity were especially appreciated. None of the readers were in total agreement with all of my interpretations and none, therefore, should be seen as necessarily endorsing any of them.

CONTENTS

Part I

THESIS AND ANTITHESIS: BODY AND MIND

Chapter

Part II

AN ATTEMPT AT SYNTHESIS

THE AMERICAN ALCOHOLIC

PART I

THESIS AND ANTITHESIS: BODY AND MIND

CHAPTER I:

THE NATURE-NURTURE CONFLICT

T HERE IS A WEALTH of theory on the nature of alcoholism. Many of these claim to be the final "scientific" answer. Unfortunately, these answers contradict one another. There is less agreement today on the nature of alcoholism than there was in the nineteenth century when scientists knew less but perhaps understood more. Today's amassing of new theories is hardly a scientific triumph, for as Francis Hsu states, "The fundamental axiom of science is to explain more and more facts by fewer and fewer theories" (29: p. 216). In contemporary alcoholic research theories seem to grow in tandem with new facts. Further, too many of the alcohologists are also suffering from an omniscience and dogmatism that is beginning to plague the behavioral sciences as a whole (30, 31). Many alcohologists have lost their perspective on the total problem because of rigorous specialization in a single discipline. Traditionally, a common scientific premise has been that "the whole is more than the sum of its parts." In alcoholic theory, too many believe that the whole is solely explainable in terms of one part. The results of such myopia can be a retreat rather than an advance toward the goal of understanding and treating the disease. Myers and Veale describe the only reasonable approach when they say, "What seems to be required for the ultimate understanding of an aberrant drinking pattern is a synthesis of information involving behavioral, physiological and biochemical research" (32: p. 132). It is time to put the alcoholic together again and examine his total being. This can only happen when the wise specialists take off their disciplinary blinders and realize that elephants and alcoholics are both explainable only in terms of the interrelationship of all their component parts.

The chaos and confusion in alcoholic research is only a sideshow in the greater arena of the nature-nurture conflict which has again flared up in a magnificent blaze. Through the eighteenth century heredity was the most accepted explanation of individual differences. However, the philosophy of the opposite side of the coin had been crystallized by John Locke before the end of the preceding century with his definition of man as a "tabula rasa"—a "blank slate" whose nature is totally determined by the environment. This *environmentalism* was compatible with the growing liberal philosophies which were eventually to castrate the power of the nobility as well as negate the belief in genetic determinism. Building on the basic assumptions of Locke, John B. Watson (33) sired *behaviorism*, the psychological branch of environmental determinism. Today many behaviorists tend to define man as a mindless automaton totally controlled by his environment. Other students of human behavior, following the mode set by Freud, concentrate entirely on the inner world of the mind that is supposedly shaped primarily by the external environment. However, both are agreed that biological correlates of human behavior are irrelevant. During and after World War II it became a patriotic duty to accept psychocultural determinism in order to refute Hitler who had endorsed racism and genetic determinism. In this environment, the behaviorists and environmentalists, led by B. F. Skinner (34, 35), began their climb up the peak of ultimate answers and planted their flag.

However, although regarded as undemocratic and perhaps even Satanic, all those in the field of biology and behavior did not confess their sins and convert to goodness and behaviorism. A few kept on working and slowly evidence supporting a non-behaviorist viewpoint began to appear from such fields as endocrinology, behavioral genetics and ethology. Konrad Lorenz (36, 37) and his colleagues demonstrated clearly that our contemporary subhuman relatives have instinctive behavior and biological drives, and unless the concept of evolution is purely a myth, we probably have some biological determinants in our own makeup. The psychocultural determinists scoffed and rejected the evidence. They accept some degree of biological determinism in other animals but perceive man as a thing apart, almost as a special creation. These specialists see man as having a mind and behavior so miraculously freed from its biological nature as to resemble a Christian soul released by death from all biological involvement.

The philosophical, ideological and political implications of the nature-nurture controversy today are so great that each extreme is using its opposite as a target for violent attack. Chapple speaks of the "unfortunate" atmosphere hindering biological research on behavior because of the "implied stigma of 'inherited' differences which many people would not accept" (26: Preface, ix). George Watson also mentions the disciplinary loyalty of psychotherapists ". . . holding back investigation and therapy in the field of the biochemistry of mental illness." He adds, "Of course, psychiatrists have a vested interest, emotional and financial, in their particular field of practice, as do all physicians" (38: Forward, xi). The reverse prejudice is also obviously true. Jellinek (4: p. 105) cites Steck as pointing out that, ". . . proponents of the biological methods look down upon the psychological methods and this is dangerous . . ." Unfortunately, when there is an exchange of ideas in any area of the nature-nurture debate, the arguments are frequently prejudiced and emotional rather than rational. Daniels and Houghton mention this in relation to the currently heated debate on I.Q., "It would, however, be an exaggeration to grace this interchange with the label of 'scientific debate' because, with both groups, the evidence was selected to prove a stance to which for quite other reasons, each group was already committed" (39: p. 71).

The lack of scientific confirmation of one or the other stance in the nature-nurture controversy can cause anxiety in the individual making a stand. This anxiety seems to be of lesser degree among the adherents of the nature school, for they have behind them a long history of successes in biology and medicine. The nurture schools, however, lack *hard* evidence for much of their philosophy and more strongly feel the threat of their opposites. Having made a stand, many of the environmentalists and behaviorists feel they cannot afford to yield an inch. Any threat to their ideology is likely to cause them to reaffirm their position.

It is all too human for those who have adopted such a posture to reassure themselves by creating a dogma with an accommodating folklore. I encountered an example of such behavior a few years ago that I found fairly amusing as well as educational. I had consulted an eminent analyst for help in interpreting an obscure piece of ethnological and psychoanalytical literature out of France. The analyst was charming and most helpful and I am deeply indebted to him for interpreting the article for me. I also found him to be one of those ardent disciples of Freud with the same ability to reinterpret the Master as Christians do the words of Christ. I had commented on the fact that Freud had explicitly stated that ultimately all mental illness would prove to have a physical etiology. His reply was, "I know Freud said it, but of course we know that he didn't mean it."

The verbal ballet to protect dogma was also performed before me on a second occasion. In a professional seminar a psychiatrist had repeated his conclusion that alcoholism is always the product of repressed homosexuality, and that alcoholic intoxication in these addicts is frequently accompanied by overt homosexual behavior. I commented that in the large alcoholic sample with which I was working, this did not seem to be true. I had noted both latent and manifest homosexuality but in no greater proportion than that of the general population. "Aha!" said the psychiatrist, "That proves my point. An alcoholic will always hide his inherent homosexuality behind a normal facade. Therefore, a normal sex life in the alcoholic is a confirmation of his latent homosexuality."

Such analogies to medieval theology have been noted by others. Marvin Opler is referring to such disciplinary astigmatism when he states that, "Approaches to problems like alcoholism or the schizophrenias have consequently been marked by numerous confusions, by an air of the mystical" (40: p. 128). George Watson speaks of "The creation of this fairyland aura around the psyche . . ." (38: p. 14). Biological determinists are capable of an equivalent mystical dogmatism and some make claims that boggle credulity. Examples are seen in some of the current nutritionist schools which try to explain everything from mental illness to global warfare by the single factor of malnutrition.

Nowhere is this subjectivism in the nature-nurture conflict

more obvious than in the attempts to explain and treat mental illness. Chein defines the two approaches, each going away from the other, when he speaks of ". . . the movement to physiologize all of psychology and the movement to build a stimulus-response psychology around the empty organism" (41: p. 124). In the United States, however, the behaviorists have dominated the field. Following the philosophies of Watson and Skinner, their basic assumption is that "irrational" and "inappropriate" behavior is purely the result of bad learning and therefore can be unlearned. However, within the context of that philosophy, the conflicts are astounding. The psychiatrists differ so among themselves that Asimov concludes that ". . . there are almost as many schools of psychiatry as there are psychiatrists" (42: p. 320). This inability to achieve a unified theory led George Watson to state, "What these basic conflicts in belief and practice mean is that there is simply no foundation of scientific fact to support all of these contradictory schools of psychotherapeutic thought" (38: pp. 5-6). The in-fighting between the various behaviorist schools again produces an emotionalism that does not contribute to a feeling of scientific objectivism. Heim notes this in the conflict between the Eysenckian approach and that of psychoanalysis. She concluded that ". . . these two extreme persuasions are actually held with an uncompromising emotional intensity more suited to religious than to scientific doctrine" (43: p. 348).

The lack of a sound scientific base is most clearly seen in psychotherapy's failure in treating mental patients. As Asimov notes, ". . . it has produced no spectacular cures and has not notably reduced the incidence of mental disease" (42: p. 320). Berelson and Steiner, after reviewing a number of massive studies of psychotherapeutic efficacy, conclude that, ". . . it cannot even be considered established that psychotherapy on the average improves a patient's chances of recovery beyond what they would be without any formal therapy whatever" (44: p. 287). Recoveries from neurosis are certainly known but do not seem to be necessarily the result of psychotherapy. Eysenck points out that, ". . . roughly two-thirds of a group of neurotic patients will recover or improve to a marked extent within about two years of the onset of their illness, whether they are treated by means of psychotherapy or not" (45: pp. 322-323). George Watson also cites the inadequacy of psychotherapy in the treatment and rehabilitation of the mentally ill (38). There is strong evidence, therefore, that psychotherapy is no better or worse than alternate means of helping the mentally ill. Peters of the University of Pennsylvania, for example, concluded a five-year study with the conclusion that psychiatrists and probation officers are equally successful in the rehabilitation of sex offenders (46). A dramatic psychiatric failure is chronicled in a recent book, *In A Darkness,* by James Wechsler (47) who recounts the total failure of eight psychiatrists and five hospitals to aid his schizophrenic son. The book is, to quote one reviewer, ". . . a staggering damnation of the psychomedical field" (48). All this is not to say that psychotherapy is a total waste of time, but rather that its value is more akin to aspirin than to penicillin. Therapy can make the pain more bearable by teaching the patient to accommodate to his illness. As Pitts points out in respect to one affliction, ". . . psychotherapy has little effect on the symptoms of anxiety neurosis, although it may influence the patient to accept his condition" (49: p. 69).

The failure of the psychotherapies may well be their insistence on denying any biological involvement in mental illness. Jellinek 4: p. 82) cites Bowman, who as early as 1939 asked, "Will psychiatry have to reorient itself to a physiological approach to many of the problems which heretofore have been regarded as purely psychological?" In 1972, George Watson states, "The failure to distinguish between psychochemical behavior and motivated, meaningful behavior is at the bottom of the chaos in psychotherapy" (38: p. 13). However, each extreme of the nature-nurture dichotomy assumes that if its opposite is involved at all, it is only as an insignificant by-product of the primary cause. The mental determinists assume that should there be any physiological correlates of behavioral problems these are but minor symptoms which will automatically correct themselves as the mind is set in order. The biological determinists claim, as Wallace points out in Hsu's book on *Psychological Anthropology,* ". . . that an adequately functioning brain will be able to adapt to, or reduce, environmental pressures, and the chronic mental disfunctions are therefore predominantly the consequence of a chronic physical disfunction which existed prior to, or independently of, the organism's embarrassment by environmental pressures" (29: p. 261). This division and the resulting chaos in psychotherapy is especially visible in regard to schizophrenia, homosexuality and alcoholism. All three, as a consequence, lack adequate definitions, verifiable etiologies and a favorable prognosis.

Schizophrenia, for example, lacks a valid definition. Asimov states that, "This word (schizophrenia) covers such a multitude of disorders that it can no longer be described as a specific disease" (42: p. 321). Sarbin concludes that "schizophrenia is a myth" (50). Nonetheless, our mental hospitals are full of schizophrenics. Moreover, few of them leave the hospitals, for the success of psychiatry and psychoanalysis in treating this undefinable illness is practically nil. This failure may be a product of seeing schizophrenia as merely the mental reaction to emotional deprivation in childhood.

A small group of heretics, however, have always considered schizophrenia to be primarily a biological problem. Recently, Arnold Mandell and Jacques S. Gottlieb have associated schizophrenia with enzyme deficiencies. Such announcements inevitably meet with rebuttals from the nurture camp (51). Another approach, referred to by Goldfarb and Berman, is the work of Hoskins and others indicating that schizophrenia may be due to adrenocortical malfunction (52: p. 422). D. W. Woolley, on the other hand, according to Hoffer and Osmond, suggests that schizophrenia may be due to an imbalance of serotonin in the brain (53: pp. 70-71). Another biological possibility, cited by Cheraskin *et al.* (54: p. 201), is to be found in the work of Derek Richter who believes schizophrenia may be due to "an impairment of the homeostatic control mechanisms situated in the hypothalamus." Whatever the physical correlate, for years many have seen strong indications that the ultimate genesis of the malfunction is genetic. Mazur and Robertson (28: p. 60) refer to the research of Leonard Heston which seems to demonstrate a clear genetic basis for schizophrenia. Clausen states that if an identical twin becomes schizophrenic, the chances are two to three that the other will too (55: p. 162). The genetic hypothesis is further strengthened by the work of Moskalenko in Russia with seventy-four families with a history of schizophrenia (56). Further, recent work at Harvard Medical School has shown a correlation between schizophrenia and genetically transmitted Klinefelter's Syndrome (57).

Any reasonable approach to schizophrenia in view of the range of mental and constitutional factors referred to above must involve a synthesis and this is becoming increasingly obvious to a number of individuals. Mandell *et al.* state, "It has become gnawingly apparent that major mental illnesses such as schizophrenia or manic-depressive disease are complex psychobiological phenomena made up of genetic, developmental and psychosocial parameters. They are no more likely to have a single cause than do such traits as height, weight, personality or intelligence" (58: p. 72). Joseph Schwab expressed basically the same idea when he said,

> In the end we'll probably discover that there is a chemical deficiency, perhaps a serious and radical deficiency, which creates a state of susceptibility to, and gives direction to psychological states and circumstances. So a 'bad' family may be indispensable to one kind of schizophrenic symptomology, but would not affect a person who did not have the chemical deficiency (59: p. 16).

Mazur and Robertson also see a synthesis as the only meaningful answer and conclude that, "Apparently, not only schizophrenia but also the lesser schizoid behaviors are genetically based. Perhaps the social environment determines whether a 'genetically primed' individual will be schizophrenic, or simply schizoid, or normal" (28: p. 62). An understanding of these views about schizophrenia is directly pertinent to studies on alcoholism. Every etiological factor postulated for schizophrenia has also been named in the development of alcoholism. Further, in both cases I believe science will validate multicausality rather than the current monocausality of either the psychological or the biological determinists.[3]

----

[3] A most significant work has just been published on this affliction: David Hawkins and Linus Pauling: *Orthomolecular Psychiatry: Treatment of Schizophrenia.* San Francisco, W. H. Freeman and Company, 1973.

The theories of homosexuality likewise beg for a synthesis, for at the moment interpretations here are as rampant and contradictory as they are for schizophrenia. There is even valid debate today on whether homosexuality should be labelled as a disease. Numerous homophile societies are currently arguing that their sexual customs be re-defined as an alternate but acceptable way of life. On the other hand, most law courts hold homosexuals to be neither acceptable nor ill, but rather classify them as sexual criminals. As such, many of them apparently suffer indignities and cruelties out of keeping with any pretense of our being a humanitarian nation (60). Aside from the moral and legal interpretations of homosexuality, scientific explanations make up a confused morass of contradictions. A recent abstract of an article by Saghir and Robins sum these up by stating, "Years of research and debate over the root causes of homosexuality have produced little more than a fairyland (sic!) of hormonal, genetic and psychological theories" (61).

The most common of these theories on homosexuality is psychiatric and derives from Freud. Bergler states this position when he writes:

> The homosexual pervert is a person who has failed in overcoming the trauma of weaning. He identifies unconsciously the breast with the penis and seeks in the other homosexual the reduplication of his own defense mechanisms: escape from breast via identification with the penis and escape to man from woman as the source of original disappointment (62: p. 446).

How this oral interpretation relates to the frequency of anal sex in homosexual behavior is a conflict that I have never seen logically resolved.

From the biological side, other interpretations are also available. Recent research has apparently revealed a difference in the testosterone of male homosexuals from that of heterosexuals. No significant hormonal difference, however, has been demonstrated in female homosexuality (63). If indeed a positive correlation exists between male homosexuality and hormones, some interesting questions may be raised. For example, if a heterosexual male is coerced into habitual homosexual behavior, will there be a noticeable hormonal change? James Hoffa has reported that forty-five percent of prison inmates practice homosexuality (64). It is doubtful that this many were homosexual upon their incarceration. Has the sexual experience of the prison altered their hormonal system and if so, will this carry over into their lives following their release? An answer to this question would also shed light on the body-mind relationship in other areas of behavior, including alcoholism. In the meantime, however, it has been demonstrated, at least in some cases, that homosexuality can be *cured* by a purely biological approach. Psychosurgeon Fritz Roeder has reversed homosexuality by operating on the hypothalamus of seven patients (65). At Tulane, another homosexual was converted to heterosexuality "by electrically stimulating (the) pleasure center in his brain" (66).

There is good evidence then that homosexuality, like schizophrenia, may be a psychobiological phenomenon. It is also cogent to a discussion on alcoholism as so many psychiatric theories attempt to link the two into one syndrome. Homosexuality also resembles alcoholism in the vagueness of the dividing line between *normal* and *deviant*. Is a man a homosexual if he only occasionally seeks fulfillment with his own sex? Is a person an alcoholic who usually drinks in moderation but on rare occasions seems to *lose control?* Do such *occasionals* differ in bodily functions from *real* alcoholics, confirmed homosexuals and *normals?*

Whatever the answer to these questions, the monocausal behaviorist theories are being questioned on many fronts beyond those dealt with above. As but one example, an abstract of an article by Eric Schopler says of autistic and psychotic children, "Research is beginning to indicate that such disturbances may be linked to genetic, constitutional and biochemical predispositions in the child" (67). The same may be true of alcoholism, for as Von Wartburg says, "Evidence for an important role of biological factors in the etiology of alcoholism has been found in recent years" (68: p. 20). Nonetheless, psychology and psychiatry still dominate the alcoholic field and are most reluctant to cede any portion of that field to the biologically-oriented researchers.

CHAPTER II:

THE BLURRY WORLD OF ALCOHOLISM

W HILE INTERPRETATIONS OF schizophrenia and homosexuality are varied and numerous, those on alcoholism are legion. It would be a physical impossibility to resumé the literature which presents this plethora of interpretation. Bergler (62: p. 434) cites Jellinek who in 1942 estimated "that papers and books on the subject of chronic alcoholism in all its aspects 'may number roughly 100,000.'" The number of such publications has grown astronomically in the thirty years since that statement was made. Unfortunately, the range of opinions expressed in all these works tend to confuse rather than enlighten. Thomas commented on the lack of agreement found in the library of alcoholism by stating, "Much has been written on the subject, with opinions varying almost as widely as men differ in their reactions when intoxicated" (69: p. 65). To further confuse the picture, many of the specialists take positions which are as dogmatic as the utterances of fundamentalist ministers. In the field of alcoholic studies the extremes of the nature-nurture debate are clearly visible.

However, from the beginnings of alcoholic research many have warned against the simplistic approach of either biological or psychocultural determinism. All of the more knowledgeable and sophisticated writers on alcoholism today argue for a multi-causal origin of alcoholism. Landis and Bolles, for example, wrote,

> Addiction has been attributed to many factors: personality, heredity, general constitution, psychotic or psychopathetic tendencies, environmental factors, occupation, physiological tolerance and the drinking customs of the community. No single one of these determines the addiction but rather a constellation of several of them brings it about (70: p. 227).

Likewise, Alexander states, ". . . psychodynamic factors (of

alcoholism) can only be evaluated properly in the light of sociological and biological factors" (71: p. 136). In the same vein,
Moore's view is that, ". . . to look at alcoholism as exclusively a
social problem or a biological problem results in a myopic view"
(72: p. 173). Berreman, realizing the complexity of alcoholism
concludes that, "No simple monistic theory can, therefore, be
expected to account for it" (73). Cantanzaro agrees when he
writes, "Alcoholism is an extremely complex illness which involves
psychiatric, physical, sociologic and cultural areas" (74: p. 31).
Ruth Fox concurs with, ". . . alcoholism probably has its origins
in numerous interrelating factors" (75: p. 331). One could go
on citing such authors for pages, all arguing for a recognition
of multicausality. At the same time, however, others see the
problem as being far simpler and argue for a single cause in
alcoholic etiology.

Generally speaking, those claiming a monocausality in alcoholism have had a minimal exposure to those afflicted with the
disease. Others, however, argue for a simplistic cause because
of a limited vision produced by a near-religious and ego-
supporting devotion to a single discipline. Such dogmatists
exist in both the nature and the nurture camps and their
discipline-dictated blinders are usually quite obvious. Their
narrow field of vision can probably be explained in part by the
Sapir-Whorf hypothesis from anthropology. This states that
one's language can structure perception and thereby affect
one's view of reality (76, 77). Likewise, it is not too improbable
that deep immersion in a particular discipline will strongly affect
one's perception. In just this way, certain religions can condition
one to witness the miracle of God in every living thing and certain
disciplines educate the specialists to see a monolithic monocausality in all behavioral problems. Such individuals would
perceive ultimate causes in a simplistic view more like a primitive
ethnoscientist than as a scientist (78, 79).

Such discipline-limited vision is, of course, a matter of degree
and varies from one person to the next. However, it is extremely
common and even strongly affects those who formally acknowl-
edge a multicausality in the etiology of alcoholism. This is to
be expected as one does use the perceptions and tools with which

one has been trained. This also works against a rounded presentation on alcoholism. A publication by the Christopher D. Smithers Foundation points to this problem by stating,

> The etiquette of American alcoholism literature demands that the psychiatrist should acknowledge that physiopathological, cultural and social elements have a role in the genesis of alcoholism. On the other hand, the physiopathologist is required to admit the existence of social, cultural and possibly some individual psychological factors. With few exceptions, however, specialists, after having made the prescribed bow, proceed to formulate their theories of causes exclusively in terms of their respective disciplines. Thus, the idea that presents itself to an omniverous reader of the alcohol literature is usually that alcoholism is an economic, a psychological, a physiological or a sociological problem, to the exclusion of the other aspects (80: pp. 12-13).

Thus, the alcoholic is viewed by the anthropologist as a product of an anxiety-producing culture, by the sociologist as a statistical deviation from a norm, by the psychologist as an inadequate ego and by the biologically-oriented as a malfunctioning body.

However, any mature social scientist is aware of such limitations peculiar to his own discipline. He also realizes that he probably picked that discipline to satisfy some idiosyncratic need which also affects his perception and analysis. He also jokes about it. One may, with some degree of truth, facetiously separate the major social disciplines by the following description: All social scientists are mentally ill and the discipline they choose reflects the attitude they take toward their illness: psychologists seek to cure themselves, sociologists try to change society to conform to their neurosis, and anthropologists seek a society that will tolerate theirs.[4] Another version of the same theme states that anthropologists like people, sociologists prefer statistics and psychologists love neurotics. On the other hand, it has been my impression that dogmatists are rarely able to joke about their profession.

Such discipline-based variation in perception and under-

---

[4] I believe the genesis of this fable was a comment by Dr. Isabel Kelly during a visit at her home in Tepepan, Mexico, many years ago.

standing[5] is basic to the different interpretations of alcoholism. Further, especially in the antagonistic opposition of the nature and nurture approaches, the distance between them is constantly increasing because of the growing incomprehensibility of material outside one's own field. The accelerated accumulation of data and concepts is producing a deluge of literature written in an increasingly esoteric vocabulary. Indeed, it is even difficult to keep up with the literature in any specialization within any of the major disciplines. Very few are able, therefore, even to attempt to master a cross-disciplinary approach. Those that do try find themselves facing a linguistic problem as they encounter the ever growing technical vocabularies which distinguish each field. Most physiologically-oriented scientists are unable to interpret what one of them described to me as the "folklorish jargon" of the social sciences. Most social scientists, on the other hand, are totally lost when they try to enter the complicated world and vocabulary of endocrinology and molecular biology. As a result, specialists in the physical and the psychocultural sciences are coming to represent *two cultures* which are rapidly losing the ability to converse with one another. The inability to comprehend or communicate with other viewpoints tends to further accentuate disciplinary blinders and is conducive of further absolutism and dogmatism.

While this growing disciplinary provincialism is preventing a holistic view of alcoholism, a frequently unconscious and unscientific prejudice blurs the vision of some investigators and therapists. These individuals are part of a larger sociocultural community and are frequently unaware of how indoctrinated they really are with popular prejudices. Such prejudices, despite massive educational programs, still assign the alcoholics to a very low position in any scale of social desirability. A recent study, for example, showed that the public rated alcoholics as more undesirable than the mentally retarded or ex-convicts (81). The stigma of alcoholism goes far into our historical past and rests upon the Christian definition of man as a possessor

---

[5] The most devastating overview of the myopia, dogmatism, and esoteric verbiage in the social sciences is Stanislav Andreski's: *Social Sciences as Sorcery* (London: Andre Deutsch, 1972).

of free will. This conflicts directly with the many schools of determinism in the study of human behavior. The abandonment of the concept of free will is described by Linsky (82: p. 702) utilizing an article by Glock (83): ". . . there has been a shift over the last hundred years from a view of man as governed almost entirely by free-will, and therefore responsible for his situation, to a more deterministic image in which man's behavior is viewed as shaped in large part by forces beyond his control." I have encountered a fair number of determinists who in fact deny any free-will, and yet when they loosen their disciplinary girdle, attribute it to alcoholics. One such person was a staff member of a mental hospital in which I was consulting. He had frequently and strongly expressed his determinist views. However, one afternoon after a pleasant luncheon he stated, "I wish we could keep the damn alcoholics out of the hospital. The bastards are perfectly normal once they sober up and they could stay that way if they wanted to." His concept of determinism was suddenly as absent as Seneca's when he said, "Drunkenness is nothing but a condition of insanity purposely assumed."

Despite the determinists' denial of a totally free will, a more subtle assumption of it is basic to most schools of psychotherapy. The psychiatric belief that once shown the light, the mentally ill can recover, implies the patient's active participation and decision-making in his own rehabilitation. This is especially observable in alcoholism. Björk, for example, says of the alcoholic that ". . . the individual is responsible for his illness, at least to a certain degree" (84). Strupp repeats the same premise as basic to all psychotherapy. "The view that man is largely responsible for his own neurotic suffering has important assumptions for the practice, the goals, and the philosophical assumptions that underlie modern psychotherapy" (85: p. 37). Further, some assumption of free will allows the therapist an explanation of his failures, putting the blame on the patient rather than on his own inadequacies. For example, a therapeutic disaster in treating an alcoholic was explained to me by the clinical psychologist in charge of the case by, "He really didn't want to get well." Another therapist freed himself from any responsibility in several failures with alcoholic patients by explaining that "They simply found drunkenness too attractive a way of life to abandon."

Some alcohologists have openly dropped all attempts at using any form of determinism to explain alcoholism and have returned that affliction to the realm of morality. They do this by disclaiming any possibility that alcoholism may be a disease. As the term disease implies a force attacking the patient, free will is not involved and the victim is not to be blamed. The removal of alcoholism from the disease category accomplishes the opposite. Verden and Shatterly are examples of this moralistic revivalism. They also bring into their writing the suspense of a Hitchcock spy movie and hint darkly of an unholy alliance between Alcoholics Anonymous and the School of Alcohol Studies in a plot to spread the disease myth and thus protect the alcoholic from judgment. These authors, therefore, conclude that the only function of the disease concept of alcoholism is ". . . protecting the compulsive drinker from moral condemnation" (86: p. 331).[6] This is a dogmatism of another color, but one equally disastrous to objectivity. Such writers as Verden and Shatterly see alcoholism as merely a naughty habit which can be untaught in the same way that a little boy who picks his nose in public can be re-educated into respectable behavior.

Such moralistic debates on the semantics of alcoholism are not very constructive. However, much of the confusion in that field does indeed rest on a matter of definition. Basic to all research and therapy is an adequate taxonomy of the alcoholic. Fairly acceptable definitions of alcoholism and its varieties have been offered by the World Health Organization (87), Jellinek (4), Keller (88) and others. These definitions, however, are all primarily in terms of behavior and are vague enough in some of the areas to leave vast room for debate and disagreement. Its basic nature has not been agreed upon. As one example, specialists still argue on whether alcoholism is a disease in itself or merely the symptom of a deeper psychological or physical

---

[6] Others have picked up the refrain of this moralistic theme. Peter B. Dewes states: "The only apparent advantage of classifying alcoholism as a disease is that it protects the alcoholic from punishment." (*Quart. J. Stud. Alc.* 33:1046 Comment on David Robinson: The alcoholist's addiction), *Quart. J. Stud. Alc.,* 33:1045-1047, 1972.

malfunction. Thus, Osborn states, ". . . alcoholism is more a symptom than a disease" (89: p. 60). Tiebout, on the other hand, had concluded ". . . that alcoholism is a symptom which has become a disease" (90: p. 54). A few place alcoholism totally within a physiological frame while others define it as a mental disease. Commonly, all these factors are combined into a vague totality. The resultant confusion led Bjurulf and his colleagues to admit that "It has proved difficult to find a generally acceptable definition of alcoholism" (91, p. 393).

Lacking a nondebatable and specific definition, there is a major problem in accurately classifying the alcoholics in a society that ranges from teetotalers to individuals who are rarely if ever sober. This is the common linguistic problem of trying to carve discrete units out of what is really a continuum. Without objective and specific criteria such linguistic segmentation into meaningful units is next to impossible. As we cannot stand vagueness in a mechanized and bureaucratic world, we rely on *experts* to draw such lines of demarcation for us. However, at best, such delineations are largely arbitrary. Examples are to be found in our official definitions of "poverty," "middle class" and "old age." The arbitrariness of such classifications stands out clearly in our courts when psychiatrists confront each other over whether another individual was "sane" or "insane" during the commission of a crime. Currently, as a by-product of heart transplants, legal debate rages over a definition of the "moment of death." Even the definition of "death" is undergoing modification. By the older code that states a man is dead when his heart stops we find some unacceptable situations. In a case of heart-transplant, the recipient would be legally dead by this definition and the buried donor would be alive.

Similar obscurity exists in the labeling of an alcoholic. If either the geneticists or psychological determinists are right in stating that the alcoholism is merely a response to an earlier condition, can an individual be labeled an "alcoholic" before he takes his first drink? If alcoholism is defined in terms of alcoholic consumption or its resultant effects, is a rehabilitated member of Alcoholics Anonymous really an alcoholic? And of critical importance is the classification in "borderline" cases. As Mazur and Robertson point out, ". . . the lines between the nonaddicted heavy drinker and the alcoholic are vague" (28: p. 142). As a correlate of the vagueness of the term alcoholic is the lack of homogeneity among those lumped together by the term. As Mayer and Myerson state, ". . . there is no single alcoholic but rather a variety of alcoholics . . ." (92: p. 627). Popham and Schmidt go further and conclude that ". . . far greater variation may be expected within the alcoholic population than between it and the community at large" (93: p. 17).

This variation within the *alcoholic population* raises serious questions in evaluating the results of research. As Pokorny and his colleagues point out, "There is no assurance that the so-called alcoholics of one study are comparable to the alcoholics of another" (94: p. 699). Pokorny also co-authored another review pointing out the "biased sampling" that can result from this vagueness of definition (95). While some are thus questioning the reliability of alcoholic samples, I have seen no criticism of the selection of *controls* or *normals* used for comparative analysis in these studies. I believe many of these are as inadequate in their definition as the alcoholic samples. Such controls range from *other patients* and *hospital staff* to *college students* and *volunteers*. It is as serious a mistake to assume a meaningful norm or homogeneity in these arbitrary nonalcoholic samples as in the alcoholic ones. There is also the unspoken assumption that the control group is *normal* and therefore *mentally healthy*. The Midtown Manhattan Study (96), however, found the norm in that city to be anything but mentally healthy. A typical sample from this area, assuming the study to be correct, would include some *well* individuals but also an enormous percentage of *impaired* and *incapacitated* personalities.

The mere fact of the wide range of variation in both the control and the alcoholic samples allows one to question the methods of classification used for either. One expects some variation in any random sample of the general population but would hope that the *scientific* label of alcoholic rested on more than one shared trait. However, expert disagreement easily leads an observer to suspect that the alcohologists have merely corralled everyone who has ever had a drinking problem and are now desperately but unsuccessfully looking for another common trait to justify their earlier diagnosis of *alcoholism*. So difficult is this task that Thomas has despaired of any generalizations on the alcoholic and states that ". . . one must regard each case as an individual problem" (69: pp. 77-78). However, on the whole problem of individual variation within psychiatric categories, Opler has said,

> For although it is questionable or at least assumptive to state that 'parts of illness' (like alcoholism) or over-generalized categories (like the schizophrenias) are illness entities, neither do they melt wholly as phenomena into isolated atoms of experience limited exclusively to the individual case (40: p. 128).

From the empirical evidence of those with any valid experience in alcoholic research and therapy, I think we can conclude that there is an entity based on more than one trait that has been labeled "alcoholism." Although there is enormous variation between alcoholics, this range of differences will shrink when we recognize the significant variables and sharpen the focus of our definition. Were each case of alcoholism really wholly idiosyncratic, none would rightly be worthy of scientific investigation for science is primarily concerned with regularities and generalities. However, in the meantime, all research on alcoholism will suffer from the vagueness of the concept itself.

The looseness of the classification has also seriously handicapped alcoholic therapy. Joan Curlee concludes from her own work that, "The study also indicated a degree of variation among patients which should sound a cautionary note to those who are inclined to lump 'alcoholics' into one category, all to be treated in the same manner" (97: p. 650). The more enlightened therapists have, in fact, been flexible in their approach. Gottesfeld and Yager thus state, "To suggest that there is a unitary or single approach to therapy is to overlook the breadth of the problem" (98: p. 224). Horn and Wanberg agree and write, ". . . persons seeking treatment for a drinking problem should not be regarded as in one bag, so to speak, ready, willing and able to respond to one kind of treatment" (99: p. 656). However, such receptivity to variation is an unbearable burden to the dogmatists. It has been all too common a practice in psychotherapy in general to force the patient into the theoretical framework favored by the therapist (100). Chafetz notes this practice in alcoholism and speaks of "The caregivers who tend to cling to their stereotyped formulations and perceptions of what an 'alcoholic' is and try to motivate the patient to accept treatment modalities that 'appeal' to them" (101: p. 444). The more sensitive dogmatists profit from their mistakes and modify their approach. Such was a wise physician I know who for several years tried to rehabilitate alcoholics according to his own rigid formula of the disease. He also met with consistent failure. "I began to modify my approach," he told me, "when I realized a patient was probably correct when he informed me that M.D. did not stand for Major Deity." However, few dogmatists achieve such enlightenment and this is probably in large part responsible for the lack of notable success in alcoholic therapy.

The concept of therapeutic *success* is itself as vague as the definition of alcoholism. As Kaplan *et al.* state, "There has been no agreement on absolute criteria for success in alcoholism therapy" (102: p. 102). Pattison *et al.* also point to, ". . . the lack of well-defined criteria of what constitutes cure, recovery or successful treatment" (103: p. 610). Most therapy programs consider abstinence as the only measure of success. Some studies have regarded six months of sobriety as an adequate indication of alcoholic recovery. Others, in agreement with A.A., see success only with sobriety continuing until death. Numerous therapists also, again like A.A., distinguish between a good *sobriety*, which is characterized by a successful adjustment and maturity and a *poor* sobriety marked by social maladjustment and emotional instability. Nearly all psychoanalysts and some other therapists would define *cure* as a total return to a *normal* life which included social drinking.

Whatever the criteria, alcoholic therapy has been a colossal failure. Many reasons can be cited besides the ignorance and misconceptions of the disease on the part of many psychotherapists. In fact, more alcoholics probably seek help from physicians than from psychologists and psychiatrists combined. Most physicians are apparently totally unqualified to render any meaningful assistance. As Ward and Faillace, both M.D.'s, state,

"Most physicians' knowledge about alcoholism is inadequate, due in part to the generally poor teaching about it in medical school" (104: p. 688). Many physicians flatly refuse to treat alcoholics. This rejection of alcoholic patients may be due to an awareness of their own inadequacies, because of the frustration of consistent failure with alcoholic cases or because of their own moral condemnation of alcoholics. I have encountered several in the last category who would agree with Todd who on June 21, 1882, told the General Association of Middletown that "Every human soul is worth saving; but what I mean is, that if a choice is to be made, drunkards are about the last class to be taken hold of . . ." (105: p. 210).

An especially amazing example of such medical intolerance was related to me by an A.A. with many years of sobriety. It seemed so improbable that when an opportunity arose, I discreetly checked with the physician involved and he confirmed the event. The A.A., suffering from a kidney complaint, was referred to this physician, a urologist, by his own physician, a G.P. The A.A. began his conversation with the urologist by saying, "First, you should know that I'm an alcoholic." The urologist replied, "I'm sorry, but I don't treat alcoholics." The A.A. replied, "It's not my alcoholism that I want to see you about, it's my kidneys." The urologist repeated, "I don't treat alcoholics." The consultation was over. The A.A. told me that he at least felt fortunate that the urologist had not billed him for his visit. Such discrimination is apparently far from rare. In fact, until recently most hospitals refused to admit cases of alcoholism although some physicians did smuggle them in under a disguised diagnosis as some socially acceptable disease.

The many physicians and psychotherapists who have been willing to work with alcoholics have used a number of different approaches depending upon their own interpretations of alcoholism. These include such widely different techniques as: a multitude of psychological and psychiatric therapies, orthodox psychoanalysis, hypnosis (106, 107), aversion therapy, shock treatment, diet control and multivitamin administration, the use of amphetamines, tranquilizers and LSD (108). The only generalization one can make of these many therapies is that failure is typical and success is rare. An equivalent record of consistent failure would bankrupt a commercial corporation in a few months, yet alcoholic therapy has been compounding its inadequacy from its very beginnings.

This dismal record must reflect a failure in understanding the nature of alcoholism. From 1945 on, Jellinek postulated a physiological x *factor* along with the psycho-cultural determinants (4). Most researchers have concentrated on either the x *factor* or on the mental aspects of the disease. Few approaches have sincerely viewed the alcoholic as a total being. This task of integration in behavioral problems is by no means limited to alcoholism. As Wallace said in Hsu's anthology, "As yet, the various special lines of the new organic approach have not achieved synthesis among themselves or with the (actually older) psychosocial tradition in psychiatry and the social sciences" (29: p. 260). The ultimate answers to the problems of human behavior and deviancy await such a synthesis.

Until such time, environmental and behavioral theories will probably continue to dominate all forms of alcoholic therapy despite the consistent failure in the past. A needed stream of criticism will also accompany future failures. Tiebout twenty years ago expressed the still current view of those who find the myopia of psychotherapy responsible for its inadequacy. He wrote, ". . . the psychiatrists have labored under certain faulty theoretical assumptions which have handicapped them in coming to grips with practical issues" (90: p. 53). On the other hand, defenders of the psychocultural approach attribute these failures to an irreparable damage in the psyche of the alcoholic. Lolli, for example, has stated that, ". . . not even the deepest psychotherapy can erase entirely those traits which sustain addictive drinking" (109: p. 245).

Whether psychotherapy is an inadequate tool or the alcoholic is damaged beyond repair is a question that will be decided in the future. Adequate or not, the various psychologies and psychiatries have contributed immeasurably toward the welfare and understanding of those with behavioral problems. In the area of alcoholism these approaches have produced many valid insights into the alcoholic psyche as well as some interesting interpretation of the etiology of alcoholism.

CHAPTER III:

THE ALCOHOLIC'S MIND

At one time it was held that all alcoholics shared a common and definable personality which was responsible for their aberrant drinking behavior. This view has never been substantiated and few hold to it today. As Lawlis and Rubin state, "Numerous studies have attempted to identify characteristics of an 'alcoholic personality' but differences among the findings have left the validity of the concept open to question" (110: p. 318). Popham and Schmidt concur and write that "The 'alcoholic personality' has persistently eluded discovery and studies of the social characteristics of alcoholics have failed to show that they differ remarkably from nonalcoholics" (93: p. 16). Tiebout (111) and Wexberg (112) flatly state that there is no prealcoholic personality that can explain the development of the disease. However, there is general agreement that alcoholics tend to share certain traits which make them susceptible to the affliction. Lisansky says, "Certainly it is true that the test literature has not yielded evidence for the 'alcoholic personality'; but it is also true that we cannot reject the idea that personality factors play a very significant role in determining who will become an alcoholic and who will not" (113: p. 13). Trice more explicitly states that "A combination of these traits makes for a maximum readiness for alcoholism" (114: p. 46).

A knotty problem has been raised at this point. Is it possible to tell with certainty whether such traits are in fact part of the cause or merely the product of pathological drinking? As the McCords put it, "It has been virtually impossible to separate the characteristics of alcoholics that may be the result of alcoholism from those that may be the cause of, or at least precede, its emergence" (115: p. 413). Likewise, Edwards observes that "In assessing the personality of the alcoholic, there is the difficulty of distinguishing behavior which is the manifestation of the basic personality and aberrant behavior which is the consequence of drinking" (107: p. 235). Sutherland *et al.*, likewise note that the distinguishing alcoholic characteristics ". . . may be effects rather than causes of alcoholism" (116: p. 557).

Jellinek (117) recognized the possibility of both a pre-alcoholic and a postalcoholic constellation of personality traits. I concur in this. As I shall point out later, many alcoholics do indeed share certain observable traits before the onset of drinking. It should be fairly obvious also that uncontrolled drinking will set up certain common behavioral defenses against a hostile social reaction to drunkenness. This defense pattern will of course vary from culture to culture. For example, I am quite sure that the alcoholic defense syndrome in Mexico and the United States is recognizably different. Further, I believe that the defensive traits are far more easily observed than the earlier personality *shortcomings* which contributed to the alcoholism.

In any study of etiology, however, these early causative traits are the most significant. Most environmentalists and behaviorists see the genesis of alcoholism in the nature of the relationship of the individual to his parents. The columnist McCabe has noted, "that human beings are something more than the sum of their parents is wisdom which prevailed in pre-Freudian days" (118). However, today many descriptions of alcoholism see its origin in an ". . . imbalance in the parents: a dominant, protective mother and a distant father" (119). Other studies describe an autocratic rather than a "distant" father. Further, as Catanzaro (74) points out, a large number of surveys have demonstrated that many of the childhood homes of alcoholics had generally unfavorable environments and some were definitely psychopathological. Many of the alcoholics I know confirm the hypothesis that alcoholism is frequently the aftermath of a painful childhood. These alcoholics also commonly carry a poorly suppressed hatred of their parents. A number of psychotherapists seem to believe that if the alcoholic can openly recognize and express this hostility he is well along the road to recovery. However, if maturity is rational understanding, such therapists err if they do not continue this approach until the alcoholic can understand the parents' behavior. I have witnessed several most unfortunate confrontations between alcoholics and their parents when therapeutically released hatred erupted to produce irreparable damage to all concerned. As Menninger has pointed out, the destructiveness of such parents is rarely calculated. He said, "Although there are exceptions, as a general rule parents of alcoholics . . . are peculiarly unseeing with regard to the sufferings of their children. . . . Such parents little realize the suffering silently endured (often unconsciously) by well-appearing, well-regarded children" (120: p. 163). This is perhaps appropriate in a larger sense today as each generation is blaming the other for the state of the world. Such accusations seem especially infantile when they come as moralistic diatribes from behaviorists or environmentalists who are berating the parental generation. By their own premises, the parents' parents are in turn responsible for their behavior. And this line of guilt then relentlessly goes back to their first erring couple. This is also the Christian concept of original sin which seems to serve primarily as an historical guilt-reducing mechanism. It is a commonly used explanation, however, and a recent article expounds on the shortcoming of the "parents as scapegoats" theme in relation to psychotic children (121). Biblical and behavioral explanations may attempt to explain origins but of themselves will not make the world a happier place nor cure the alcoholic. In contrast to this historical approach many therapists concern themselves only with the patient's present psyche and circumstance. The interactionists and many of the Gestalt approaches thus regard the past as irrelevant. The same opposition of methods is to be seen in anthropology between the historical and the functional approaches. In both psychological and anthropological problem-solving, an exclusive concern with either the past or the present fails to produce a complete picture of any situation.

Whatever approach is taken to alcoholism and despite the debate on whether it is a moral or a medical problem, most psychotherapists classify the alcoholic as *mentally ill*. Here again, however, one can enter an ideological and semantic briar patch. Some authorities such as Szasz (122, 123) claim mental illnesses are merely social myths. This linguistic debate depends in part on what one means by *mental illness*. Moore defines it as merely "defective functioning in life" (72: p. 173) and would therefore include alcoholism within its boundaries. Debate does not end here even among those who accept this definition. The question then arises as to whether it is a neurosis, a psychosis or a thing apart. Menninger, who held to the theory of a unitary alcoholic personality, spoke of the "alcoholic neurosis" (120). My own experiences with alcoholics lead me to agree with Landis and Bolles who stated, ". . . some alcoholics are definitely neurotic; some are psychotic; and some are neither neurotic nor psychotic. . . . Alcoholism occurs in some persons who show no other evidence of mental abnormality, or rather, show no consistent and characteristic difference from normal behavior, save alcoholism" (70: p. 226).

Whether classified as mentally ill or merely as deviant, there is still no agreement on what personality characteristics distinguish the alcoholic. The psychological search for these has relied heavily on various tests. Lisansky has clearly demonstrated that not only have these tests failed to identify the existence of an alcoholic personality, but they have also provided no more than leads as to what traits or characteristics are even significant (113). Other approaches have been no more successful in naming the key personality traits which produce alcoholism. These approaches are many and include the intensive digging of psychoanalysis, the lengthy questionnaires of sociologists, observations of therapists from innumerable schools of thought and the writings of alcoholics themselves. From these combined approaches, however, a number of alcoholic traits have been identified even if there is no general agreement on their rank importance or significance.

From the massive list of such traits, Catanzaro has listed those which are most commonly named as being of greatest significance to alcoholism. These are:

> (1) a high level of anxiety in interpersonal relations; (2) emotional immaturity; (3) ambivalence toward authority; (4) low frustration tolerance; (5) grandiosity; (6) low self-esteem; (7) feelings of isolation; (8) perfectionism; (9) guilt; (10) compulsiveness; (11) angry over-dependency; (12) sex-role confusion; (13) inability to express angry feelings adequately (74: p. 38).

Whether Catanzaro stopped at the number 13 because it is symbolic or whether he merely got tired of listing them is unknown. He certainly could have gone on into far higher numbers had he cared to, for as Gottesfeld and Yager say, "The generalizations in descriptive terms of the personality features of the alcoholic are too numerous to warrant complete elaboration" (98: p. 223). Catanzaro's list, however, is a significant one and I doubt if merely extending it would improve our understanding of alcoholism. As Trice wrote of such traits, "In and of themselves, they do not equal the disorder" (114: p. 46).

If these traits in themselves fail to explain the pathological drinking of alcoholics, it becomes difficult to know where to go for the answer. The alcoholic himself seems unable to provide it. The Big Book of A.A. states, "Some drinkers have excuses with which they are satisfied part of the time. But in their hearts they really do not know why they do it" (124: p. 23). Karl Menninger had come to the same conclusion years earlier when he said, "It is literally true that the alcoholic, as he himself says, does not know why he drinks" (120: p. 168). Ludwig, using a sample of 176 male alcoholics, found that a significant number ". . . simply have no comprehension (or are not willing to share their reasons) about the cause of their drinking" (125: p. 94). On the other hand, when the alcoholics do give reasons, these produce no commonality to provide an understanding of the desire. As Landis and Bolles state,

> There are many 'reasons' given for alcoholic addiction but, for the most part, these reasons are only rationalizations which state what the drinker hopes to achieve through the use of the beverage. Reasons such as escape, revolt, relief from tension, relief from anxiety, outlet for social and gregarious tendencies, or inflation of the ego are commonly mentioned. These reasons may be meaningful in describing a specific case, but they offer no basic explanation of the craving or compulsion to drink that develops in certain people and not in others (70: p. 228).

In other words, as Selden Bacon points out, asking why the alcoholic drinks may be as pointless as asking, "Why don't worms jump higher?" (126: p. 63).

However, I believe it is safe to say that the alcoholic drinks to fill a need. More specifically, I would agree with Chafetz that this need is an attempt to regain an equilibrium and homeostasis (101: p. 445). Alcoholic drinking may thus be an attempt at a self cure. Ludwig found this reason given by 25 percent of his sample (125: p. 94). Moore expresses the same idea, "Alcoholism is used as an adaptive technique, a form of self-treatment. . . ." (72: p. 173). Menninger had also defined the reason for the alcoholics drinking in the same manner (120: p. 162). All of my alcoholic sample agreed that, at least at first, alcohol "did something" for them, and made life more bearable. An expression frequently heard around A.A. about alcohol is, "The hell of it is that it works—at least for awhile." The alcoholic is pursuing an escape from an undefined pain and finds a specific medication in ethanol. Jo Coudert speaks of "the exquisite relief" that alcohol provides (127: p. 72) and Alexander refers to "the magical effect of alcohol" (71: p. 135). Lillian Roth, in describing her own experiences with the disease speaks of her "first lesson in the witchcraft of alcohol" (128: p. 104).

Most alcohologists would agree that the *magic* of alcohol is that it reduces tensions and stress. There is some good evidence today to demonstrate that alcohol does in fact ameliorate physically-induced stress in humans. For example, the work of Keatringe and Evans (129) is cited by Harold Kalant,

> . . . a dose of 75 cc. of absolute alcohol, corresponding to about 5 oz. of whiskey, gave a very significant protection to human subjects against the severe stress of immersion up to the neck in cold water, and suggested that this treatment might be of great advantage as a prophylactic for sailors about to abandon ship in cold water (130: p. 70).

The British Navy may have erred by giving up their daily ration of rum. But though alcohol may relieve physical stress, it is very dubious if this plays any significant role in alcoholism. Research with rats, at least, has consistently demonstrated that they increase their alcohol intake when exposed to psychological stress but not to physiological stress (131, 132, 133). The earlier classical studies by Masserman had already demonstrated the alcoholic potential for tension reduction on "neurotic" cats (134, 135). More recently, Anisman's research indicates that alcohol will also lower the emotion of "fear" in rats (136).

Such animal research may give us some promising leads but does not in itself warrant making conclusions about human behavior. In fact, the limitations of both the observers and the laboratory conditions may cast doubt on the results even for the animal species under study. Chapple points out that testing any animal in a laboratory can yield valid results only when we know the creature's natural behavior. "It is not informative," he states, "to study variations of behavior unless we know beforehand the norm from which the variants depart" (26: p. 4). Some of the laboratory experimenters in alcoholic behavior of goldfish, dogs, monkeys, apes and other creatures apparently lack a complete knowledge of their normative behavior in either free or caged conditions. Such ignorance seriously affected many experiments on alcohol selection under differing conditions. Myers describes a common error resulting from this shortcoming discovered by Gillespie and his co-worker,

> In relation to two-bottle tests for ethanol preference, Gillespie and Lucas (137) reported that in 20 out of 25 rats, preference for 15 per cent ethanol was determined entirely by the positions of the drinking tubes: the so-called 'alcoholism' of rats, which preferred 15 per cent ethanol was 'cured' simply by changing the position of the ethanol dispensers (138, p. 487).

An equally negating procedure is to make overly simple correlations of human and nonhuman behavior. Mazur and Robertson warn "That caution is in order when generalizing findings from one species to another . . ." (28: p. 99). A few pages later (p. 108) they charmingly explain that "There are pitfalls in generalizing from chickens to humans since their differences go well beyond the discrepant use of eggs." Nevertheless, used with care, animal research can give some invaluable leads for further investigations into human behavior and alcoholism. In some instances, however, experimentation on humans will not duplicate the results of laboratory animal research.

Such a failure to replicate a human equivalent to results from animal laboratories is found in the recent doubts raised about the concept of alcohol as a tension reducer. As Cappell and Herman have shown in their review article on "Alcohol and Tension Reduction," much of the evidence for this hypothesis is ". . .

negative, equivocal and often contradictory" (139: p. 33). Most
of this "contradictory" evidence, however, appears to me to be
based upon the extremely naive research that is so typical of
much of the laboratory work being done on the human response
to alcohol. In much of this work the basic error of the animal
labs is duplicated: the assumption that responses of free and
caged individuals are identical. Most of the subjects in these
experiments were *caged* in the sense that they were institutional-
ized in hospitals or jails. Even those who were volunteers were
caged in the sense that a laboratory is a highly artificial and
restricted environment. The limitations on experimental validity
are the same on caged humans as they are for caged animals as
described by Julian Huxley:

> . . . it has become clear that animals do not reveal the higher
> possibilities of their nature and behavior, nor the full range of their
> individual diversity, except in . . . conditions of freedom. Captivity
> cages minds as well as bodies, and rigid experimental procedure
> limits the range of performance. . . . (140: Forward, viii).

Much of the laboratory research testing human responses to
alcohol strikes me as being as meaningful as dropping a legless
lion in the Serengeti Plains to test its hunting ability.

These experiments have administered alcohol in settings and
by schedules that are totally alien to either normal or alcoholic
drinking. In one study ". . . the patient goes to the nursing
station at an appointed time, receives his alcohol and drinks it
there" (141: p. 317). The authors, however, are fortunately
aware of the fact that the scheduling ". . . of one drink an hour
is not only different from the customary drinking patterns of
the patients but is actually aversive" (141: pp. 321-322). Another
experiment along these lines imposed an equally unnatural pattern
on its alcoholic subjects: "Five dosage levels of alcohol were
administered at 90-minute intervals on each of two days of
drinking . . . on an empty stomach . . . (and) the subjects were
instructed to finish each drink in 30 seconds" (142: p. 345).
Such drinking would be as natural for an alcoholic as eating
underwater would be for a chicken.

Equally simplistic assumptions are made about identifying
normative alcoholic reactions to ethanol by experiments in ab-

normal settings. As one example, an experiment was made to test the hypothesis that ethanol tends to improve the alcoholic's self-concept (143). It is my opinion that the conditions in this project would more than negate any positive value of the alcohol. Hospitalized alcoholics were used as subjects and it has been my observation that such subjects invariably feel stigmatized and would feel acute anxiety and guilt at the very thought of drinking. The alcohol was followed by tests to measure self-perception which in this circumstance must have been extremely stress producing. Lastly, blood alcohol levels were regularly checked which would probably cause anxiety in a normal drinker. In other words, self-concept was being measured under a set of conditions guaranteed to prevent any improvement to the negative images the human guinea pigs must have already created of themselves. Alcoholics feel shame about their drinking and this would be extreme in a punitive environment that drunkenness had taken them into. To be asked to drink under examination while in such circumstances would make the alcoholic extremely self-conscious and increase his feelings of inferiority and inadequacy. Yet, this particular alcohologist was amazed to find that the alcoholics' self-images did not consistently improve. An equivalent experiment would be to invite incarcerated homosexuals to perform sexual acts before their keepers to see if this experience increased their sense of normalcy.

Other *controlled* experiments along these lines strike me as being equally inadequate. One of these, for example, checked the effect of alcohol on anxiety levels. The experiment did not confirm the hypothesis of an anxiety-releasing property in alcohol. However, the sample probably explains the negative results. These were "paid volunteers selected among inmates incarcerated for drunkenness" (142: p. 355). One-half of these actually showed a rise in anxiety after drinking. This seems only natural in a person who had experienced the trauma of arrest as the direct result of drinking. I would hazard a guess that the other half of the sample had adjusted to the stigma of arrest because of prior experiences. Sometimes the findings of such projects appear to me to be too obvious to warrant subjecting alcoholics to a drinking experience. The same researcher mentioned above, for example, made the "notable finding" that ". . . alcoholics know far less about their drunken selves than about their sober selves. . . ." (142: p. 355). When one aspect of alcoholic drinking is alcoholic amnesia, how could one expect any other conclusion?

Despite the evidence of such *scientific* experiments as these, I do not believe that the hypothesis that alcohol can reduce anxiety and tension has been destroyed. A psychiatrist I have known for some years commented on such studies, "Any conclusion that alcohol does not relax the drinker," he said, "could only be reached by a teetotaler or someone accustomed to stronger chemicals." With him I would agree that empirical evidence is frequently more reliable than the results of inadequate laboratory experimentation. A parallel can be seen from the 1930's in regard to the effect of cigarettes on health. During that period several old-fashioned aunts assured me that if smoking could cause shortness of breath and discomfit the lungs the smoke was injuring me. However, I had the comfort of a physician-professor who assured us in class that "There is not an iota of scientific evidence to show us that smoking can have any serious consequences." Likewise, in respect to the effect of alcohol, inadequate scientific experiments are not necessarily more valid than the empirical observations of the drinking public.

All alcoholics report immense relief from the first few drinks. In fact, despite hangovers, many alcoholics young to the disease experience a relief from tension for several days after a crisis-free drunk. Advanced alcoholics who have suffered psychologically and socially from their imbibing still experience a temporary relief when they begin drinking. However, for them the resultant drunk shortly becomes an anxiety-producing experience. This is undoubtedly due to the fact that they know from past experience that their immediate future has become unpredictable and liable to end in tragedy. Many alcoholics also report a conscious anxiety in mid-drunk that their supply of alcohol may be cut off. This pattern was even reported from laboratory studies by Gottheil *et al.* who found that ". . . with continued drinking, the early gains are quickly lost and give way to steadily increased dysphoria and distress" (144: p. 326). I also strongly suspect that biochemical correlates accompany this increasing discomfort.

If we can assume, then, that alcohol can at times relieve tension and anxiety, the question may be raised as to the nature and sources of these discomforts. In reply, environmentalists respond that our sociocultural setting is responsible. The behaviorists have a variety of other possible answers.

Many in the psychoanalytical schools state that the tension is an orally-based neurosis. Further, they see the alcoholic using his beverage to retreat from neurotic discomfort to the pleasurable security of infancy. Lolli, for example, posits that through drinking the alcoholic regains a blended physical and emotional pleasure associated with maternal contact and a full and warm tummy (145). Radó sees the alcoholic thus returning to an infantile bliss so total in blending of mind and body as to be labeled an "alimentary orgasm" (146).

This desire to regress is usually associated with an oral frustration deriving from infancy. Too early a weaning, psychoanalysis postulates, creates an insatiable oral drive (120, 147, 148, 149). Therefore, as Lolli says, alcoholism rests upon ". . . the revelation that alcohol can give him exactly what milk gave him" (109: p. 213). Menninger, who held strongly to the oral thesis, states that alcohol '.' . . supplies the oral love symbolically, in the form of precious liquor taken by mouth, the 'mother's milk' which was so much craved; and actually in the form of conviviality and sentimentality which accompanied social drinking" (120: p. 131).

If one is to consider the oral hypothesis at all, I find some fiction more reasonable than the psychoanalysts. Stuart Cloete, in his novel *The Curve and the Tusk*, writes of the difference in weaning African and white children,

> It is only the swiftly weaned white child that cannot remember, even if it has had the comfort of the breast, for its time there is too short. Or, perhaps when it is bottle-fed, it does remember, and turns back to the bottle again as soon as it can, to the Coca-Cola bottle and the beer bottle which, in its hands, have the same feel as the mother substitute on which it was raised. Nor is this all; the abstract love of the bottle may continue in such children so that everything that comes out of a bottle is good, whisky and gin, vitamins and sauces, soft drinks and poisons. So the bottle on which they began their lives, being contrary to the law of nature, may end them in alcoholic graves or in death from an overdose of veronal (150: pp. 54-55).

Oral needs, according to psychoanalytic theory, explain more than alcoholism. As has already been mentioned, it is also described as the basis of homosexuality. Many theorists thus see homosexuality and alcoholism as functional equivalents. The orally frustrated, by such theories, seek alternatives for the mother's nipple: the male sexual organ or a bottle. Others, however, see latent homosexuality and alcoholism as being possibly a single entity. Bergler, for example, states, "Since alcohol addiction has an oral basis too, the coincidence of drinking and homosexuality is possible" (62: p. 446). Others state emphatically that the two deviancies always go together. However, valid doubts on this interpretation have been raised for many years. As early as 1942 Thomas stated that ". . . to believe that all inebriates are homosexual is erroneous" (69: p. 77). He then goes on to point out that "Poorly sublimated tendencies occur in many individuals who are not alcoholic." In 1950, Prout and his colleagues were able to identify homosexuality in only four cases in a sample of one hundred hospitalized alcoholics (151). In 1951, Botwinick, after studying alcoholics in Kings County Hospital in Brooklyn, concluded ". . . that insofar as the tests in this study measure homosexuality, latent or otherwise, homosexuality cannot be an essential factor in alcoholism, although it may play a dynamic role in individual cases" (152: p. 272). The McCords, using their Cambridge-Somerville sample, state, "We are forced to conclude . . . that our research does not support the belief that alcoholics have latently homosexual personalities" (153: p. 32). Since that time, increasing opinion by qualified individuals has turned against the alcoholic-homosexual hypothesis (154: p. 19).

The entire *oral* explanation, I believe, is a rather weak one. The McCords found the oral correlation of alcoholism as inadequate as the homosexual explanation. They state rather that "Boys who had demonstrated oral tendencies did not become alcoholic more often than boys who lacked these tendencies" (153: p. 31). It seems probable that if there is any validity in the oral syndrome at all it must be associated with active alcoholism rather than as a trait carried over from childhood.

Psychoanalysts would reply to this by stating that the orality of alcoholism represents a *regression* to infancy. I personally find the concept of regression as improbable as that of atavism. Even if one accepts the concept of the oral regression hypothesis, it fails to explain why alcohol was the choice rather than milk or gluttony. Further, there is always the possibility that the oral drive is a product of biological rather than mental malfunction, for it is also symptomatic of diabetes. As Alexander points out in relation to that disease, ". . . from the early beginnings of life, an extreme oral-demanding attitude can be observed, an attitude which may not be fully explained by psychological experiences in the family" (71: p. 139). The compulsive consumption of certain foods by alcoholics closely parallels the cravings of the oral diabetics. As Gottesfeld and Yager point out that ". . . the alcoholic consumes large quantities of coffee and shows a great demand for glucose and other carbohydrates" (98: pp. 222-223). The possibility of a simple biological answer is therefore not impossible. However, if such is eventually provided, it will not be as satisfactory to some as the older mysticism of analysis. It has frequently impressed me that one of the primary functions of psychoanalysis is that it can be used to replace theology in a materialistic age crying for a dogma that will account for every mystery of life.

Aside from its basic premise, however, the oral hypothesis does include some behavioral definitions that do seem to apply to large numbers of alcoholics. These traits include being dependent, childlike, passive and immature. The dependent aspect has especially been cited by alcohologists and Blum does a very capable summary of those who see dependency as ". . . a predisposing element in the genesis of alcoholism" (155: p. 265). While admitting the dependency factor, I question whether it is in every case present prior to the disease. I have known several alcoholics who developed the disease late in life and had by then gained enormous economic and professional power and totally lacked any evidence of a pathological dependency. When alcohol finally *flattened* these, they indeed became dependent. Again the psychoanalysts would explain this by the miracle of regression. I think the explanation is simpler. These alcoholics ended up in hospitals and all patients are, by definition, dependent.

Tremper also has pointed out that the dependency concept in alcoholism may be the result of social imposition rather than an inherent part of the disease (156). Most sick people are dependent but the dependency is a by-product of the illness. Also, as with any quality, the question can be raised as to where on a continuum it becomes pathological. To be human is to be dependent. Evans-Pritchard, for example, cites Radcliffe-Brown, who stated ". . . that religion is everywhere an expression of a sense of dependence" (157: pp. 74-75). Yet, all psychiatrists would not necessarily regard priests as suffering from a pathological dependency any more than the religious would see the analysts' reliance on Freud as a manifestation of an immature dependency. It seems probable to me that dependency will be classified as patthological in those areas where the culture or the therapist proscribe it in normal behavior. The American core-value of self-reliance (158), which is usually defined in economic terms, is not violated if one is ill through no fault of one's own. However, the moral condemnation of alcoholism, which pervades both popular and therapeutic minds, does not excuse the alcoholic his dependency, but rather makes it into a character defect to explain the pathological behavior. The positive feedback between alcoholism and economic need continues to increase the dependency. As Charles McCabe has written in his lovely column, "There is nothing more antipathetic to making money than drinking spirits" (159). Therefore, while many alcoholics are indeed *dependent* before the beginning of pathological drinking, others develop this trait as a result of the disease.

Having classified the alcoholic as dependent, many alcohologists therefore conclude that he is "infantile" and wants "to be treated like a child" (120). This attitude is explained by the statement that the individual has chosen alcoholism ". . . as a substitute for emotionally mature adaptation" (155: p. 264). Therefore, the *immature* alcoholic uses alcohol as the inappropriate response to situations calling for adult reason. This last statement is undoubtedly true. The reasons for it, however, are unclear to all but the psychoanalysts. Freud saw the pattern of inappropriate responses beginning in childhood, apparently after the trauma of too early a weaning. In this interpretation, Freud's letter to Fliess (160) is quoted by Blum (155: p. 263), "It has occurred to me that masturbation is the one great habit that is a 'primary addiction,' and that the other addictions, for alcohol, morphine, tobacco, etc., only enter into life as a substitute and replacement for it." The relativity of all judgments is seen in the contrasting views of masturbation. Colin Wilson seeing it from another angle could conclude that "Absurd as it sounds, masturbation is one of the highest faculties mankind has yet achieved" (161: pp. 30-31). Whether "the primary addiction" or "the highest faculty," no analyst has advocated regressing the alcoholic to masturbation which would certainly be far less harmful to him than ethanol.

While many psychiatrists have followed Freud by interpreting the alcoholic as questing for the security of his premasturbation infancy, as many see him as self-destructive. The fact that alcoholism is wasteful has been noted by all who have witnessed it. Somerset Maugham commented on this in "The Vessel of Wrath" which portrayed the alcoholic Ginger Ted. The "Controleur," wrote Maugham, "liked the reckless way in which Ginger Ted squandered the priceless treasure of life" (162). Some alcohologists interpret this wasteful and self-destructive behavior as a manifestation of masochism and state that the alcoholic continually seeks self-inflicted punishments (155: p. 265; 75: p. 333). Leslie Osborn commented on the biological oddity of such behavior when he wrote, "From the viewpoint of biology it is surprising to find any organism deliberately hurting itself . . ." (89: p. 59).

Others see alcoholism as going beyond masochism and actually being a form of total self-destruction. Ryback has expressed one common interpretation when he stated that "In a sense, alcoholism may be viewed as a socially accepted form of suicide" (163: p. 1010). Blum cites the enormous numbers of studies which see alcoholism as "slow suicide" (155: p. 265). However, it was probably Karl Menninger who is best known for dealing with this approach. He wrote, ". . . alcoholism is chosen or substituted as a kind of lesser self-destruction serving to avert a greater self-destruction" (120: p. 181). If one accepts this hypothesis, it should today be extended and one would conclude that all cigarette smokers are consciously pursuing a slow suicide. I think this is improbable. Likewise, Cutter and his associates found that while some alcoholics are suicidal, others are not (164). My data is in agreement with this conclusion. More specifically, I found that most alcoholics in the early stages of the disease were pursuing life rather than death. However, there can be no doubt that the alcoholic in the advanced stages often feels life to be hopeless and would welcome death. I strongly suspect, therefore, that in the Cutter study an analysis would show the suicide-prone individuals to be those most advanced in the disease.

Whether interpreted as *oral* or *suicidal,* all alcohologists agree that the alcoholic lacks the ability to cope adequately with most aspects of life. Several have interpreted this inability in terms of a lack of power. This definition would be in agreement with alcoholic *childishness, dependency* and the feeling of hopelessness that may lead to suicide. If the aggressive drive is inherent to social mammals and essential for a successful life way, as the ethologists and psychoanalysts claim, its lack would certainly create a malfunctioning individual. The "oral character," as Lowen points out, "has a weak aggressive drive" (165: p. 370). This lack of aggressiveness, in my opinion, outweighs all other components of the oral hypothesis.

Alfred Adler was probably the first to describe alcoholism as a mechanism to achieve a sense of power as a compensation for a profound feeling of inferiority (166). A recent book by David McClelland picks up the drinking-for-power theme again (167). As this book states, "The studies reported in this volume gradually led to the formulation of the hypotheses that drinking serves to increase power fantasies and that heavy liquor drinking characterizes those whose personal power needs are strong and whose level of inhibition is low" (167: p. 276). I am in agreement with the power hypothesis which is also sanctioned by our popular culture. The general agreement on it is reflected in jokes about the drunk who "can beat any man in the house" and "feels ten feet tall" after a few drinks. Alcoholic-derived bravery has long been known as *Dutch courage*. In fiction, readers of P. G. Wodehouse will know that Bertie Wooster had discovered the same principle nearly two decades ahead of McClelland. Bertie, terrified at an upcoming dinner with the dreadful Trotters, accepted one of Jeeves' "Specials." "The effect was magical. That apprehensive feeling left me, to be succeeded by a quiet sense of power. I cannot put it better than by saying that as the fire coursed through my veins, Wooster the timid fawn became in a flash Wooster the man of iron will, ready for anything" (168: p. 12).

One of McClelland's colleagues, Sharon C. Wilsnack, agrees with him only on male drinkers. She concluded that ". . . drinking does not increase feelings of power in women but can temporarily enhance feelings of womanliness" (169). The same distinction was made in 1967 by Catanzaro who said: "One of the biggest conflicts present in many alcoholics revolves around their manliness, womanliness or lack thereof. Over and over again in therapy, alcoholics expand the theme that alcohol makes them feel like the real he-man or she-woman they always wanted to be" (74: p. 40). I obtained equivalent responses from most of the alcoholics whom I interviewed in depth. Again in such analyses, word traps are easy. A woman drinking in quest of *womanliness* is drinking for one type of traditional power. Further, to achieve a desired sense of power certainly contributes to tension reduction. Moreover, drinking for power is far too great a generalization to cover all instances of drinking and overdrinking. Many drink merely as a rite of social conformity. Others get drunk to achieve oblivion rather than in the pursuit of power. And, as I have already indicated, advanced alcoholics may drink in the hope of death.

CHAPTER IV:

THE ALCOHOLIC'S BODY

W HILE BEHAVIORISTS WERE explaining alcoholism by such concepts as tension reduction, oral frustration and power questing,
others were seeking to explain the disease in biological terms.
The behavioral and environmental dogmatists have replied by
ignoring or denying any such possibility. In 1960, for example,
Lolli stated that "No differences as yet have been found in the
bodily structures or functions between addictive drinkers and
other men or women." However, Lolli does admit that "Such
differences may exist" (109: p. 211). Eleven years later Verden
and Shatterly express the same verdict more strongly when they
said that, "Despite numerous attempts to establish a physiological
or biochemical explanation of compulsive drinking, no such
causes have been isolated" (86: p. 331). Because of the lack of
the positive identification of a specific biological factor, Verden
and Shatterly thereby reject even its possibility and pontificate
that

> . . . the placing of 'alcoholism' within the physically-construed
> medical model of illness has worked a detrimental effect on the
> public's conception of alcoholism, the alcoholic's understanding of
> his own condition, and has created a hindrance to the advancement
> of scientific knowledge concerning alcohol abuse (86: p. 335).

This somehow reminds me of the early carping about research
on the source of yellow fever by the *informed* who knew that it
was due to an unidentified swamp miasma. As I have already
indicated, the behaviorist approach has also failed to explain
alcoholism and such dogmatic adherence to an unproven psychocultural thesis has also created a hindrance to the advancement
of scientific knowledge.

The more experienced and knowledgeable specialists in
alcoholism, even though they emphasize the behavioral aspects,

44

realize that there must be a biological base to the disease. Ruth Fox, for example, states, "We must not lose sight of the fact that there is surely an underlying biochemical disturbance in alcoholism" (75: p. 328). No one with any experience in the alcoholic field can deny that many differences have been identified in the alcoholic's physical being.

As with psychological traits, however, the question can validly be raised as to whether these differences contribute to the alcoholism or are products of it. Some of these, as Claeson and Carlsson point out, are clearly the result of heavy drinking. Specifically, these authors identify ". . . liver disease, alcoholic cardiomyopathy, alcoholic myopathy and polyneuropathy" as by-products of "excessive drinking" (170: p. 317). Other traits are not so easily identified as preceding or following the onset of alcoholism. As an example, Kalant (130: p. 81) uses some of the findings of Olson and his associates (171). These researchers find alcoholics to be deficient in the conversion of tryptophane to urinary 5-hydroxyindoleacetic acid but are unable to demonstrate whether this condition exists before the beginning of alcoholism. Further, the interrelation of physical and mental factors in any area of human behavior makes research along these lines most difficult. As Mazur and Robertson point out, ". . . it usually is not possible to distinguish a particular biological mechanism or even a set of mechanisms which can be associated with psychological states or social behavior" (28: p. 156). Nevertheless, for years significant findings have pointed to the probability of biological factors in the etiology of alcoholism. I do not think this work can be ignored.

The earliest biological determinists labeled alcoholism as a hereditary defect. As early as 1867, as Hawkins points out (172: p. 14), Charcot (173) believed that heredity played a role in alcoholism. The first formal study of the genetic factor in alcoholism, according to Cruz-Coke (174: p. 335), was that of Legrain (175) in 1889. Dr. Benjamin Rush, an early American pioneer in alcoholism, also saw a possible hereditary factor in pathological drinking (176). From those times to the present, continuing studies have indicated a strong probability of a genetic factor in the disease. As Partanen and his colleagues point out (177:

p. 131), Kroon in 1924 and Amark in 1951 both concluded that heredity is a major factor in alcoholism. Kalant (130) has noted that many of the so-called nutritional determinists also see an ultimate hereditary factor behind alcoholism.

The psychocultural determinists have either ignored this genetic research or tried to explain it away. As many have noted, the fact that alcoholism frequently runs in families does not confirm an hereditary hypothesis. Wexberg states, "The fact that it often clusters in families can be explained by the theory emphasizing environmental influences" (178: p. 118). Thus, the onus would go onto the parents as bad models rather than as the sources of defective genetic material. As Blum says of this explanation, "Patients are said to identify with these inadequate models" (155: p. 265). Karl Menninger firmly stated the position of the behaviorists when he said, "Alcoholism cannot possibly be an hereditary trait" (120: p. 177). Landis and Bolles deny that there can even be an inherited tendency toward alcoholism (70: pp. 227-228). The McCords report from their study that ". . . evidence for a hereditary explanation of the disorder is lacking"(153: p. 28). Roe and Burks (179), in a study of foster children of alcoholics, found that none of these became alcoholic, which strongly bolstered the behaviorist denial of a genetic factor.

While the psychocultural determinists were disproving the genetic hypothesis, others were selectively breeding strains of rats that manifested an hereditary predisposition to excessive alcohol consumption (180, 181, 182). At the same time, some therapists were concluding that only heredity could explain the etiology of some of their alcoholic cases. Catanzaro, for example, describes two observations which suggest ". . . a high degree of genetic biological determinancy for alcohol" (74: p. 35). One of these is that some of his patients were literally alcoholics from their first drink. Most therapists have encountered such alcoholics and I found a sizable number of them in my sample. Secondly, Catanzaro describes the reverse phenomenon: several of his patients consciously set out to become alcoholic but could not make it. These would seem to lack a genetically endowed ability to join the unhappy ranks of alcoholics.

Despite the reasonableness of observations like Catanzaro's, specific studies on alcoholic heredity have failed to show uniformity in the resulting evidence. At one point, for example, Cruz-Coke seemed to offer fairly solid proof of a genetic binding of color-blindness and alcoholism (174). Smith and Brinton, however, then demonstrated that such color blindness is probably temporary and secondary to alcoholism (183). What was needed, as Wexberg pointed out in 1950 (178), were valid twin studies. Several of these have since appeared. Eysenck found a very strong correlation of heredity and alcoholism in his study of twins (17: p. 126). Partanen and his colleagues (177) cite several other twin studies which indicate a positive correlation. Further, their own work on twins seems to be overwhelmingly in support of the genetic hypothesis. If one ignores the complex Finnish definition of alcoholism which includes such social consequences as arrests, the authors conclude that their study ". . . shows significant heritability" (177: p. 128) in the etiology of alcoholism. In 1972 a study of half-siblings by Schuckit, Goodwin, and Winokur (184) comes to the same conclusion.

Actual biological examination of alcoholics by Denes de Torok at first seemed to strengthen the genetic argument when he announced that his study of two hundred alcoholic patients demonstrated that they lacked ". . . entire sets or parts of chromosomes" (185). However, in a 1972 publication de Torok writes,

> The question arises as to whether the observed irregularities have to do with alcoholism-proneness or whether excessive alcoholic consumption over a period of years has induced changes in the studied victims. While the question cannot be answered with absolute certainty, it is suggested that the chromosomal aberrations are likely to be secondary, consequential changes rather than causative ones (186: p. 99).

Although the genetic studies are thus open to question, they do offer sufficient grounds for skepticism of the psychocultural dogmas.[7] Even assuming that personality is the primary cause in

---

[7] The case for a genetic basis of alcoholism has been greatly strengthened by the research of Donald W. Goodwin, M.D. as reported in his paper "Is Alcoholism Inherited?", delivered at the Third Annual Conference of the National Institute on Alcohol Abuse and Alcoholism, Washington, D.C., June 20-22, 1973.

alcoholism, genetic factors are not automatically ruled out. Insel, in a recent study of grandmothers and grandsons in London, concluded that the personality similarities "can better be explained by genetic or biochemical process" than by environmental factors (187). From ancient Greece to the present, some have postulated that heredity determines both one's physical form and an associated personality. In the 1940's, for example, Sheldon wrote extensively on the correlation of physical type and personality (188, 189, 190). He, incidentally, believed that *mesomorphs* (muscular types) were the most prone to alcoholism. On the other hand, Lecomte in 1950 claimed that the individual with a *pyknic* (fattish) constitution was the most likely to become an alcoholic (191).

Even if the genesis of alcoholism has not been confirmed as biological, some of its behavioral manifestations seem to be better explained by body than by mind. One example of this is the phenomenon of alcoholic amnesia or *blackout*. At one time nearly all behaviorists explained this in purely psychological terms. This was sharply brought home to me some years ago while attending a seminar of alcohologists. My suggestion that such blackouts might be primarily a biological fact was greeted with a solicitous concern for my ignorance. Today, however, the work of Ryback appears to strengthen the possibility that the blackout is primarily physical in nature. Working with goldfish, Ryback found good evidence for a neurophysiological or neurochemical basis for alcoholic amnesia (192: p. 605). Working with humans, Ryback has taken cognizance of the fact that many have suggested hypoglycemia as being a significant factor in blackouts (193: p. 623). However, he does not second this interpretation, but instead concludes

> . . . that alcoholic amnesia and the Korsakoff memory deficit can both be explained, respectively, by acute and chronic disruption of the limbic system, especially that portion from hippocampus to cortex. With alcohol amnesia there may be an acute disruption of electrical activity either by direct suppression, by occult seizure, or by blocking of hippocampal output (193: p. 628).

In a later work (163), however, Ryback accommodates his interpretations slightly toward the behavioral approach. Here, though maintaining the blackout as physiological, he postulates that this condition may be actively pursued by the alcoholic to fulfill certain psychic needs. This is an interesting hypothesis, but it runs directly counter to all I know about alcoholism.

While just one aspect of alcoholism such as the blackout is difficult to understand, the tasks of explaining the whole syndrome in biological terms seems overwhelming. However, a number of attempts have been made. As Jellinek (4: p. 86) points out, one of the oldest biological theories is that of alcoholism as an allergy, first presented in 1896 by Toulouse. The allergy theory was revived by Silkworth in 1937 (194) and through his influence on Bill Wilson adopted into the formal philosophy of A.A. It also led to attempts to develop anti-alcoholic serums (195) which, however, failed to be of value. Herbert Karolus (196) did in fact find alcoholics showing allergic reactions to various grains such as rye and wheat from which distilled beverages are manufactured. However, no specific allergy to ethanol has been demonstrated in the disease of alcoholism. Block even denies the possibility of this and bluntly states that ". . . alcoholism is not an allergy" (197: p. 29). Randolf (198), on the other hand, described alcoholism as the product of a "masked food sensitivity," which would relate it to the allergy concept. Further linguistic confusion is created by the fact that many authors use the term "allergy" as a metaphor for "psychological allergy" (4: p. 80). Others use the word allergy in the alcoholic literature as an analogy (70: p. 229). This is the usual use of the word by the more knowledgeable A.A.'s.

Another approach has been to define alcoholism as the product of an inadequate metabolic process. Perhaps the best known of these *nutritional* theories is that of Roger Williams (199, 200, 201, 202, 203). He maintains that the alcoholic inherits a metabolic defect which produces a craving for alcohol because of nutritional deficiencies. Specifically, he sees these deficiencies as due to the lack of certain enzymes. He has further stated that these deficiencies could be corrected by nutritional supplements. Vitamins and other supplements do indeed seem to help many alcoholics in abstaining from drinking. Smith and his associates, for example, found that the megavitamin approach with alcoholics produced ". . . a decrease in desire for alcohol and a reduction of tension, hostility and insomnia . . ." (204: p. 384). O'Malley and his co-workers also found ". . . a diminished craving for alcohol . . . in many patients receiving vitamin supplements. . . ." (205). In recent years impressive claims have been made for Niacin (Vitamin B₃) in the rehabilitation of both schizophrenics and alcoholics (203: p. 174; 206: pp. 67-72). Glutamine likewise seems to reduce alcoholic preference in both rats and human alcoholics (130: pp. 78-79; 203: pp. 172-174). Alcoholics also seem to have low levels of magnesium (207; 203: p. 174) and calcium. Calcium imbalance, it is believed, in itself may cause behavioral abnormalities and is one possible explanation of the phenomenon known as "arctic hysteria" (29: pp. 265-270). Calcium is probably involved in the resemblance of alcoholism to anoxia that has been noted by O'Brien (208: p. 190). He also found the administration of calcium of great benefit in the treatment of alcoholism (208, 209).

Low calcium levels may also be a factor related to the frequency of hypoglycemia in alcoholics. As early as 1943, Voegtlin and his associates found "seriously deranged" carbohydrate metabolism in the majority of 303 alcoholics tested (210: p. 164). It should be noted that these impressive results were from using a four-hour test and hypoglycemia frequently does not show up until the fifth hour. The longer test, then, probably would have shown an even higher incidence of hypoglycemia. In 1971, Cheraskin and Ringsdorf stated that "Evidence provided by six-hour glucose tolerance tests in alcoholics show that hypoglycemia exists in from 70 to 90 percent" (206: p. 57). At least 90 percent of my alcoholic respondents who were tested also proved to be hypoglycemic. Several of these had earlier been diagnosed as diabetic on the basis of a simple blood-sugar test, but the longer test in each case demonstrated the error of the earlier diagnosis. I have unconfirmed reports of alcoholics being diagnosed as diabetic on the basis of the simple test and later going into shock as the result of insulin therapy.

We do not know if the hypoglycemia is a condition that existed prior to the alcoholism or merely as a product of it. I suspect that in a large number of cases it did in fact precede pathological drinking. Many of my respondents reported hypoglycemic symptoms before they began drinking. Such traits included chronic exhaustion, sudden periods of sweating and acute anxiety. The brain itself is strongly affected by drops in blood sugar as glucose is critical to its normal functioning. Any drop in glucose levels therefore probably creates a *need* for it or a near equivalent. Alcohol perhaps satisfies this need and possibly more rapidly than sugar itself. It may be literally true that "Candy's dandy but liquor's quicker." As early as 1941, Tennent pointed to the large number of studies which showed that ". . . alcohol of itself may cause an increase of sugar in the blood" (211: p. 271). In 1951, Pansini and Casaula from their own research concluded that alcohol perhaps enhances the utilization of sugar (212). In the same year, Lovell and Tintera noted a delayed negative effect on blood sugar levels that may explain the *hooking* mechanism of alcoholism. They reported that "The consumption of alcohol produces an initial hyperglycemia but shifts quickly to hypoglycemia" (213: p. 5). Nitzuleczu and associates also noted that alcohol ". . . has the tendency to lower blood sugar levels in many experimental animals and in healthy and diabetic human subjects" (214). In 1963, Dr. Frederick G. Hudson of San Francisco informed me that his research uniformly showed an ultimate blood sugar drop in alcoholics after the initial relieving experience. It seems quite possible then that the alcoholic experiences a relief when he begins drinking, but at the same time inaugurates a mechanism which will shortly drop his sugar level and thus recreate the need for more alcohol.

If the alcohol thus creates the need to drink more, one may ask why the alcoholic may feel a compulsion to imbibe when he has been sober for any period. I believe that many alcoholics suffer from perpetually low blood sugar with all its associated negative effects. Others have a metabolic system which triggers a drop in blood sugar under any form of stress. The probability that psychic discomfort can produce hypoglycemia has been demonstrated in rats by Paolino of Purdue and DeFeudis of Indiana University. They found that isolating mice for four to

five weeks decreased glucose uptake in the brain by 70 percent
(215). Simple exhaustion is likewise a correlate of low glucose
levels and Lolli points out that ". . . a certain business executive
finds that his late afternoon fatigue is relieved by a glass of
sherry which lifts his blood sugar" (109: p. 22). The same lift,
of course, could be obtained by eating candy, although the effect
would not be felt so quickly. As George Watson says, ". . . if
you think you need a drink, you don't need a drink; you need
ATP (energy) derived from acetate through the breakdown of
blood sugar, fat, and protein" (38: p. 105).

The fact of a certain functional equivalence of alcohol and
sugar has been shown in a number of rat studies. Many of these
show that rats will increase their appetite for alcohol when under
psychological stress. However, it has also been demonstrated
that these same rats will prefer a sugar solution to alcohol if
given the choice (216). Mardones and his colleagues (180) and
Rogers and McClearn obtained similar results (217) with rats
and mice respectively. Alcoholics have also discovered sugar
as an alcohol substitute, although its results fall far short of the
effects produced by ethanol. Many have noted, as did Voegtlin
and his associates in 1943, ". . . the craving of alcoholics for sugar
between sprees and their avoidance of sweets during the drinking
phase. . . ." (210: p. 163). However, I have known many
alcoholics who have tried to slow down their drinking rate by
forcing themselves to eat a piece of candy or a lump of sugar
between each drink. All found the practice *revolting*, and none
reported any success in this attempt to moderate their alcoholic
consumption. However, I have rarely witnessed an alcoholic
sober up who did not experience a powerful need for sugar in
some form during the first sober months. Others have told me
that sugar consumption ameliorates the anxiety of *dry drunks*
and weakens the drive for a drink during these periods. However,
in the long run, most alcoholics find that a steady diet of sweets
does not successfully relieve their discomfort. This is due to the
unfortunate fact that sugar, like alcohol, produces an eventual
hypoglycemic reaction. Most of the sober alcoholics I know
who have investigated the subject or received competent medical
advice find they are most comfortable on a high protein diet free

of most sugars and carbohydrates. Hypoglycemia is thus a major factor in alcoholism, but certainly not the only one. The significance of hypoglycemia in general has been largely ignored by the medical profession, although many of the reading public have profited by self-diagnosis and reliance on a hypoglycemic diet. This is reflected in the massive reissues and sales of Abramson and Pezet's *Body, Mind and Sugar* which first appeared in 1951 (218). Recently, hypoglycemia has reversed itself from being a medically ignored condition to practically a fad and laboratories are crowded with patients receiving glucose tolerance tests.

The significance of metabolic variation between populations may also be suggestive. It is conceivable that genetic factors affecting the utilization of sugar and alcohol may predispose certain populations to alcoholism. This is at least indicated in the study by William Hood of recent changes in the diet of Tarahumara Indians who are coming increasingly under the influence of the dominant Mexican culture (219). With these changes in nutrition, the Tarahumara are developing ". . . an inordinate appetite for refined sugar and distilled spirits." Hood resumés his research by stating, "In short, a metabolic advantage, probably genetic, is converted to a serious disadvantage by exposure to high caloric concentrates, with an expectation of obesity, diabetes and ischanic heart disease." If this proves true, there will also be an increase in alcoholism. Hood sees the political implications of genetic research referred to earlier. He realizes that "Raising the specter of genetic difference is considered heresy at worst and poor taste at best. . . . But science leads where it will go, not necessarily where we want it to go." An alternate explanation, however, may be applicable. The psychic stress of accelerated acculturation in itself could produce low blood sugar levels and thus create the taste for sugar and alcohol.

It is conceivable, however, that diet in itself could help explain regional differences in the incidence of alcoholism. I have long been struck by the fact that alcoholism accompanied by behavioral problems is most common in an alcoholic crescent from European Russia through Scandinavia and Finland, England and Ireland, and into North America. France, Italy and Spain have addictive drinking, but unlike the areas mentioned above, are not greatly bothered by drunken behavior. The cultures of the alcoholic crescent are also heavy milk and sugar consumers. In the U.S. especially, children are practically bathed in a surfeit of sugar in soft drinks, pastry and candy while accepting the idea that "every body needs milk." Lactate is a by-product of gluconeogenesis and its body levels could possibly be affected by a heavy intake of milk, sugar or both. It has also been demonstrated that lactate by itself will produce anxiety and may be of major significance in alcoholism (49). It may well be that there is a correlation between lactate levels and the presence of lactase, the enzyme responsible for the digestion of milk. Genetically, lactase is primarily limited to the white population within the alcoholic crescent (220). The correlation of lactase to the dairying cultures shows its presence to be a result of natural selection through long periods of time (220, 221). The milk cultures of such dairying countries will encourage massive consumption of the cows' product from infancy to death. Both adult consumption and the substitution of cow for human milk in infancy may be involved in altering human metabolism. The lack of mother's milk may deprive the infant of factors essential for an adequate development. It has long been known that a baby raised on human milk has a higher tolerance to certain diseases. Moreover, at the Ninth International Congress of Nutrition held in Mexico City, it was reported that "bottle feeding in lieu of breast feeding may produce an individual who will suffer obesity for life" (222, 223). Thus, the milk that everybody needs may be only that of its own species. The lack of mother's milk with an extension of drinking cow milk into adulthood may be major factors in producing both alcoholism and obesity.

France, Italy and Spain have never become obsessive milk-drinkers like the Scandinavians and the Americans. Like the Chinese, they seem to believe that God intended cows' milk for calves. They also are primarily wine consumers. In both their wines and their *sweets*, they also have shown a preference for natural fruit sugars, unlike the cultures of the alcoholic crescent which emphasize refined sugar. While Americans are eating candy, these southern Europeans prefer fructose. As McLaughlin puts it, "Among the French, the Italians, the Jews, there is a sort of racial obsession with fruit" (224, p. 38). These also are the ethnic groups that have no major problem with drunken behavior. Although entirely speculative, one might theorize that excessive use of refined sugar, cow's milk and distilled alcohol is conducive to alcoholism associated with drunken behavior. On the other hand, alcoholic addiction without drunkenness may go with fructose, and avoidance of milk (but not cheese) and wine drinking. Fructose in itself seems to negate some of the intoxicating effects of alcohol (225) and may conceivably modify the metabolic process to mitigate against drunkenness.[8]

A faulty metabolism by itself is seen by some biological determinists as an adequate explanation of alcoholism. Specifically, a dysfunction in the endocrine system is the crucial explanation in many theories. Tintera and Lovell, for example, describe a basic hypoadrenocorticism leading to hypoglycemia which produces a craving for alcohol (213). Goldfarb and Berman are in agreement that the adrenal anomalies precede alcoholism (52). Smith also concurs (226). Wexberg, on the other hand, sees hypoadrenocorticism as secondary to the alcoholism (178). One of the reasons for the disagreement on hypoadrenocorticism as cause or effect is in a definite identification of the appearance of its first symptoms. The syndrome as a whole involves the interaction of the pituitary, adrenal and gonadal systems and alcohol is known to affect all of these. For example, Gottesfeld and Yager (98: p. 223) and others have pointed out that in the alcoholic, the testicular tissue shows degenerative changes. All of the adrenogonadal steroids, which are affected by alcohol, strongly affect body hair growth and distribution. Smith, along with Tintera and Lovell, points to the rare occurrence of baldness among alcoholics as well as their sparse body hair as proof that the condition preceded alcoholism. Wexberg, however, attributes this hair pattern to the alcoholism itself. I find myself unable to agree with Wexberg. As is generally acknowledged, alcoholism may take up to twenty years of consistent drinking to manifest

---

[8] A newspaper reports (*San Francisco Chronicle*, Feb. 1, 1973, p. 2) that researchers at Lynn Hospital, Massachusetts, have discovered that intravenous fructose quickly sobers up drunks.

itself. Certainly partial or complete baldness could be expected in large numbers of these individuals before they become alcoholic. If alcoholism itself produced abundant head hair, the bald pates would vanish under a new healthy head of hair as the disease developed. More specifically, however, I asked large numbers of alcoholics who fit the Lovell-Tintera definition if their head or body hair distributions differed before and after the onset of alcoholism. The response was uniformly no, and most reported a consistent pattern and amount of body hair from postadolescence to the present. If hypoadrenocorticism is indeed a primary factor in alcoholism, a specific in its treatment should be adrenocortical extract (ACE). Some have indeed reported consistent and effective results using this approach (227). On the other hand, on the use of ACE, the McCords state that ". . . these experiments have not met with marked success" (153: p. 24).

Other glandular malfunctions have been noted in relation to alcoholism. Kalant (130: p. 78), for example, cites Goldberg (228) who found hypothyroidism in two-thirds of his alcoholic patients and he believes that this condition preceded the onset of alcoholism. Increasingly, the hypothalamus is being named as the ultimate source of a series of interlocking malfunctions that produce alcoholism. Jellinek (4: p. 101) points out that Smith (229) finally concluded that the alcoholic adrenal malfunction actually originated in the pituitary or the hypothalamus. Roger Williams in his last publication states ". . . that alcoholism probably results from an impairment of the cells in the appetite-regulating mechanism in the hypothalamus region of the brain" (203: pp. 170-171). Kalant (130: pp. 80-81) describes the work of Kissen and his co-workers who concluded that all the abnormal biological functions associated with alcoholism are ". . . regulated in one way or another by hypothalamic centers which can be influenced by emotional and environmental stresses, constitute a source of discomfort which the alcoholic learns to relieve by the intake of alcohol." The work of Segal and his associates at the Moscow Psychiatric Research Institute further reinforces the probability of hypothalamic involvement in alcoholism (230).

Valles bluntly states that ". . . the direct action of alcohol in the hypothalamus produces chronic alcoholism" (231: p. 56).

Valles' position that alcohol itself produces alcoholism is strongly reinforced by the work of Myers at Purdue. He gave intracranial injections of ethanol to rats which had never been exposed to alcohol. As a result of the injections these rats thereafter showed strong preference for alcohol over other beverages (232, 233). In effect, by this simple treatment Myers had converted *normal* rats into *alcoholic* rats. Myers, therefore, concluded that ". . . a new biochemical theory of alcoholism may have to be evolved with its primary focus on a metabolic aberration of the central nervous system" (232: p. 241). Later experiments by Myers and Veale showed that acetaldehyde, paraldehyde and methanol also produced an increase in alcohol preference. They note that as acetaldehyde is a by-product of alcohol metabolism, it "may play an important role in the alcohol disease state" (234: p. 111). Dahl has noted that acetaldehyde may cause psychological modifications as well (207). Redmond and Cohen, working with rats, found that males produce far more acetaldehyde than females, thus making possible the hypothesis that a male preponderance in alcoholism may be sex-linked (235). Later, Myers and his co-workers infused ethanol, acetaldehyde and paraldehyde into the cerebral ventricles of rhesus monkeys. Again they found that ethanol, and to a slighter extent acetaldehyde, increased alcohol preference. They could thus conclude that ". . . the effect on drinking of elevating the cerebral levels of ethanol does not appear to be species-specific" (236: p. 433). In resumé, Myers and Veale state,

> It would therefore appear that a constant elevation in the level of intracranial alcohol, for a prolonged period of time, is the main causal factor in the development of the strong alcohol preference. . . . Alcohol probably acts directly on one or more of the structures which form the walls of the cerebral ventricles and comprise the so-called 'drinking-emotional circuit' within the limbic system (32: p. 153).[9]

---

[9] A recent article by Candace B. Pert and Solomon H. Snyder identifies the opiate receptors in nervous tissue (Opiate receptor: demonstration in nervous tissue. *Science, 179*:1011-1014, 1973).

Myers also notes the strong probability that as a correlate of

58	The American Alcoholic

alcohol-induced cerebral alterations, imbalances of biogenic amines may play a major role in alcoholism. Specifically, he found a positive correlation between serotonin levels and alcoholic thirst and that a reduction in the serotonin removed the apparent need for alcohol. He and his colleagues have reported that orally administered p-chlorophenylalanine (p-CPA) drastically reduced preference for alcohol in both *drinker* and *nondrinker* rats. This negative reaction to available alcohol continued even after discontinuation of p-CPA. The function of p-CPA is to reduce serotonin levels and thus a direct relationship would seem to exist between serotonin level and appetite for ethanol (32, 133, 237, 238, 239). However, as the authors state that "Since whole-brain serotonin values return to normal within 16 days after the administration of p-CPA, an entirely different biochemical system may thus be involved in the resultant rejection of alcohol after administration of p-CPA" (237: p. 1470). In another publication, Myers hypothesizes that the alcoholic thirst or lack of it ". . . may be found to be controlled by a delicate balance in the presence and subsequent release of the endogenous biogenic amines" (138: p. 495). Thus, alcohol-induced cerebral impairment may cause an imbalance of the biogenic amines as reflected in part by a high serotonin level with an accompanying discomfort which motivates the consumption of alcohol. Blum, Wallace and Geller have also noted the possibility that disruption of normal biogenic amine functions by alcohol itself may contribute to alcoholism. They say, "Ethanol can alter monoamine metabolism in the normal brain. This change might result in an imbalance of certain inhibitory monoamines, such as glycine, and thereby play a significant role in the development of alcoholism" (240: p. 294). It therefore seems probable that alcohol in itself can create malfunctions and discomforts which more alcohol can temporarily relieve. I strongly suspect that the alcoholic malaise syndrome includes low blood sugar as well as biogenic amine imbalances. As ethanol temporarily elevates blood sugar, so it also works to correct the biogenic amine imbalance. Specifically, it has been demonstrated that alcohol, like p-CPA and reserpine, lowers serotonin levels (133: p. 380; 241: p. 74). Further, ethanol appears to be even far more effective in lowering serotonin in man than it is in rats (241: p. 77).

The biogenic amine imbalance combined with low blood sugar could well account for many of the emotional factors in alcoholism. There is today no doubt but that the biogenic amines relate to the emotions and are significant in abnormal behavior (242, 243). The biological correlates of emotions have been totally ignored by most behaviorists and environmentalists. Chapple comments on this, "Many non-biologists, in fact, still appear to believe that emotions operate in a world independent of the human body and are not physiological" (26: p. 59). In the same volume he defines emotions as ". . . the physiological and biochemical systems whose adaptive or maladaptive changes are an integral part of all behavioral patterns" (26: Preface, xi). There can be no doubt but that the role of the amines in the functioning of the central nervous system and resultant feelings and behavior is critical. However, the exact role of the amines has not as yet been specifically defined (242: p. 24). Continuing research, however, is beginning to clarify the role of such amines as serotonin in both alcohol and drug addiction (245).

Certain rough correlations of the amines and emotional states, however, have been known for some time. Although much work has been done in serotonin with valuable results, the full range of its effects on emotion and behavior have not yet been defined. Some believe that it produces a generalized "central excitation" (242: p. 24). Janov cites some work which tends to associate depression with low serotonin values (246: p. 102). In working with cats, MacDonnell and his co-workers found ". . . that serotonin is a potent suppressive agent in the modulation of affective defense at least at the level of the hypothalamus, a region rich in serotonin (244: p. 760). When their cats' serotonin levels were dropped, they became very nasty cats from our viewpoint. When they received intracranial serotonin they became placid. MacDonnell and Fessock also found that p-chlorophenylalanine enhanced the evoked response of predatory cats, implying a relation to the lowered serotonin level (244). Drops in serotonin, at least in cats, therefore seem to enhance aggression.

Serotonin, however, is only one of a multiplicity of physiological correlates to emotions and behavior. The roles of epinephrine (adrenaline) and norepinephrine (noradrenaline) are also highly significant. Funkenstein and his associates have described an epinephrine response to anxiety and a norepinephrine response to anger (247). Schildkraut and Kety describe a similar correlation.

> Increased epinephrine excretion seems to occur in states of anxiety or in threatening situations of uncertain or unpredictable nature in which active coping behavior may be required but has not been achieved. In contrast, norepinephrine excretion may occur in states of anger or aggression or in situations which are challenging but predictable and which allow active and appropriate behavioral responses to the challenge (242: p. 23).

Further, these authors cite the fact that injections of epinephrine produce ". . . subject symptoms resembling anxiety." Hoffer and Osmond (248) are of the opinion that the tension-producing mechanism of epinephrine may be stimulated by adrenochrome which may thus be a factor in the etiology of alcoholism. Because adrenochrome, like serotonin, has an indole nucleus similar to the hallucinogens, it may play a role in abnormal alcoholic behavior. It has also been postulated as a major factor in schizophrenia (249: pp. 3-4). Hoffer and Osmond speculate that in schizophrenia adrenochrome converts into adrenolutin and thus sparks the symptoms of the illness (53: pp. 51-54). The parallels between theories of alcoholism and schizophrenia have already been mentioned and there may be common factors in the development of each affliction. In both diseases, however, it is probable that no single biological factor determines emotional response, but rather a combination of interrelated factors.

As Pitts has pointed out, an increase in epinephrine also produces an increase in lactate and both are associated with anxiety. In fact, Pitts defines an anxiety-neurotic as one who is characterized by a chronic overproduction of adrenalin. Further, he postulates that ". . . alcoholism may be symptomatic of anxiety neurosis in men, and when it is, the alcoholism makes it difficult to diagnose anxiety neurosis" (49: p. 71). Some supporting evidence for this hypothesis is provided by the work of

Hobson who thus reviewed his research: "Anxiety levels of recovering alcoholics were tested by eye-blink conditioning. They were more anxious than normal nonalcoholics but less so than diagnosed anxiety-neurotics" (250: p. 976). The fact that this sample of alcoholics was less anxious than the anxiety-neurotics could be a function of the masking of the neurosis mentioned by Pitts due to an optimism produced by the fact that they were recovering, the possibility that the anxiety neurotics in Hobson's sample were extreme cases, or the possibility that alcoholics simply tend to be low-grade anxiety-neurotics.

I, personally, am very impressed by the possibility that alcoholics represent a type of anxiety neurosis. The major portion of my alcoholic sample manifested most of the primary symptoms of anxiety neurosis. Such an hypothesis would also bring together in a meaningful way most of our biological and behavioral information on alcoholics. I know of no description of the alcoholic that does not at least describe him as an anxious person who is unable to cope realistically with existence. In McClelland's terms, the alcoholic lacks "power" and therefore feels inadequate. His sense of inadequacy would prevent him from a realistic approach to life-problems. His failure to deal adequately with these problems would create anxiety which in turn would make him feel powerless and inadequate. This positive feedback on a behavioral level would be marked by the biological correlates of such responses. In short, the alcoholic exists in a stressful environment that he cannot handle.

Since the time of Cannon (251) and Selye (252), we also know that stress is a two-sided coin with both psychological and physiological symptomology. In 1942, Cannon demonstrated how fear inspired by black magic or witchcraft could so profoundly alter bodily functions that death resulted (253). Many American behavioral and environmental dogmatists will agree in such mental initiation of a psychosomatic phenomena. However, they then refuse to consider the possibility that one's physical state can affect one's psyche and emotions. In Europe, on the other hand, students of behavior have tended to stress the physical aspects of abnormal behavior while ignoring all psychological factors. Thus, in 1952 C. J. Jung wrote, "The dogma, or intellectual superstitution that only a physical cause can be really valid still blocks for the psychiatrist the way into the psyches of his patient. . . ." (254: p. 1). European psychiatry, because of its equal though opposite emphasis, is no more advanced than that practiced in America. In fact, explanations of behavior cannot rest on the basis of an either-or situation but must rest upon a holistic, interactional approach. As Mazur and Robertson put it,

> The day-to-day functioning of these biological attributes is not just a consequence of genetic instructions, however, they also depend on stimuli from the physical and social environment. It is at this level that most of the interaction between the biological and social environment occurs, with effects in both directions: biological on the social and social on the biological (28: p. 91).

The denial of either physical or psychological factors in alcoholic research can only hinder any meaningful progress. The psychological aspects of alcoholism have long been obvious. However, as Fabre and his colleagues have said, "It is conceivable that much of the morbidity of alcoholism is secondary to alcohol-induced endocrinopathy" (255: p. 483). While accepting the role of psychocultural factors, therefore, I must agree with Mazur and Robertson who ". . . predict that within ten years a significant segment of social psychology will be centered around hormone studies" (28: p. 160).

Accepting both psychological and biological correlates, then, alcoholism may be defined as a *stress disease*. The alcoholic lacks both the psychocultural and biological means of maintaining homeostasis. He has, however, sought in alcohol a chemical means to reduce the stress and anxiety of his condition. That condition is in large part physical. Some of the perimeters of the biological correlates have already been outlined, but exactly how each of these relates to the rest we as yet cannot say. As Chapple stated on stress research, "The field has become so vast that no single person has appeared to integrate the knowledge of today as Cannon earlier did" (26: Preface, xi). The answer, when it comes, will probably be the product of many corresponding minds.

What we do know, however, is significant. The biological uniqueness of the alcoholic has already been demonstrated in many laboratories and in a rough way the various findings interlock to show a relationship of the malfunctions. The "general adaptation syndrome," to use Selye's terms, has broken down and its "stress-fighting mechanism" fails to perform adequately (252). A pathological alcoholic axis runs from the cerebral areas, the limbic system, the hypothalamus and through the pituitary, thyroid, adrenal and gonadal glands. A resulting abnormal balance of the total endocrine system and the biogenic amines is accompanied by enzyme irregularity and abnormal sugar metabolism. Hypoglycemia is related to rises in epinephrine which correlates to a rise in lactate. The anxiety effects of high lactate levels go uncontrolled because of alcoholic hypocalcemia and hypoglycemia. Faulty inhibition of monoamine oxidase is also indicated. The end product of these malfunctions is a sense of discomfort and anxiety which the alcoholic has learned to relieve with alcohol. Unfortunately, the initial relief is followed by an alcohol-induced increase in the malfunctions producing increased discomfort and thus the need for the brief respite from discomfort another drink will produce.

The locus that is responsible for triggering this complex set of physiological abnormalities has not been located. However, increasing evidence is indicating that the pineal gland may be the master regulator of all systems involved in the biological aspects of normal and abnormal behavior. Descartes may have indeed been poetically correct when he identified the pineal as "the seat of the soul." Asimov refers to the work of Mark D. Atschule, who in 1957 injected schizophrenics with extracts from the pineal body which resulted in great improvement in their condition. Asimov postulated that this ". . . extract may conceivably be a hormone-like substance that controls the serotonin balance and thus acts as an arbiter of order in the brain" (42: p. 323). The "hormone-like substance" has been identified as the hormone melatonin. Work by Irving Geller has demonstrated that increasing melatonin levels in rats by depriving them of light creates a morbid appetite for alcohol (256).[10] At the Fifth International Congress on Pharmacology in 1972, Julius Axelrod gave a paper demonstrating that "Studies during the past decade have established that the pineal gland is an organ par excellence for neurochemical and neuropharmacological regulation" (257: p. 3). Melatonin emerges as involved in multiple regulatory functions ranging from biogenic amine levels to "an inhibitory effect on gonads by blocking the secretion of the luteinizing hormone." A pineal malfunction could thus explain all of the biological symptomology of the alcoholic. It may also be seen perhaps as the prime mechanism of other mental afflictions, which, in fact, often closely parallel alcoholism in some of the biological correlates. The probable high epinephrine level in alcoholics, for example, is paralleled in schizophrenics (247) and both are most likely controlled by the pineal either directly or indirectly. With schizophrenics and alcoholics both sharing a pineal-originated high level of epinephrine and serotonin, it is possible that alcoholism, by controlling these levels, is actually saving some alcoholics from psychosis. Cases of psychotic seizures in alcoholics upon being dried out are by no means unknown. Wallerstein has commented that alcoholism is, in fact, frequently a mechanism allowing borderline psychotics to avoid the full manifestation of a latent psychosis (258). I have observed a few cases where this was true, but I do not believe it to be typical.

We have clues, therefore, to the biological aspects of alcoholism. From these we may hypothesize an alcoholic syndrome originating in the pineal gland with ramifications throughout the body producing a psychic discomfort and an inability to withstand stress.

------

[10] Kenneth Blum has also demonstrated how an enforced darkness makes normal rats into alcohol consuming rats. Further, when returned to a normal environment, these rats continue to prefer alcohol to water. On the other hand, when the pineal gland is removed, rats in enforced darkness drink less alcohol than those who retain their pineal. Blum concludes that "It is possible that alcoholics may have highly active pineals." (*Science News*, *103*, No. 17:271, 1973).

CHAPTER V:

TO DRINK OR NOT TO DRINK

DESPITE THE AWARENESS of both biological and psychological factors in alcoholism, there is no definitive answer to the question of whether the alcoholic thirst is ultimately a psychological *compulsion* or a physiological *craving*. Here again the literature falls into a semantic jungle, for no one has come up with an adequate means to separate the two nor to measure the extent to which either can be an actual determinant of behavior. Mardones has defined craving as an "overpowering desire" (259) which would imply that anyone experiencing it would be unable to resist its dictates. Ludwig, however, in his study of 176 male alcoholics found less than one per cent who offered *craving* as a reason for going off the wagon. However, he does add that

> . . . it is quite possible that a far larger proportion of patients actually experienced craving than admitted it. In the process of intellectually elaborating on the 'gut level' feeling of craving, they may have misinterpreted this feeling, defined it in a socially desirable fashion, or employed an excuse which indicated to themselves and others that they were not addicted to alcohol (125: p. 95).

A more common interpretation than that of a constant or recurring craving is the concept that while dry the alcoholic may experience a psychological compulsion, but that one drink will trigger an uncontrollable craving. This philosophy is central to the thinking of Alcoholics Anonymous and is reflected in such expressions as "One drink means a drunk," or "One drink is too many and a thousand are not enough." Exactly the same belief is held by heavy cigarette smokers who have tried to give up the habit. As with alcoholics in A.A., they conclude that the choice is between total abstinence or heavy addictive use. I know several cigarette smokers who have successfully quit the habit only to relapse some years later after one *slip*. The same is true for a number of my alcoholic respondents who returned to active alcoholism after allowing themselves *one little drink*.

Several experiments of late, however, have tried to disprove the concept that alcohol by itself can create a desire for more alcohol. These experimenters are, of course, all dogmatists of either the behaviorist or environmental way of thinking. They are either ignorant of or totally ignore the physiological research that I outlined in the previous chapter. Further, they all show a naiveté about types of *alcoholism* and the degree of control alcoholics have in the earlier stages of the disease. These variations I will review later when I try to synthesize our conflicting interpretations of alcoholics and alcoholism. Further, many of these alcohologists put a heavy reliance upon the *self-reporting* of alcoholics despite the acknowledged fact that Ludwig so clearly states, "There are no objective standards to measure the truth of a subjective report" (125: p. 95). Others, including Trudy Summers (260), have also specifically called attention to the usual inaccuracies in such alcoholic self-reporting. When attempts are made in many of these projects to cross-check an alcoholic's report on his own behavior, those questioned are generally spouses or kin who, I have found, are frequently ignorant of much of the alcoholic's activities or will lie to try to maintain a good public image of him. I have the general impression that lying is most typical of the alcoholic who is reluctant to abandon drinking while alcoholics sincerely desirous of sobriety tend to be painfully honest.

One of the research experiments at Patton State Hospital in California claims to have disproved the "one drink—one drunk" hypothesis (261). Part of the conclusion rested on a questionnaire administered to alcoholic patients. The majority stated that they believed they could drink 16 ounces of liquor and stop while in the hospital, but could not do so "on the outside." I believe that this probably reflects a fairly correct estimation, but I do not agree with the authors that it disproves the concept of an alcohol-triggered compulsion. As I shall try to demonstrate later, almost any alcoholic under certain circumstances can limit his drinks just as a heavy smoker can avoid smoking during High

Mass. To temporarily master a compulsion does not mean that no compulsion exists nor that the individual is not experiencing acute discomfort. The Patton experiment, however, actually put their alcoholic sample to a drinking test. Each alcoholic patient was allowed to consume up to sixteen ounces of alcohol a day but no more. They were then carefully watched to see if any would be driven to sneak off the hospital grounds to drink in nearby bars or purchase alcohol in adjacent liquor stores. Only a small percentage ". . . found it necessary to leave the hospital to obtain more liquor." The authors admit that any patient thus leaving the grounds to drink ". . . knew that he would be transferred to a locked unit and then discharged from the hospital." The authors, in my opinion, totally fail to recognize the power of a possible craving in relation to other motivational drives. The alcoholics, it is implied, were self-committed and therefore desirous of treatment. Their desire not to lose the chance to obtain therapeutic help, plus the sharing of a possibly frustrated craving would certainly allow them to endure a high degree of discomfort. There is no indication of how advanced the alcoholism was in each patient, but as Jellinek has shown it is only in the last or "crucial phase" that the alcoholic almost loses all control to abstain after the intake of alcohol (117).

Other alcohologists, however, have come to the same conclusion as Patton Hospital—that alcohol does not trigger a compulsion or a craving in the alcoholic. Gottheil and his associates (144), for example, agree with the Patton Hospital conclusion. They, in part, use evidence of others who have doubted the *one drink—one drunk* hypothesis. These include Merry (262), Mello and associates (263), Mello (264) and Paredes and his colleagues (265). This array of support is impressive, but in science *truth* is determined by unequivocal evidence and not by ballot. Further, the evidence provided by the experiments of Gottheil and his co-workers, it seems to me, supports the opposite possibility as strongly as it does their own conclusion. Thirty-five per cent of their alcoholic sample chose not to participate in their highly contrived drinking experiments which were held within the confines of a hospital. This refusal could reflect an awareness by the alcoholics that alcohol would create more discomfort

than release in this environment so alien from their usual drinking milieu, and with an artificial and rigid schedule of available
liquor. More significantly, fifty-six percent of those who chose to
participate stopped drinking after one week. This could be
interpreted as a reaction to the discomfort caused by a constantly
rising compulsion that could not be sated by the available alcohol.
In the postdrinking week, the discomfort score of the heavy
drinkers was almost double that of the moderate and non-
drinkers. This could easily correlate with an aroused and now
blocked craving.

One shortcoming in all these experiments to disprove the
concept of craving is the undefined vagueness of the alcoholic
sample. In none of them is any attempt made to correlate
reactions to alcohol with the degree of development of the
sample's alcoholism. Far more significant is the experimenters'
too literal interpretation of the *one drink—one drunk* hypothesis.
They make the totally unfounded assumption that this concept
means that if an alcoholic takes one sip of alcohol he becomes
an automaton without a mind and is driven by forces beyond
his control to drink until collapse. This simplistic interpretation
is totally contrary to what we know of human nature and rests
on a biochemical determinism that is contrary to all theories of
the mind and of human motivation. These experimenters have
also ignored all of the literature on alcoholic progression which
indicates that a total lack of control after one drink is typical
only of very advanced alcoholism.

This misinterpretation of the one drink, one drunk hypothesis
was probably the product of listening to the formal philosophy
of Alcoholics Anonymous rather than to the actual alcoholic
experience of A.A.s. The basic premise of A.A. is that if drinking
continues, it will ultimately destroy the alcoholic. Therefore,
the alcoholic's only salvation is to practice total abstinence.
Further, every A.A. knows that in the early stages of this disease
he had considerable control of his alcoholic intake and could cut
it off under sufficient motivation. Of over 100 alcoholics that I
queried in one sample, only three per cent said they could not
quit drinking after one drink if other circumstances warranted

the discomfort they would suffer. Eighty-one percent of the sample also said that they knew from past experience that they could practice controlled drinking for an undeterminable period ranging from one day to over a year. What all alcoholics do know is that if they continue drinking, at some unpredictable time they will lose control and enter into a binge. Many have paralleled their drinking to Russian Roulette. This is precisely what an alcoholic means by loss of control. I witnessed several A.A.'s attempt to return to normal drinking and all temporarily succeeded, only to end in catastrophic drunks. None could explain what went wrong when they entered the drunk. It seems probable, however, that the physical resistance they had built up by an earlier sobriety broke down under the steady intake of alcohol. This hypothesis would seem to be supported by some of the experiments by Mendelson (266). With alcoholics to whom he daily administered alcohol, it took several days of imbibing for the craving to become noticeable.

It is also possible that the craving, in at least some alcoholics, is a cyclical phenomenon and even perhaps associated with the biological Circadian rhythms of the alcoholic. Marty Mann has commented on periods of alcoholic control which would be meaningful to this hypothesis. She stated that

> It is true with many alcoholics, even in the advanced stages of alcoholism, there are occasions now and then when their power of choice and restraint seem miraculously returned to them. They have memorable evenings when they are able to drink along with (and no more than) the company they are in; memorable days when daylong nipping is negligible and seems to have no untoward effect; memorable periods when for a few days they seem to need no more than the normal nonalcoholic drinker takes; even thrice-memorable times when they can consume their usual excessive amount and not show it (5: pp. 9-10).

Voegtlin and his associates also recognized the cyclic nature of the loss of control among alcoholics and hypothesized that this phenomenon may relate to periodic hypoglycemia. They point to ". . . the possibility that a hypoglycemic tendency might be cyclic in nature and correspond to the episodic desire of the periodic inebriate" (210: p. 180). Cutter and his co-workers doubt the absolutism of the one drink, one drunk hypothesis but do postulate the possibility of such cyclical periods of craving. They suggest that ". . . it may be possible to extinguish the craving for alcohol or to train the alcoholic to maintain abstinence during periods of craving so that moderate drinking can be enjoyed by the alcoholic at other times" (267: p. 377). This is a noble suggestion but not, I think, a practical one. In fact, I do not see how the alcohologists could train an alcoholic to recognize a "craving" when they cannot even adequately define it nor agree on its reality.

Despite such disagreement among the specialists, I am convinced that the craving is real and the alcoholics know that it is. However, like pain of all kinds, it differs in quality and quantity between individuals and within the individual through time. When present, it is never comfortable, but an alcoholic can frequently live with it without succumbing to drunkenness if other factors are strong enough to motivate sobriety. I know a few alcoholics who abstain except for the wine of Holy Communion. They agree that this frequently creates a desire for more alcohol, but it is a desire that in these circumstances they can endure. I know four others, young in the disease, who abstain except for a single cocktail or glass of wine on occasions when it would be socially embarrassing to refuse. All state that this usually establishes a craving for more but that the rewards of social acceptance in these circles is enough to motivate them to endure their felt need. All also believe from past experience that a second drink would probably destroy their ability to stop short of a drunk. One of these has told me that on several occasions when he tried this single drink approach he "had" to leave the party early to continue drinking in bars where he was unknown. In all probability these four will in time lose this ability of painful control as the disease and the craving response increases.

Many alcoholics have tried to describe to me the indescribable nature of the craving and the losing ability to resist it. They agree that up to a certain point under the right circumstances it can be endured but that the endurance period lessens as the disease progresses. Most descriptions were in terms of biological analogies. Several compared it to the ability to ignore and delay the demands of bowel or bladder. The most graphic compared alcoholic craving to the urgency of an aroused sex drive. One respondent said,

> Most of the time that I was in college I could go out with my girl and we would engage in sex play for hours but always stop short of actually performing the act. I always wanted to go through with it and she said that she did too, but we didn't for we both thought it would be wrong. One week, however, we petted every night and the desire for fulfillment grew with each encounter. Finally it was too much and without discussion or thought we went through with it. That's the way drinking is for me now. An occasional drink is like petting, but if I overdo it, the desire grows to go full hog. And for me a drunk is like an orgasm. The hell of it is, the longer I drink, the fewer are the occasions when I don't have to go all the way.

To avoid the semantic debate on whether such alcoholics have a compulsion or a craving, it could be agreed perhaps that they at least have a powerful *desire* for alcohol that is sometimes too strong to resist. This would also certainly apply to the cigarette smoker. A colleague of mine after several weeks of the agony of giving up smoking finally lit one with relief and accepted his habit. Kidding him on his lapse, I asked: "Too weak to resist a little addictive craving?" "No!" he answered in some anger. "Craving has nothing to do with it. I just needed a cigarette." Likewise, whether the cause is psychological, physical or both, the alcoholic's need for a drink can be very real.

The identification of a psychological or physical cause, however, is critical for those alcohologists who believe that the only real cure for the alcoholic is to make a *social drinker* of him. Both physical and psychological approaches have been made to achieve this and increasingly claims for success have been announced. I am personally skeptical of many of these but they cannot be dismissed without examination. In this approach again, endeavors are usually entirely psychological or physical with no thought of treating the whole being of the alcoholic.

These attempts to teach the alcoholic to drink normally are going against the major interpretations of alcoholism and a large number of most reputable scientists think that they are doomed to failure. Many specialists agree with the statements of Tiebout (90: pp. 54-55) and Lolli (109: p. 245) that psychotherapy simply lacks the ability to turn an alcoholic into a social drinker. Others believe that the physiological malfunction is so great that it cannot be corrected. Valles, for example, states that ". . . damage to the hypothalamus is the reason why the alcoholic cannot go back to social drinking" (231: p. 56). Likewise, Myers and Veale postulate that "A metabolic mechanism may even serve to sustain drinking in the absence of any grave psychiatric problem, and if the mechanism is irreversible, an individual may become incapable of ingesting small amounts of alcohol without lapsing into uncontrolled, self-regenerative drinking" (32: p. 152). Alcoholics Anonymous agrees although it does not close the door to the possibility that eventually such a complete cure will be discovered. The A.A. Big Book states that "Physicians who are familiar with alcoholism agree there is no such thing as making a normal drinker out of an alcoholic. Science may one day accomplish this, but it hasn't done so yet" (124: p. 31).

If in fact science is not yet in a position to insure such a transformation in the alcoholic, grave ethical questions are raised by such experiments. This is also true of administering alcohol to alcoholic *guinea pigs* in a laboratory setting to test their responses, but at least, few of these researchers urge the alcoholic to then go forth and drink. Speaking generally of the ethics of science, Mazur and Robertson speak of the ". . . ethical constraints which prevent one from using a technique which has a potential for harm to the persons acting as subjects" (28: p. 123). Faillace *et al.*, however, believe ". . . that to study adequately the causes of alcoholism it is ultimately necessary to conduct research in which alcohol is given to humans." They also realize that this may be walking the razor's edge of ethical responsibility when they caution that "Investigators, when undertaking this kind of research, have to consider carefully the ethics of giving a potential toxin to human subjects, especially when this is not a traditionally accepted form of treatment" (268: p. 85). Urging alcoholics regularly to ingest a potential poison outside the hospital assumes an even greater ethical consideration. If those who advocate that alcoholics return to drink have guessed wrongly, an immense amount of suffering and death will be the result. If they are wrong, history may look back on their experiments with the same horror with which we today view the U.S. Public Health Service's study which "induced" 655 syphilitics to go without treatment to "determine the disease's effect on the human body" (269). I do not doubt the sincerity of those involved in trying to condition alcoholics to drink socially; I do question their judgment.

However, psychocultural determinists believe that we are already knowledgeable enough to confine alcoholism to the definition of a correctable bad habit. Blum points out that except for Calvinist-indoctrinated therapists, psychoanalysts share this belief about the alcoholic. She states that "In general the ability to drink moderately, when and where he chooses and with whom, is regarded as therapeutic success" (155: p. 281). In the past few years an increasing number of individuals in other disciplines have come to accept this viewpoint. As but one example, Verden, a sociologist, and Shatterly, a student, have pooled their sociological and medical knowledge and concluded that ". . . the assertion that alcoholism is a disease is . . . in truth no more than a slogan" (86: p. 331). Further, they urge ". . . that no official or semi-official agencies preclude the possibility that alcoholics can drink in a socially acceptable, non-pathological manner" (86: p. 332). A midwestern farmer I know lacks Verden's training but would heartily agree with him. The farmer once informed me that "All the 'alkyholic' has to do is shape up and he ain't no different from no one else." The behavioral dogmatists believe that psychotherapy is an adequate means to *shape up* the alcoholic and make a social drinker of him. Increasingly, claims of success by this approach are being presented.

The first credible report of normal drinking by recovered alcoholics was made by Davies (270). This is a very balanced and thoroughly reliable document and Davies reports it as a fact of significance. He does not, however, urge a return to drinking as the goal for all alcoholic therapy. His article was followed by many comments ranging from outright skepticism to others offering further cases of such completely rehabilitated alcoholics (271). Since that time, numerous reports by others cite similar total cures. Most of these are referred to by Pattison *et al.* (103) and Verden (86) and need not be listed here. Some are perhaps credible. Others are not.

Unfortunately, some of the most accepted and cited reports are those of Arthur Cain. In large part his convictions, resting upon a rather emotional and shallow hostility aimed at Alcoholics Anonymous, were first expressed in an article published in *Harper's Magazine* (272). His ultimate work was *The Cured Alcoholic* (273) in which he claimed to have successfully re-habilitated alcoholics so that they could drink normally. Like so many of the *successes* reported in this vein, the report was premature. I have learned from the most reliable sources that Cain's venture ended as a tragic fiasco. This fact is apparently unknown or purposely ignored by those who quote him.

Other leaders of the back-to-drinking movement may be more accurate in their reporting but are oversimplistic in their approach. One of these is Claude Steiner who agrees with his master, Berne, that the alcoholic is a naughty child rather than a sick adult (15: p. 274). His cute and flippant style has annoyed a number of therapists who have some feeling and respect for their patients (275). One of these describes Steiner's approach as a "blood sport" (275: pp. 945-948). I would agree and firmly believe in the light of earlier comments in this book that Steiner is asking many of his alcoholics to play Russian Roulette with all the chambers loaded. If he loses some of his patents, however, he should not despair for he will always be able to find other alcoholics to play with.

A more reasoned and, I believe, sincere approach is that reported by the Sobells and others at Patton State Hospital in California (276, 277, 278, 279). Through *re-education* an attempt was made to "teach" the alcoholic to know himself and to pace his drinks. The pacing was taught at a bar where the alcoholic received an electric shock when he began drinking too rapidly. In other words, conditioned reflex utilizing electricity was used to moderate drinking rather than to produce an aversion as has been done so often in other therapies (280). The Patton experiment claims massive success in converting alcoholics into controlled drinkers. However, success is a relative thing and the premises of the Patton experiment seem to me extremely dubious.

The main assumption they make that I question is that occasional drunks are normal and that the alcoholic should accept these as a part of controlled drinking. This may be true in some subcultures but certainly isn't in others. Even if one should accept this dubious premise, the Patton experimenters completely ignore the quality of a drunk and its effect on an alcoholic. For the average heavy drinker a drunk may be an accepted and even appreciated aspect of the drinking game. For the alcoholic, a drunk represents a total loss of control and is a terrifying experience. It is my impression that the Patton sanction of drunkenness as normal merely eases the anxiety the alcoholic experiences after a blast. The alcoholic certainly seeks every sanction he can find to label himself as *normal*. Active alcoholics, lacking the Patton endorsement of intoxication, frequently operate in extremely alcoholic subcultures where they find confirmation of the belief that the symptoms of alcoholism are normal. They thus try to believe that there is no cause to worry about blackouts, the *shakes*, the *sweats* and awakening the day after in sheer terror. The definition of drunkenness as acceptable behavior is even more reassuring when it comes from the prestige of a state hospital. My own opinion is that telling the patient to accept these symptoms as nonpathological is as meaningful as telling a person that he should live with the symptoms of gonorrhea and not fret about them. A drunk by an alcoholic simply does not equate to a drunk by a normal person. The Patton assumption that reducing the number of drunks is proof of controlled drinking by an alcoholic strikes me as ridiculous. One could by extension say that if a homicidal maniac learns to control his desire to kill 99 percent of the time he is now normal.

The statistical evidence of the Patton *success* is even more dubious. In no place does the experiment demonstrate that a single alcoholic has learned to control his drinking totally. Rather, the total sample is reduced to a mass evaluation of controlled and uncontrolled days for all the alcoholics who went through the program. These are then compared to controls who at six months show only about half the success the trained alcoholics had in nondrunken drinking. This difference is probably explainable by the rigorous selection of the individuals used in the training experiment. The most likely to volunteer would be those who had suffered less from the disease. These would be individuals in whom alcoholism had not advanced to a point where all control had been lost. The therapists selected from among the alcoholics those individuals with the best motivation and home environment to succeed in their program. With these facts in mind I am not surprised by their limited success but by what I read as their dismal failure. The trained Patton alcoholics look partially successful only in comparison to the controls. Using any reasonable therapeutic scale, by their own performances they are still uncontrolled alcoholics.

A six month follow-up study of the Patton graduates lists how they, en masse, spent their days. For 40.67 percent of these days, the alcoholics were abstinent. An abstinent day does not measure any success at controlled drinking. Of the totalled time, the trained alcoholics spent 28.48 percent of the days practicing *controlled drinking*. I am really not sure what the researchers mean by controlled drinking despite long explanations. However, it seems to mean drinking without any negative objective results. No adequate check is made of the subjective effects on the alcoholics. The validity of the experiment, of course, rests on the relationship of controlled to uncontrolled drinking. These *cured* alcoholics, by the project's own statistics, were drunk on 19.28 percent of their days, in hospital for alcoholism 9.50 percent and in jail 2.07 percent. In actual drinking situations, therefore, these alcoholics lost control on over 40 percent of the occasions when they took a drink. If one includes institutionalization following a drunk as a period when the alcoholic is not in full control of life, the percentage of uncontrolled time rises sharply. This is a success rate considerably under 60 percent. In most classrooms a grade below 60 is a D. If an alcoholic is to lose control this frequently I believe it somewhat ludicrous to classify him as a *controlled drinker*. The Patton success rests more on a dubious definition of *controlled drinking* than on an actual modification of alcoholic drinking patterns.

It would be as reasonable to classify as a *good swimmer* the individual who drowned every second time he entered the water.[11]

In fact, from my own data I would hazard the guess that these alcoholics would have had less uncontrolled drinking had they not been exposed to the experience of the Patton training program. The Patton belief that being able to avoid a drunk about 40 to 50 percent of the time is normal and a demonstration of controlled drinking would certainly encourage the alcoholic to go to it. I collected biographies from 30 alcoholics on their drinking patterns the year before they entered A.A. In each case I spent over twenty hours in interviews with each alcoholic and in most cases interviewed families and spouses at length. I came to know these alcoholics well and was trusted by them. I firmly believe that my evidence is as reliable as that in the Patton reports. In typical alcoholic pattern these A.A.'s had all been trying to control their drinking the year before entering A.A. Their record, by Patton standards, was an overwhelming success. Their accumulated total in days showed over 49 percent abstinent days, as against Patton's 40.67 percent. This in itself demonstrated little but an ability to abstain. However, my sample revealed controlled drinking on over 39 percent of the total days (vs. Patton's 28.48 percent). By controlled drinking I mean that they stopped drinking at two drinks or less, suffered no blackout, and displayed no antisocial behavior. My sample was drunk on under 10 percent of its days, as compared to Patton's 19.28 percent. More significantly perhaps, while Patton's controlled alcoholics spent 2.07 percent of their time in jail on drunk charges, mine spent .0000913 percent (one alcoholic for less than one day). Patton's graduates were in hospital for alcoholism 9.50 percent of their time, and mine for .0005475 percent (one alcoholic for six days). However, such statistics to me mean little. The significant thing

---

[11] Dr. Sobell, who has been extremely generous in sharing both his published and unpublished findings with me, has sent me his one year follow-up. As was to be expected, the percentage of successes has dropped dramatically. At the same time, San Mateo County in California has adopted this technique to "re-educate" drunk drivers (*San Francisco Chronicle*, March 4, 1973, p. 1). This may work well for the occasional tippler but, I believe, will be tragic for alcoholics and other motorists and pedestrians.

is what alcohol does to alcoholics. All of my sample suffered massive anxiety, feelings of inadequacy, fear and dread throughout their attempts at controlled drinking. When they gave up the uncertain battle, their reaction was uniform—an enormous sense of relief. Several commented on the freedom from fear as almost ecstatic. Most also commented on the relief at realizing they'd never have to endure the pain of stopping after one or two drinks. One explained,

> One highball and every cell in my body screams for more . I can't explain it but it hurts like hell. It's just not worth it. And I know if I take a second I'll completely lose the ability to stop. I don't know if it ups the desire or downs the willpower, but two drinks and I'm on my way to a drunk. I could go back to a drink a day for a while, but each time would be sheer torture. Why do it? And I know one day without fail I'd get drunk. Then it would be Dante's Inferno for a week or two. No thanks.

I must conclude from my own evidence and that of decades of alcoholic research by others that the alcoholic simply cannot be taught to be a social drinker. Some reports of success, such as those from Patton Hospital, rest on dubious assumptions and peculiar statistics. Others may seem to be more reliable. The seemingly successful report may rest largely upon *retraining* alcoholics early in their disease when they in fact still have considerable control. Any sample of alcoholics today will contain large numbers of alcoholics who have not as yet suffered much from the disease. With the increasingly abundant publicity on the disease, more and more alcoholics are recognizing its early symptoms and are asking for treatment. On top of this, although alcoholism still carries an enormous stigma, it is becoming more and more acceptable. This in part has been due to the large number of eminent individuals in politics and the arts who have been willing, at great personal sacrifice, publicly to tell of their own recovery from alcoholism. This has helped immensely in making alcoholism more acceptable. As one A.A. said to me, ". . . they've given the disease a little class." The acceptance of the diagnosis of alcoholism is also made easier when it no longer threatens job security. The Civil Service Commission, for example, on July 27, 1971, issued orders that alcoholics were to be treated as ill and given sick leave for treatment and rehabilitation (281). Many industries had earlier established the same policy. I have no doubt that many non-alcoholic drinkers have misinterpreted their own neurotic symptoms as alcoholism and thus found their way into alcoholic samples. Alcoholics who have only entered the early stages of the disease and nonalcoholic problem drinkers misclassified as alcoholics would be especially susceptible to the back-to-booze therapies. They will also produce the successes. The non-alcoholic problem drinkers may indeed be re-educated. The real alcoholic will see his remaining control as evidence that the therapists who urge drinking are right and that A.A. and its *allies* are merely using malicious and false propaganda for some unsuspected subversive reason to deprive alcoholics of their rights. After therapeutic training they will for some time demonstrate a limited control. However, the disease will run its course and they will in time enter the critical phase of total helplessness.

Most therapists simply do not realize how far some alcoholics will go to convince themselves and others that they are really able to control their intake of alcohol. A local member of a Santa Barbara alcoholism team recently recounted to me her visit to a very sick patient in an alcoholic ward. She asked the patient if he thought he had a problem. He said he wasn't sure. He was then asked if he'd ever been hospitalized before because of alcoholism and he admitted this was his sixth such visit to a hospital. He also mentioned that two of these stays were in a well-known California State Hospital. "But honey," said the visitor, "isn't that where they teach you to drink socially?" The patient brightened up. "Yes it is," he said, "I've been through the course twice."

Nonetheless, the concept that abstinence represents the only reasonable treatment for alcoholics is being increasingly attacked at both the professional and the public level. The popular press continues to report professional opinions sanctioning the back-to-booze therapies. This has beyond any doubt had a negative effect on many who would ordinarily have sought therapies based upon abstinence. The publicly cited authorities are frequently so eminent as to warrant the alcoholic's thinking twice before giving up alcohol. Dr. David H. Knott, for example, is the director of the Alcohol and Drug Dependence Clinic at the Tennessee Psychiatric Hospital and Institute and a highly regarded scientist in the area of alcoholic research and therapy. He is quoted in a newspaper as saying, "Once an alcoholic, always an alcoholic is a myth. . . . The concept is not only misleading but also relieves the patient from accepting responsibility for his own action due to his 'biological affliction'" (282).

However, despite the many claims to the contrary, I cannot foresee any massive success in turning addicted alcoholics into social drinkers. I do not deny that this has probably happened on occasion, but its frequency is about the same as the remission of terminal cancer. To abandon the proven abstinence approach for a drinking therapy in alcoholism would be as reasonable as to send all cancer victims to Lourdes in lieu of any medical treatment. Moreover, doubt can be cast on most of the claims of the alcoholic-into-social-drinker transfiguration reports. As Kalant has said of alcoholic treatments, "The surprising beneficial effect of any therapy in the initial period of its trial is explained by the enthusiasm of the therapist combined with insufficient length of follow-up" (130: p. 86).

Kalant's evaluation also applies equally well to the biological determinists who, while scoffing at the re-education approaches, believe that the alcoholic's metabolism can be restored to allow social drinking. As Keller notes, "Williams, Smith, and Randolf . . . have each suggested that correction of the hypothesized defect should constitute a cure for alcoholism and allow the alcoholic to resume moderate drinking" (283: p. 10). Williams specifically stated that diet and megavitamin therapy could overcome the alcoholic defect and make the alcoholic into a social drinker. He tested his hypothesis on an inadequate sample of alcoholics for too short a period and announced his "cure" (200). A number of alcoholics, many of whom had been sober for years, tried social drinking by his formula and disproved its validity.

More powerful medications than vitamins have been proposed for years to correct the alcoholic's biological malfunction. As early as 1939 amphetamines were seen as a specific for alcoholism

(284). Many believed that the amphetamines could balance the alcoholic metabolism and give him the ability to drink normally. I encountered several alcoholics who indeed became social drinkers for various lengths of time by taking ever increasing doses of Benzedrine® or Dexedrine®. In one case an alcoholic drank without intoxication for three weeks and another for just over two years. In all of these cases, however, eventually the amphetamines failed to prevent intoxication and the alcoholics found themselves with a double addiction, unable to give up either the alcohol or the amphetamines. Four of my sample found themselves going on week-long benders combining alcohol and amphetamines which prevented sleep and usually without any food source but the alcohol. All four ended up with temporary but extreme paranoid-like seizures. In 1963, Walter Little, recognizing the role of epinephrine and sugar metabolism in alcoholism, announced a cure which consisted of adding massive amount of vitamin B-1 to a regular Dexedrine dosage. Further, he states that this therapy allows social drinking (285). This promising cure was apparently still-born.

Other attempts to curtail intoxication by metabolic alteration have also been attempted. Five alcoholics of my acquaintance had tried preventing intoxication by large doses of thyroid. An initial success was produced in three cases but none of these lasted over a month. Another alcoholic, with the cooperation of his physician, drank for a period without intoxication by using massive doses of triiodothyronine. His controlled drinking lasted for four months when he gave up the thyroid dosage because of *discomfort* in the throat and a truly spectacular gain in weight. Four days later he was drunk.

In Europe considerable success has been attributed to apomorphine in controlling alcoholic craving and at times allowing a return to social drinking (286, 287). Feldmann believes that the apomorphine acts directly on the hypothalamus correcting the "biochemical disturbances present in alcoholic patients" (288). Pattison *et al.* (103: p. 621) note that in a later publication by Morsier and Feldmann (289), 15 percent of an alcoholic sample of 500 were able to return to social drinking following treatment with apomorphine. I am unaware of any attempts to use apomorphine to control alcoholic drinking in this country, although Schlatter and Lal (290) did find that it significantly reduced craving. The limited European success with alcoholic controlled drinking may be associated with the typical French type of alcoholism which implies addiction but not intoxication.

Another approach to moderating alcoholic drinking is to chemically force the drinker to limit his intake or become ill. This differs from the abstinence approach of antabuse which produces alarming symptoms with the smallest ingestion of alcohol. Calcium cynamide allows the drinker to consume one or two drinks with no ill effects but if he drinks more he becomes ill. This approach is today used in Japan (291, 292) but has apparently not been tried in the U.S. However, for a while it looked as though an equivalent American treatment was possible using metronidazole (Flagyl®). The first reports on its value to alcoholism in 1964 (293) stated that it limited the craving and the intake of alcohol. However, from that time to the present contradictory reports on its efficacy have appeared in the literature. In 1966 Semer *et al.* (294) confirmed many of the earlier results and concluded that metronidazole offered great promise. However, in 1967 Goodwin's study (295) was unable to confirm that metronidazole reduced desire or produced a disulfiram-like reaction on alcoholic intake beyond a few drinks. Fried in 1970 (296) tended to accept the original optimistic opinion and in laboratory work found that metronidazole inhibited alcohol dehydrogenase, thus giving some insight into its specific function. In the same year, Strassman *et al.* tested metronidazole on social drinkers and found ". . . that intake of a therapeutic dose of the drug when combined with alcohol produces noticeable physical responses in some subjects. These reactions may make the ingestion of alcohol an unpleasant experience" (297: p. 398). At the same time, however, Rothstein and Clancy found ". . . no evidence that metronidazole in any way aided the treatment of our patients." Moreover, six of their 29 ". . . metronidazole-treated patients developed an acute functional psychosis. . . ." (298: p. 447). In other words, metronidazole is still far from proven in aiding alcoholics to achieve either abstinence or controlled social drinking. Several of my alcoholic correspondents had read the original popular report on this drug (299) and have reported to me the attempts of some of their friends who took it with the aid of cooperative physicians. None of these succeeded in becoming social drinkers for more than a few days and one died in the attempt to prove he could now drink like other men.

Another approach to allow alcoholics to drink socially is to find a chemical means to block the effects of alcohol. Geller and his associates found that Diethanolamine-rutin (D-R) did in fact block the intoxicating effect of alcohol in rats (300). This led one popular writer to postulate that if such a block could be discovered for humans it would constitute a boon for the treatment of alcoholism (301). Dr. Geller has told me that his research has not produced any such human analogy. Moreover, it is doubtful if any such block to intoxication would in itself solve the problem of alcoholism. It would make it possible for the alcoholic, if he wished, to conform to societal drinking demands. However, it would not solve the emotional problems which may inaugurate destructive drinking.

Undoubtedly the most promising chemical approach being investigated today is propranolol hydrochloride, available commercially as Inderale®. Propranolol seems to block the intoxicating effects of alcohol and also relieves the anxiety which is so typical of the alcoholic. Pitts has pointed out that double-blind experiments in London and South Africa have confirmed the anxiety-releasing property of propranolol (49: p. 75). Jack Mendelson and his co-workers at Harvard have been testing propranolol on alcoholics and it seems to block the effects of alcohol on humans as effectively as D-R does on rats (302, 303, 304). Mendelson has told me that to date this alcoholic antagonism has been demonstrated only on amounts of alcohol that would represent "the average intake of a social drinker at a cocktail party." He is now testing the effects of propranolol against the massive intake of an alcoholic's usual consumption. Should propranolol indeed prove to be an effective antagonist of alcohol, it will indeed be a most promising tool in dealing with alcoholism. In breaking an addiction it is always more effective to negate the effect of a drug than merely to cause an adverse reaction. By lowering lactate levels (49), acting on the biogenic amines and blocking some of the symptoms of hypo-glycemia propranolol also seems to deal with some of the major correlates of anxiety and perhaps even addiction itself. However, great caution should be maintained before seeking a cure-all in propranolol. The early reports on amphetamines and metroni-dazole were just as promising.[12]

Like the amphetamines and metronidazole, both apomorphine and propranolol are said to affect both the psychological and the somatic aspects of alcoholism. The amphetamines and metronidazole have failed to live up to their early promise. Apomorphine and propranolol remain to be fully tested. Any approach which fails to deal adequately with both the mental and physical aspects of alcoholism is probably bound to fail. I am personally convinced that even if a chemical means is found to work on both the mind and body of the alcoholic, considerable psychological repair will still be advisable in most cases. It is true that some assume that correction of one part of the body-mind unity will automatically correct the correlate. Janov, for example, believes that his psychologically induced "primal scream" will also correct the biological malfunctions associated with neurotic tendencies (246). More specifically in relation to anxiety, it has been demonstrated that through "transcendental meditation" lactate levels can be dropped dramatically (305). This concept is, of course, the basis of "biofeedback" which is gaining in popularity with both scientific and lay individuals (306). It is also the basic assumption behind psychoanalysis. In cases of advanced alcoholism, however, so rare are proven cures allowing a return to normal drinking that one must assume that the biological malfunction is too great to be rectified by any amount of mental manipulation.

Despite my doubts that we can now achieve so total a cure as to allow alcoholics to drink, reports of such successes continue

---

[12] I have just learned informally that propranolol fails to block the intoxicat-ing effects when alcohol is administered in large amounts. At the same time, lithium, which is so effective in treating manic-depressive conditions, is proving of value in the treatment of alcoholism .(Nathan S. Kline, M.D. and J. C. Wren, M.D.: "Evaluation of Lithium Therapy in Chronic Alcoholism." Paper delivered at the Third Annual Conference of the National Institute on Alcohol Abuse and Alcoholism, Washington, D.C., June 20-22, 1973.)

to pour in. Pattison and his co-writers show that an averaging of all projects claiming alcoholic rehabilitation to social drinking shows a four to ten percent success level, depending on how one defines one's sample (103: p. 630). It is my contention that this is about the range of nonaddictive, incipient or symptomatic alcoholics one would obtain in any group of problem drinkers labeled as *alcoholic* by our inadequate though traditional techniques. It has also been my experience that frequently individuals are self-classified as alcoholics for reasons that have no relation to problem drinking. In my sample of members of Alcoholics Anonymous I concluded that nearly five percent could not be classified as alcoholic by any criterion except their own self-labeling. They were merely lonely and neurotic individuals dreadfully in need of acceptance by a caring group. In return for this acceptance they found wearing the label *alcoholic* a very small price. Further, in the criminal courts and before parole boards many violators of the law have found that to confess to alcoholism and to express a desire for rehabilitation creates a more lenient judgment of their cases. A number of my sample were individuals on parole or probation who were free only on the provision that they regularly attend A.A. meetings. Four of these to my definite knowledge had never had any problem with alcohol and had play-acted the role of *alcoholic* to obtain its maximum legal payoff. This is the probable reason behind the "spontaneous remission" of many "alcoholic" ex-convicts (307).

Another failure in sampling which has contributed to the belief that alcoholics can be trained to drink socially is the naive assumption that the term *drunk* and *alcoholic* are synonymous. The confusion is due to the enormous range of *problem drinkers* included under the rubric of *alcoholic*. In large part this rests upon Jellinek's monumental study *The Disease Concept of Alcoholism* (4). Undoubtedly the most thorough scholar of alcoholism to date, I believe Jellinek inadvertently misdirected alcoholic research by his classification of alcoholic types. He was so all-inclusive in this classification that he included several types that in fact are not addicted nor the victims of any alcoholic craving. He admits that his classification is "arbitrary" because of its broad scope (4: p. 41). In fact, he specifically attributes craving to only two of his types, the "gamma" and "delta" (4: p. 40).

Jellinek's "alpha" alcoholism is one of the most common in America. He defines it clearly:

> Alpha alcoholism represents a *purely* psychological *continual* dependence or reliance upon the effect of alcohol to relieve bodily or emotional pain. The drinking is 'undisciplined' in the sense that it contravenes such rules as society agrees upon—such as time, occasion, locale, amount and effect of drinking—*but does not lead to 'loss of control' or 'inability to abstain.'* The damage caused by this species of alcoholism may be restricted to the disturbance of interpersonal relations. There may also be interference with the family budget, occasional absenteeism from work and decreased productivity, and some of the nutritional deficiencies of alcoholism, but not the disturbances due to withdrawal of alcohol. *Nor are there any signs of a progressive process.* . . . This species of alcoholism cannot be regarded as an illness per se (4: p. 36).[13]

He continues with "Alpha alcoholism is sometimes called problem drinking . . ." (4: p. 37) but states his intention not to use the terms "problem drinking" and "problem drinker" in the book. Others have used such terms as "reactive," "secondary" and "symptomatic" for Jellinek's "alpha" (308: p. 256).

This classification of the alpha as alcoholic rather than as a problem drinker, I believe, has had catastrophic results on sampling in alcoholic research. The alpha suffers no compulsion and can stop at will. He obviously is an excellent subject for rehabilitation and any adequate psychotherapist should be able to return him to social drinking if behaviorist theory on habit formation is valid. However, every sample and collection of alcoholics that I have seen undergoing therapy or who were serving as research objects has included a large number of alphas who are regarded as the equivalent of the addicted alcoholics. At the time Jellinek wrote his book he estimated that "at least ten to fifteen percent" (4: p. 38) of the A.A. membership were alphas. At the time I did my primary research on A.A., I estimated the number of alphas as closer to twenty-five percent.

---

[13] Emphasis is Jellinek's.

My impression is that the percentage of alphas in hospital collections is even higher and those in jails and prison would be over fifty percent of the alcoholics.

Jellinek's beta alcoholic is likewise nonaddictive and free from craving. His inclusion within the ranks of the alcoholics is based entirely upon alcohol-derived physical disabilities such as "polyneuropathy, gastritis and cirrhosis of the liver." These, as Jellinek points out, ". . . may occur without either physical or psychological dependence upon alcohol" (4: p. 37). I believe the justification for including the beta within the alcoholic ranks is even weaker than the case for the alpha. However, Jellinek's "gamma" and "delta" are true alcoholism with craving, addiction, and withdrawal symptoms when desired alcohol is denied (4: pp. 37-39). The gamma is the periodic alcoholic and the delta is the truly addicted alcoholic who is dependent on a certain daily intake of alcohol to function. In the popular culture, the best image of the delta is W. C. Fields. Jellinek's "epsilon" (4: p. 39) is defined as "periodic alcoholism" and he equates it to the older term "dipsomania." He calls it ". . . the least known species of alcoholism." However, I would tend to include it within the bounds of gamma alcoholism which is also characterized by periodic benders. Block says of the epsilon, "These drinkers are just as alcoholic as those in the other classification, even though they do not drink at all between binges. Once they start drinking, however, they have no control and they continue until they are taken in hand or until they lose consciousness" (197: p. 34). This description would equally fit the advanced gamma alcoholic.

In other words, the different species of alcoholics may share no more than an abuse of alcohol. To equate alphas and deltas probably makes as much sense as an ornithologist equating the albatross and the ostrich. A Criteria Committee of the National Council on Alcoholism has issued a set of *Criteria for the Diagnosis of Alcoholism* (308). One valid purpose of this document is ". . . to prevent overdiagnosis" (308: p. 249), an important and needed move. However, apparently as a result of an attempt to keep the committee in agreement, their contribution is less instructive than Jellinek's classification in separating addictive from nonaddictive alcoholics. The committee does indeed state that "Reactive, secondary, or symptomatic alcohol use should be separated from other forms of alcoholism" (308: p. 256). The report, however, does not give any absolute criteria for such a separation nor any valid means to distinguish between the addicted and the nonaddicted alcoholic. By their criteria and rating system, every one of Jellinek's species clearly emerges as alcoholic. It is not surprising then that the committee agrees that a return to social drinking is possible for some alcoholics (308: p. 255). Fortunately, this list of criteria is not presented as a dogmatic finality but as a basis for further deliberation. As Frank Seixas, Medical Director of the National Council on Alcoholism, has said elsewhere:

> It is intended that the committee will continue its deliberations, obtaining through large cooperative studies, experience ratings in utilization of the criteria. Thus, it is hoped that agreed-upon areas will increase, some of the currently necessary ambiguities will diminish, and failures to diagnose alcholism will become rare, as will the far currently smaller segment of the population who may be inaccurately given the diagnosis (309).

The vagaries and catch-all nature of any definition of alcoholism is complicated by humanistic and semantic consideration. Today legal, employment, insurance and medical advantages go to an *alcoholic* but not to a *drunk*. As anyone suffering from a pathological overuse of alcohol is obviously sick, humanistically all such individuals should be called *alcoholic*. However, at a therapeutic level, the inability to separate alcoholics who are primarily biologically driven from others who are psychologically motivated can result in failure and catastrophe.

On the level of therapy it would be wise to reconsider the recommendations made by the Alcoholism Subcommittee of the World Health Organization which were first published in 1952, reprinted in the *Quarterly Journal of Studies on Alcohol* and later published in a slightly modified form in Pittman and Snyder's *Society, Culture and Drinking Patterns* (310). Jellinek summarized a basic part of those recommendations by stating that

> The Subcommittee has distinguished two categories of alcoholics, namely, 'alcohol addicts' and 'habitual symptomatic excessive drinkers.' For brevity's sake the latter will be referred to as non-

addictive alcoholics. Strictly speaking, the disease conception attaches to the alcohol addicts only, but not to habitual symptomatic excessive drinkers (310: p. 357).

Thereby, Jellinek reconfirms his earlier pronouncement that only the gamma and delta are addicted alcoholics. I believe it is therapeutically unfortunate that he did not leave the "symptomatic excessive drinker" outside the ranks of alcoholism. He and others experienced in the alcoholic field, however, recognized the difference between primarily psychologically originated overdrinking and alcoholism with biological correlates. These two major typologies call for different therapeutic approaches regardless of the semantic debate over whether they should both be covered by the term "alcoholic" or be separated more realistically as alcoholics and sick symptomatic drinkers.

The difference is especially critical in the problem of whether or not attempts should be made to teach alcoholics to drink. It should be obvious that alpha alcoholics can be re-educated into social drinkers. The beta alcoholic usually has such massive alcohol-induced damage by the time he is diagnosed that it would be medically ridiculous to even consider drinking for him. I am convinced that delta and gamma alcoholics are so metabolically inadequate that they can never drink normally again. The experiments of the back-to-booze movement, I believe, in large part get their positive results from alphas (i.e. symptomatic drinkers), and other nonaddicted imbibers within their sample. Thus, they indeed can prove that they have taught an *alcoholic* to drink again. However, when they then apply their techniques to addicted alcoholics they can only fail. A few experimenters have claimed to use only gamma or gamma and delta alcoholics in their sample. However, purely on the basis of psychological and behavioristic criteria it is extremely difficult to separate the addict from the symptomatic and I sincerely doubt if any of these experiments are using purely addicted samples.[14]

---

[14] Recent work (R. L. Rosenhan: On being sane in insane places. *Science*, 179:250-258, 1973) has clearly demonstrated the inadequacy of our standard techniques of psychiatric classification. In this study, it was demonstrated that twelve mental hospitals could not distinguish between the mentally well and psychotics. To separate symptomatic drinkers from addicted alcoholics is a far more difficult task.

Further, as I have already indicated, addicted alcoholics who are young in the disease have considerable control and for a period may seem to respond well to an education in social drinking. Eventually, however, they will fail. These facts by themselves could invalidate the general applicability of all the laboratory tests on tension relief, craving and controlled drinking. If alcohologists must persist in their attempts to teach alcoholics to drink socially, I think it would be wise if they excluded from their experiments all alcoholics having any of the biological criteria for diagnosing alcoholism listed by the Criteria Committee of the National Council on Alcoholism (308). Attempts have been made to find simpler and specific biological tests to identify addictive alcoholism (311, 312), but to date none exist.

The entire semantic and therapeutic jungle would be greatly clarified if we simply modified our terms and used *alcoholic* to refer to individuals who drink in response to a psychobiological drive and *symptomatic problem drinkers* to categorize those who overdrink primarily for psychosocial reasons. Recognizing this distinction, I believe that the focus of most of our research should be to find a definite test for the true alcoholic and then a means to correct his biological failing. In the meantime, standard psychotherapeutic techniques could perhaps be refined for returning the nonaddicted symptomatic drinkers to normal alcoholic imbibing. Even these, however, may have biological malfunctions which are associated with their neurotic behavior, although of a type that does not produce craving and addictive drinking. Increasingly specialists in human behavior are coming to realize the importance of the body in all behavior. Recently, for example, Jean Piaget at the City University of New York ". . . predicted that psychoanalytical theory—the whole school of training and therapy deriving from Freud—would be exposed as 'mythical' by studies on hormones and the way the brain functions" (313).

PART II

AN ATTEMPT AT SYNTHESIS

CHAPTER VI:

THE CULTURAL MILIEU:
THE ANXIOUS AMERICAN

IN VIEW OF THE ideas expressed in the preceding pages, I do not think that we will make any further progress until we come up with a more meaningful interpretation of drinking pathology. The first step must be a means of segregating the alcoholics from the ranks of the problem drinkers and devising appropriate but different therapies for the addicted and the symptomatic drinkers. Secondly, we must recognize that mind and body are parts of a single entity. The false body-mind dichotomy has existed from the earliest days of Western society although there have always been individuals who spoke out against the falsity of this splitting of human nature. Janov was aware of this when he wrote, "What should be clear by now is that one cannot cure the mind and body separately" (246: p. 82). The unity of mind and body is recognized increasingly today by many writers including Eysenck (17: p. 340), Chapple (26: p. 137), Watson (38: p. 15), Valles (231: p. 54), Lowen (165: p. 33), Perls (314: p. 8) and many others. Specifically, in relation to alcoholism, Lovell and Tintera speak of "This medically useless philosophy of 'mind-body' dualism. . . ." (213: p. 1). More broadly, Fox (75: p. 334) quotes Leon Greenberg as saying, "Unless or until we understand the sociological, psychological and physical causes and effects of emotions like hate and love, we cannot understand alcoholism."

In the hope of stimulating some thought toward a more meaningful and comprehensive view of alcoholism and problem drinking, I will present my own very hypothetical interpretation of these afflictions. It will become obvious that if there is anything novel in my approach, it is merely the attempt to synthesize. Most of the basic ideas, concepts and categories I have borrowed from other writers. Alcoholism itself I see as a product of a multitude of interacting causes all of which contribute to its genesis and development. It is my conviction that by psychological and sociocultural approaches we now have the means to help most alcoholics maintain an adequate life based upon abstinence. A total biological cure is not yet available and the true alcoholic is no more able to metabolize ethanol than a diabetic can handle sugar. Nonetheless, this biological inadequacy is in part a product of the psychological history of the alcoholic which is in turn strongly influenced by his sociocultural environment. All of these factors must be understood if we are to clearly define alcoholism and improve the available therapies. The best we can do at the moment is to give the alcoholic the psychological means to handle stress without escaping into alcoholic drinking.

If one accepts alcoholism as a stress disease, one may question the origin of the stress. Catanzaro states that it may be of either internal or external origin (74: p. 41). This sort of dichotomy is not too realistic, for unless an external stress is internalized it does not in fact exist for the individual. However, some writers emphasize one or the other. For example, Eric Berne (315), as Pattison *et al.* point out (103: p. 626, f.n. 10), ". . . ignores the intrapsychic drives and conflicts that 'hound' the alcoholic. . . ." The same is largely true of his disciple Claude Steiner (15, 274). Traditional psychoanalytical approaches, on the other hand, are concerned only with the "intrapsychic drives and conflicts." More realistically, Ward and Faillace say that alcoholism ". . . should be viewed as a complex interactional process between individual factors and the social field" (104: p. 684). However, with the alcoholic, 1 believe the inner conflict to be primary. Thus, I find myself in agreement with Menninger who years ago described the alcoholic as having ". . . an unseen inner conflict aggravated but not primarily caused (as many think) by external conflict" (120: p. 168).

However, it should be obvious that the reasons for overdrinking probably differ from individual to individual. Some drink heavily because of inner stress and anxiety while others do so as a response to environmental stress. I believe Edwards to be correct when he says that the overdrinker responding primarily to environmental stress has a far better chance for recovery than the neurotic alcoholic who drinks to ease internally-generated malaise (107: p. 235). In fact, the individual who overdrinks solely to relieve a stressful situation is what I have defined as a situational drinker. If he does not experience a craving and a biological addiction, he is not alcoholic. The true alcoholic is driven by an internal psychological stress with all of its biological correlates.

The alcoholic also, of course, responds to environmental stresses. However, as long as he believes that this is the only reason for his drinking, he will fail to recover, for he carries the primary cause within himself. The A.A. experience has long recognized this fact and the futility of the *geographic cure*: moving to a new environment to escape stress and hopefully to return to social drinking. This attempt at a self-cure never works. When therapeutic philosophies assume that the alcoholic is simply a product of his immediate environment they are also committed to failure. An example of this recently ended in tragedy in San Francisco. An alcoholic policeman was put on disability pay by the City Retirement Board after a hearing in which two psychiatrists testified that he had taken to drink "because of the 'social tensions' on his job" (316). The obvious assumption was that, freed of these tensions, he would recover. The police department resisted the order by firing him for his drinking. He filed suit in court to collect his pay but the case was never heard. On September 28, 1972, he was found dead at a steam bath (317). A coroner's report showed that he died of "alcoholic poisoning" (318). The police response has been to inaugurate a "crackdown on drinking" by suspending those found guilty of the malfeasance of having an "alcoholic problem" (319). Environmentalists would, of course, state that this man overdrank and died because he was still suffering environmental stress. However, the stress of a working policeman is different from the stress of being unemployed and suing for redress. This alcoholic, like all alcoholics, could not handle external stresses regardless of their structure. The reason, I am convinced, was his incapacitation because of internalized stresses. Further, the environmentalists, in my mind, fail to understand behavior when they assume the human to be a standardized robot responding predictably to all environmental cues. To borrow a description from Julian Huxley who used it in a different context, in explaining alcoholic behavior the environmentalists are guilty of the ". . . intellectual misdemeanor of 'mechanomorphising' it and reducing it to the false oversimplification of a mere system of reflexes" (140: p. ix).

To ignore the environment, however, would lead to an even more erroneous interpretation of human behavior. We live our lives in a sociocultural milieu that is as significant to our behavior as water is to a sardine. No behavior is really understandable without reference to both biological and environmental determinants. As P.L. Broadhurst has generalized for all animal behavior, "The point is that there are few aspects or items of behavior which are solely innate, or solely learned. Most are due to both inborn, genetic endowment—heredity in a word— and to acquired, developmental forces—environment in another word" (320: p. 69). The human animal is likewise molded by both of these forces and from their congress emerges his mind, a semi-independent entity whose freedom is limited by both biological and psychosocial influences.

The alcoholic mind, then, is in large part a product of its environment. If we assume that the alcoholic psyche is characterized by stresses, it is reasonable to assume that these are internalized from the cultural environment or are the product of an inadequate functioning in society. It is then a reasonable assumption that, other things being equal, the best seed-bed for alcoholism is a stress-laden society that fails to provide adequate and available means to discharge the resultant anxiety. It is my opinion that nontraditional and industrialized societies undergoing rapid culture change are especially stressful. Further, for a number of reasons, the United States appears to be outstanding among such societies in the maintenance of a high stress level. It is today typical for the American to experience stress and anxiety. He has also learned to reduce this tension in part by alcohol. Some who are more deficient in the means to cope become problem drinkers. Others, equally handicapped, become biologically addicted and constitute our alcoholic population. The American alcoholic has always impressed me as being an exaggerated caricature of the typical American failings. He is the epitome of the great American anxiety and the classic fulfillment of our negative values.

The generalized American anxiety is the product of many historical streams leading up to the present. It is characterized by a proliferation of values without an adequate over-all source to resolve value conflicts. It rests to a large degree on the "future shock" (321) of a way of life changing more rapidly than the average citizen can adjust to the new ways. For many the end result is a loss of meaning as seen in the "death" of God. The great American anxiety reflects also the loss of permanence as seen in our divorce rates and fantastic residential mobility. It is also the end product of a long history of increasing alienation that has been noted from the time of Rousseau to the present (322, 323, 324, 325). One immediate result of alienation is the proliferation of an ever increasing deviancy (326, 327), including alcoholism. So prevalent is deviancy in our society that many of the previously rejected *life-styles* are now in the process of being presented as acceptable, or at least tolerated, alternatives to the more traditionally-defined ways. Homosexuality, as an example, is being politically pushed by homophile societies toward a legalized status.

The homophile societies in part reflect a constant pattern in American life—the quest for community. There appears to be an almost innate need in all social mammals to belong to a small, personalized and structured group. There is an enormous sense of worth and security in belonging to a caring group that both loves and protects. Most primitive and folk people belong to such groups and these are sufficiently small so that one knows all other members personally, and in large part interacts with them as known individuals rather than as strangers filling socially defined roles. In the larger and more complex societies of civilization there usually remain stable and truthworthy equivalents as in the primary group represented by the family in traditional

China. However, in the typical city most of our sociocultural
patterns adapt us to interacting with strangers in a largely
impersonal way. With the breakdown of family and community,
America is today indeed becoming "a nation of strangers" (328).
Our deep need for acceptance has led us to develop the
chameleon-like ability to blend in and conform in any temporary
relationship with others. In Riesman's terms, lacking either
tradition or inner values to guide our relationships, we have
become "other-directed" (329). We tend to seek acceptance
from others by trying to live up to their expectations of us
rather than by an inner mental compass or a tradition. At best,
this in itself is an unfulfilling existence and one that can only
result in a deep sense of alienation and of being alone. Increasingly large numbers of Americans feel themselves at any one
point as merely players in socially assigned roles such as teacher,
policeman, plumber, Black or driver. The great need to belong
to a caring primary group in this type of environment is
enormous. Like the primitive, we each seek to belong to a group
we care for and that cares about us. We long deeply to be thus
intimately associated with others who share our values, our
belief in the meaning of life and the difference between good
and evil. We need people we respect to applaud us one way
or another when we have fulfilled certain shared values. This
need in America has produced a proliferation of voluntary
associations seeking to provide *brotherhood, sisterhood* and other
caring and personalized relationships. We have become a nation
of joiners in a multitude of available organizations serving as
substitutes for the primitive band. These include such diverse
bodies as hippie communes, Elks, Masons, Rotarians, Moose and
the deluge of such power-seeking groups as Communist cells,
The Birch Society, Blacks, Women's-Libbers and homophile
groups. One of the most successful attempts at forming a society
based upon a common experience, mutual care and group support
is the society of Alcoholics Anonymous.

All of these attempts at creating a meaningful small community rest largely on creating a simplified and absolute system
which is sanctioned by some higher meaning or deity. This in
turn is an unconscious quest for the reliability and predictability

of the primitive and folk systems. It also represents an escape from the conflicts and uncertainties of the contemporary American system. To fully understand the differences between such folk structures and the confusion of many sophisticated civilizations, one must examine the differences in the ratio of "alternatives" and "universals" (330). In any society, a part of its cultural totality consists of universals, that is to say there is only one known or accepted form available. Thus, when the Aborigines of Central Australia wanted to travel in the days before European contact they had but one universal mode—walking. On the other hand, in every society, in some areas of behavior, alternatives are available. Thus, in the U.S. we have an enormous number of alternate ways of travelling ranging from walking to jet aircraft. A historical fact is that as one moves from primitive to civilized, the alternatives increase and the universals decrease. One may diagram any society by an outer circle representing the total culture and an inner circle indicating the relative presence of alternatives and universals. Thus, the difference between a primitive or folk society and a civilization would be diagrammed:

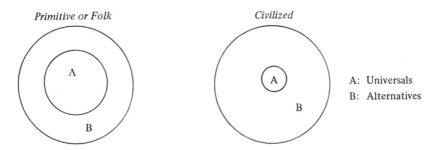

Primitive or Folk   *Civilized*

A: Universals
B: Alternatives

The significance to emotional well-being in the comparative ratio of alternatives and universals is in regard to values. For the purpose of this discussion, I will simply define a value as any behavior which a society defines as *good* and therefore rewards. For example, bravery was a value to the Crow Indians and when it was demonstrated in warfare it was rewarded with high honors. And values are as critical to human motivation as instincts are to lower forms of life. Instinct leads a salmon up a torrential river to breed, spawn and die fulfilled. The human is guided toward his fulfillment by achieving the values he shares with his primary group. When values grow numerous and begin to conflict, the human begins to experience stress. In primitive and folk systems all major values are within the core of universals and this type of stress is absent. In civilized societies the tendency is for values to multiply and drift from the core of universals into the sphere of alternatives. This is discomfitting. When these alternate values are in conflict, it is often unbearable and creates social distress and a yearning for a simplification of the value system. Occasionally the response is for the society to split, each half achieving an even greater homogeneity in its common hostility toward its opposite. An example would be the Civil War. Another response is to create a simplified and integrated value system by both persuasion and coercion. Thus, the Nazi movement resolved the anxieties of Germany after World War I by offering a unified and *meaningful* value system supposedly sanctioned by a semi-divine state and forcibly removing all who would not conform. In fact, much of recent political history can be seen in a similar structure which may be diagrammed thusly, with * representing values:

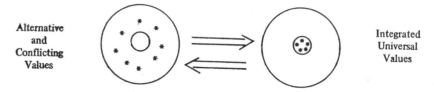

Alternative and Conflicting Values

Integrated Universal Values

Likewise, each of the great world religions, Buddhism, Christianity and Islam, appeared in periods of multiplying and conflicting value alternatives and presented a core system of integrated universal values. All three began by using persuasion, but at various times in their history resorted to coercion, Buddhism least of all, however.

The United States has from its beginnings swung from one pole toward the other while never reaching the fullest possible manifestation of either extreme. When conflicting values are multiplying, the resultant psychological discomfort produces a need for the integrated universal system. Various techniques appear to achieve this. The Un-American Activities Committee represents one approach, the moral persuasion of Billy Graham another. However, as the country swings toward universal values, one of these, the belief in freedom, begins the opposite movement. The current value confusion is creating a distrust of the value of freedom and as we begin our swing toward a more homogeneous system of values we may lack this brake to its going full-term. As early as 1941 Erich Fromm noted the felt need of an "escape from freedom" (331). Today Skinner sees freedom as a definite danger and urges it be abolished by his conditioning techniques (35). The chemist, Kenneth Clark, also sees freedom as an explosive condition needing control but, taking the opposite approach in the nature-nurture debate, urges a chemically applied leash to total freedom (332).

In the meantime, American culture has produced its own means to handle the multitudinous field of alternate values. One of these is to create a sense of unity in the face of an external enemy. The threat of Japan created a united effort after Pearl Harbor. For some decades thereafter a fear of *world Communism* served equally well although its function today is rapidly diminishing. Similar unifying processes have been used in other times, *e.g.* the fear of the Anti-Christ in Europe as the medieval unity began to crumble. It is used in a more restricted way within the U.S. today as various power movements define an enemy in the we-they dichotomy. Thus, Blacks define the White enemy and the White supremacists point to *the Black threat;* Women's-Libbers unify by hating male culture, and Republicans and Democrats owe their respective unity to a negative and threatening image of their opposites as much as to uniformity in their own ranks.

These conflicts splitting society are increasingly causing a sense of splintering within the individual, for Americans also internalize conflicting values so that their mental value system in fact resembles that of the society overflowing with a mass of competing and conflicting values. As Lowell Holmes has put it,

> The cultural pattern of the United States is one involving numerous paradoxes and contradictions. This is probably the case

in any complex civilization undergoing rapid change. . . . The interesting thing about these cultural contradictions is that the opposing attitudes and behavioral patterns . . . do not necessarily represent the views of different subgroups but are found simultaneously in the value system and behavior of the 'average' American (333: p. 199).

The columnist Charles McCabe described the same tendency when he said, "One of the infuriating things about the human mind is that it can easily hold differing and even conflicting propositions at the same time" (334). The psychocultural technique to handle this is *compartmentalization*—dividing the psyche into sections like pieces of a pie, each with its own integrated and nonconflicting set of values. Thus, although the individual does carry numerous value conflicts, they are segregated and kept from clashing by limiting the values being utilized to the role being played in any particular action. Thus, *situational ethics* can allow a man to play many roles without being aware of any conflict of belief. For example, the father can honestly lecture his son on the need to obey and respect the law about marijuana while in other roles he himself exceeds the speed limit as a driver or exaggerates a bit on expenses in income tax declarations.

As long as conflicting values are segregated by role compartmentalization no incongruity or anxiety results. However, when the separating walls collapse, bringing two roles with conflicting values into the same arena, extreme anxiety manifests itself. In the words of Leon Festinger, a "cognitive dissonance" is the result (335). A felt need for consistency will then produce an attempt either to rationalize the conflict or to resolve it by appealing to a higher authority such as a god, a minister, a psychiatrist or a court. When the higher authority cannot adequately solve the dilemma, the anxiety increases. This is currently being demonstrated on both the individual and the national level in the debate and agony over school busing. The higher authority in this case is the U.S. Constitution. However, this document defends the two conflicting values: freedom and equality. For example, a poll of San Francisco showed all minority groups as well as the majority strongly opposed to busing. Yet, busing was ordered to achieve equality. In other words, to achieve either value meant compromising its opposite.

The internalization of two conflicting values which cannot be resolved can be diagrammed by what I have called the *anxiety arrow* as follows:

In the case of school busing, one arrowhead points toward freedom and the other toward equality. Our Christian heritage, as mentioned earlier, sees man's ultimate fate as choosing between good and evil and forbids compromise. Thus, synthesis comes hard and we tend to want to find a means to totally eradicate one pole and give total victory to the other. Lacking a higher authority or a means to logically resolve the conflict, we learn to live with anxiety. All of us, with the exception of some of our integrated folk communities and religious fundamentalists, live with a heavy collection of anxiety arrows manifesting themselves from time to time. If we cannot resolve the conflict, a high level of anxiety is built up with its biological correlates including elevated levels of epinephrine and lactate. If the conflicts cannot be submerged or replaced, the basis is laid for anxiety neurosis.

We have a number of acceptable techniques for the relief of anxiety but by far the most popular is the use of chemistry. This is the natural result of a society which prides itself on its science and material progress. It is also a by-product of the American expectation of immediate results. Thus, we rely on strong purges for blocked bowels, aspirin for headaches and massive amounts of antidepressants and tranquilizers for uncomfortable emotional states. However, the original soother of a suffering psyche is alcohol. Its use is an accepted self-administered method of psychotherapy. It works. However, drinking or abstinence are also frequently structured as an anxiety arrow within the mind. Those who have been programmed with the concept of alcohol as evil as well as good fail to derive the full effect of its anxiety-relieving qualities and may instead at first experience guilt and later a heightening of anxiety. As with prohibition on a national scale, today many individuals find relating meaningfully to alcohol to be difficult when it is both the product of a taboo and a sanction. This American ambivalence about alcohol has been noted in the professional literature on alcoholism at least since 1940 (336). This ambivalence seems to be characteristic primarily of the Protestant-dominated cultures and is undoubtedly an important factor in gamma alcoholism with its associated emotional turmoil and problems of intoxicated behavior.

Ambivalence, then, is probably one of the forces contributing to antisocial drunken behavior. A number of studies have demonstrated that primitive and folk peoples who in fact encourage total intoxication rarely witness such antisocial behavior by inebriates (9, 337, 338). Their group and individual psyches are structured, as diagrammed earlier, by integrated, universal, nonconflicting value systems. Therefore, the almost ever-present anxiety arrows of contemporary Americans are rare with primitive and folk peoples. Most of their anxieties are shared and are attributed to a common cause external to the individuals. This anxiety is generally handled by group activity in religious actions, shared labor projects, warfare or group ritualized drinking. Horton (339) specifically concluded from a study of primitive drinking that the primary function of alcohol is the reduction of anxiety. However, such group drinking to relieve a shared anxiety is entirely different in function and result from Americans who drink to relieve their own individualized and distinctive anxieties. Further, all adult primitive and folk peoples who value intoxication are models for the young of proper drunken behavior. As Washburne stated,

> Thus, by the time an individual starts drinking, he has a whole series of expectations in mind about his behavior when drinking, and his behavior when drunk will follow the pattern laid down by his society. (This does not exclude possible psychological changes produced by alcohol which may affect his behavior) (337: p. 262).

MacAndrew and Edgerton came to exactly the same conclusion eight years later when they said, ". . . we have contended that the way people comport themselves when they are drunk is determined not by alcohol's toxic assault upon the seat of moral judgement, conscience or the like, but by what their society makes of and imparts to them concerning the state of drunkenness" (338: p. 165). These authors continue to state that even should alcohol be shown to biologically affect behavioral centers it would not change their opinion. In their words, ". . . if the 'worst' should happen, it would not really change the supremacy of social factors over physiological ones" (338: p. 166).

Basically, I agree with these opinions. If behavior is learned it is obvious that its manifestation will reflect what is learned, whether sober or drunk. In a primitive society with homogenous values and traditionalized social drunkenness, deviance is not to be expected. However, as I have shown elsewhere (9), when a Mexican Indian becomes acculturated to the point of abandoning his culture and entering Mestizo society, he is unable to cope with internal conflicts, a new drinking environment and the use of alcohol. While socially-proper drunken behavior was typical of his first culture, he now tends to become morose or belligerent. I do not, however, rule out the possibility that diet changes and a different set of alcoholic beverages may physiologically *short-circuit* some acculturating Indian overdrinkers to produce definitely psychotic drunken behavior. Alcohol-induced psychosis is an established fact and I have witnessed numerous alcoholics whose drunken behavior may be due to temporary alcohol derangement of the nervous system as well as to internal conflicts. Needless to say, this manifested deviant behavior is conditioned by learning, usually being the negative expression of some value. This does not, however, mean that social factors outweigh physical factors in intoxication or mental illness. One's cultural education and value system will determine how the drunkenness or mental illness is expressed. After all, a monolingual American drunk or paranoid could hardly express his feelings in Chinese or by the distress calls of a bird he had never heard.

However, the fact is incontrovertible that a homogeneous, traditional, personally defined society can develop patterns in which drunkenness is sanctioned and drunken behavior tends to reinforce social bonds rather than disrupt them. An addicted alcoholic might live out his life in such a culture and never be noticeable by his conduct until such time as alcohol-produced nervous pathologies resulted in psychotic behavior. This appears to be true of civilized as well as primitive and folk people. Although the Chinese traditionally drink very little, those in Hong Kong have added heavy drinking to their more traditional patterns. The Hong Kong Chinese usually over-drinks alone rather than in a group but his behavior is mild and not anti-social. His inner integration is intact through a drunk and he may even become addicted unknown to himself or anyone else (340).

Not only may cultures structure most drunken behavior, but apparently, may limit the incidence of alcoholism. An integrated traditional society which approves of only limited drinking will obviously have less alcoholism if overdrinking in itself can cause the affliction. The orthodox Jews, for example, drink most moderately but are also members of a supportive and integrated community. Snyder (341), cites these as the major factors in the low incidence of alcoholism among the traditional Jews. He also indicates that as Jews leave their traditional culture and the closely-knit structure of their society, they become increasingly susceptible to alcoholism. His findings, as he points out (341: p. 201) agree with those of Cheinisse (342) in France fifty years ago when he wrote,

> Judaism has in general conserved up to the present time this characteristic of collective and social ties which the other churches have lost little by little, and it is precisely this force of cohesion and concentration of the religious community which has kept the great Jewish mass from alcoholism. But wherever the traditional tie is weakened, one immediately sees the alcoholic contagion open a fissure and penetrate this milieu which previously appeared absolutely refractory.

A nutritionist might question whether the abandonment of the traditional Jewish diet might not make way for some metabolic factors as well in the etiology of alcoholism in deculturated Jews. The low rate of alcoholism in Italian culture is likewise in part the result of an integrated value system, strong familial and community ties plus the fact that alcohol is regarded as a food rather than as an intoxicant (343). Again, a contributing factor may be nutrition.

Unlike the traditional Chinese, Jew or Italian, the American lives with a belief in progress rather than tradition and his collapsing family and community structures are leaving him an alienated and lonely individual. Increasing unresolvable inner conflicts increase his anxiety level while he has been led by the *American dream* to expect an eventual utopia of total happiness and bliss. He has also learned that alcohol will ease the anxiety, serve as a *social lubricant* which facilitates a sense of social cohesion, and at times creates a temporary illusion of a utopian bliss. His approach to alcohol has been strongly influenced by the American equation of bigness and goodness. As a people we have, at least until recently, treasured things for their size. He stands in awe of the tallest building, the enormous gap of the Grand Canyon, marvels at the size of the King Ranch, and respects Alaska for becoming the largest state. He also treasures the double martini, the *Texas-sized* jigger glass and the *two-hour cocktail hour.* He believes that anything worth doing is worth doing in a big way. Therefore, a man is highly admired when he can be described as one who works hard and plays hard. And his anxieties because of his drinking are also frequently of jumbo proportions. He also eats big so that obesity is a major problem. However, he does not eat wisely and any number of books indicate that a surfeit of the *wrong* foods and a neglect of essential nutrients may contribute to the prevalence of many pathologies including alcoholism.

The American delight in drinking is also influenced by the high value we place on adventure. Probably in part a heritage of our frontier days, this adventurous bent is nourished by our fiction, movies and television. Further, a favorite adventure is to skirt the thin borderline between culturally defined propriety and sin. Thus, the shocking sight of a see through blouse in public, or a proper citizen sneaking in to see a bottomless show are both regarded as adventuresome. The attempt of entertainment to expose the female body to the absolute millimeter of legality has been a traditional and adventuring quest. In fact, the recent removal of nearly all restrictions on physical display and sexual exhibits has almost destroyed one of America's favorite games. Part of the syndrome of the American sexual game has always been alcohol and few American men can conceive of engaging in the sport of seduction without alcohol as an accompaniment. And, like sexual display, it is regarded as adventuresome to drink to the very edge of a limit. Thus, to drink until the last millisecond before bars legally close is fun and adventurous. Also, to drink to the edge of drunkenness without quite crossing the line is seen as an exciting goal.

If approaching a tolerated line is an adventure, crossing it is often regarded as high adventure. Thus, the pursuit of drunkenness is for many as thrill-producing as was seduction before the onset of today's *new morality*. The degree of adventure is always directly related to the lessening degree of control in the hands of the player. Thus, the gambler, the parachute jumper and the drunk are all playing with the goddess of fortune. When all of the player's control is lost, including an objective view of reality, he passes into a new subjective existence which, depending on one's viewpoint, may be described as the height of spiritual attainment (344, 345, 346) or psychosis.

The quest of another reality underlies much of our semi-religious drug culture. In a recent book, Andrew Weil even postulates that man has a normal drive to achieve such "altered states of consciousness" (347). I believe that it would be valid to say that such a *trip* would be rated a psychosis if it was one-way, but an altered state of consciousness if it was a round trip and the tripper could meaningfully relate his experience to his everyday existence.

Many cultures certainly endorse the pursuit of truth or power by entering into such a subjective reality and then returning. Such cultures see the five senses as barriers between the self and a greater truth or power and so seek to break through. Borrowing from Nietzsche, Ruth Benedict (348) named such cultures "Dionysian," after the god of wine. Other cultures tend to regard anything beyond the five senses as best left alone and cling to an objective reality and to predictability. Benedict termed these cultures "Apollonian." Except for the recent developments of our mystic and drug-oriented subcultures, Americans have preferred to leave this other-reality to the psychotics, early Christians and Oriental mystics. However, using the terms loosely, one may state that Americans have tended toward the Apollonian goal in their work-a-day world and sought after the Dionysian in their play. The predictability and reliability of good accounting typifies the ideals of the American mundane world. In all play total control is given up and varying elements of chance are introduced, such as in parlor games, or athletics, gambling on cards or on whether a theater ticket will prove to be worth the price. Reality is left behind in Disneyland, T.V., movies and Las Vegas. An element of danger is present in drag racing, scuba diving or riding on a roller coaster. Excessive drinking above all can be regarded as pointed toward a Dionysian goal for as one heavy but not addicted drinker said to me, "Booze is beautiful! It brings beauty into my world, fills me with power and leads me on fascinating and unpredictable adventures." The heavy drinker also has the added adventure of trying to approach but stop short of true alcoholism. The alcoholic unwillingly approaches but tries to stop short of insanity. He often avoids this by another trip—death.

CHAPTER VII:

THE AMERICAN ALCOHOLIC: I

WITHIN THE TURBULENT, shifting mass of American values, alcoholics abound. The most common species of this being is the one already described and called the gamma by Jellinek. In the earlier stages of his disease, the gamma is frequently a daily drinker. As alcoholism advances he becomes increasingly aware of his loss of control in regard to both his intake and his behavior after the first few drinks. As blackouts and regrettable drinking experiences increase, he becomes aware that something is wrong. He generally begins, at this point, to limit his drinks and at times can do this for varying but unpredictable periods. Finally, after an especially stressful drunk, he decides to abstain. This he can frequently do for a considerable period of time but inevitably he again drinks. Occasionally, especially if he has been abstinent for some time, he finds he can control his drinking for days or weeks. But inevitably he gets drunk once again and usually when he least expects it. After one or more drunks he once more swears off all alcohol and the pattern repeats. He now becomes a cyclical drinker with periods of sobriety interrupted by binges, each of which continues until a point of exhaustion is reached. Segovia-Riquelme and his associates have therefore labeled this type of addiction "intermittent alcoholism" (349). The period between drunks varies from alcoholic to alcoholic. These cycles are roughly predictable for any one alcoholic although their timing may be drastically altered by stressful incidents or situations. The length of each drunk also follows a fairly regular pattern for each alcoholic. Large numbers drink on *one night stands* while others drink excessively for several days or even weeks. Generally, the longer the binge period, the longer also is the sober portion of the cycle. Unlike drug addiction or delta alcoholism which require a daily intake of the chemical addictive, the gamma becomes subject to short-term addictive periods which disastrously punctuate his life until he achieves death or a lasting sobriety.

The more knowledgeable and experienced specialists in alcoholism have long noted that there are two subspecies of gamma alcoholism. One of these, which I shall follow Fox in labeling as "primary" (350), is neurotic from childhood and manifests the symptoms of alcoholism early in his drinking career. The other, which Fox calls "secondary," shows a more normal childhood and usually drinks for many years before any major signs of alcoholism are noticeable. The primary, I believe, rests on a hereditary base while the secondary is acquired. The primary is the product of an inherently weak constitutional system which is severely damaged by psychological stress or disease during childhood. The resulting psychophysical condition is one resembling anxiety-neurosis. The secondary alcoholic is the product of physical damage produced directly by years of heavy drinking. The secondary's personality is not necessarily neurotic and most, if not all, of his psychological aberrations are the direct result of his alcoholism.

Ruth Fox has clearly described this distinction between the two alcoholisms. She states that

> Primary addicts are those persons who have been emotionally maladjusted since childhood. Alcohol has seemed a godsend to them, helping to solve temporarily their basic social and psychological problems. They usually have become alcoholics at a very early age, and they are more difficult to treat than the secondary addicts since they have never used the more mature avenues of self-expression. They tend to have the emotional equipment of a child. When every difficulty has been met by evading it through alcohol, they have developed few other, more mature techniques of living. They must be helped to grow up.

Fox describes the secondary alcoholics as

> . . . those persons, not obviously neurotic in their early life, who have slipped in later life into pathological drinking through some kind of habituation process. They are often persons of great talent and ability who have for years been heavy social drinkers. To their dismay, they find they have lost control. Having once stepped over

the borderline into alcoholic drinking, they can never resume drinking in a controlled fashion (350: pp. 164-165).

The same distinction between these two types of alcoholism has been noted by others. In 1949, Tintera and Lovell, who attributed alcoholism to adrenal malfunction, likewise distinguished between the early alcoholic in whom hypoadrenocorticism leads to alcoholism and the late alcoholic who is adrenally damaged by a massive and continued intake of alcohol (351). In 1950 Landis and Bolles noted the difference between those who became alcoholic because of an inadequate personality structure and those who became alcoholic as a result of years of heavy drinking (70: p. 229). Earlier, Knight (352) had separated "essential" from "reactive" alcoholics in roughly the same way. However, as I interpret him, his reactive would combine elements of the secondary with the situational overdrinker. Diethelm also has identified a dichotomy and says, "Alcoholism which starts in early adult life occurs most frequently in psychopathic personalities and in immature and dependent individuals" (353: p. 291). In view of the shared observations of these and others, I propose that Jellinek's gamma classification be either replaced by or subdivided into primary and secondary alcoholics.

My own field experience has also made clear to me the differences between these two modalities of alcoholism. The primary is distinguishable by the early manifestation of alcoholic symptoms following his first encounter with ethanol. This I attribute to a genetic susceptibility. However, I am by no means supporting an absolute genetic determinism. As Mazur and Robertson have stated,

> Substantial evidence indicates that an individual's behavior is influenced by his genotype. This does not mean that the genes immutably predetermine behavioral characteristics. On the contrary, genetically based behaviors appear to be greatly modifiable through interaction with the physical and social environment (28: p. 62).

At no level of vertebrate behavior is a genotypic determinism absolute. If it were it would be impossible to train jungle beasts to perform for circus audiences. No behavior can be properly interpreted then solely in terms of heredity. In this regard, Chapple resumés Sewall Wright's conclusion that one may not ". . . assume that environment and heredity are independent of each other . . . the genes are the ultimate physiological and behavioral agents, and the phenotype is the resultant of the interplay of environment and the genotype" (26: p. 136). Chapple could therefore rightly conclude that "The extreme environmentalism of Watsonian behaviorism is as fallacious as its counterpart in rigid advocacy of genetic predestination" (26: p. 137).

Inheritance, however, appears to be a major factor in primary alcoholism. In fact, evidence is mounting to demonstrate that genetic factors are involved in variations of all drug reactions (354). What the primary inherits, of course, is a predisposition to breakdowns in the nervous and metabolic systems and not alcoholism *per se*. The primary's weakly structured defenses break down quickly after exposure to alcohol and the first symptoms of the disease appear. These early manifestations of alcoholism may take place at any period ranging from the first drinking experience to months or even years later. The variation in the appearance of alcoholic symptoms rests upon such variables as the degree of the genetic weakness, psychological and physical wear and tear before the onset of drinking and the actual drinking situation. Generally speaking, primary alcoholism is always recognizable at the latest after five or six years of regular drinking. This is in notable contrast to the secondary alcoholic who may enjoy from fifteen to fifty years of controlled drinking before the onset of the disease. The age of the individual at the time of the first alcoholic symptoms does not in itself offer any clue as to whether it is of the primary or secondary varieties. I encountered several primaries who had grown up and resided in abstinent settings in the Midwest and Texas who were not even exposed to alcohol until middle age. However, following their first drinking experience, the disease bloomed rapidly. I even met one old gentleman who took his first drink on his 70th birthday and was committed to the state hospital for acute alcoholism three months later. I am sure there are primaries in abstinent religious subgroups who have never touched alcohol and so live out their lives as anxiety-neurotics rather than as alcoholics.

The length of controlled drinking the primary demonstrates depends in part on the stresses placed on his genetic weaknesses before his first exposure to alcohol. This damage may be in part nutritional through his own inability to adequately metabolize a surfeit of cow milk and an absence of mother's milk, or an excess of refined sugar. Five of my sample had actually experienced drunkenness before the onset of puberty and this experience may have affected their susceptible natures as thoroughly as alcohol did Myer's rats. Others had experienced severe physical illnesses in infancy and childhood which may have contributed to their alcoholism. The overwhelming number of my cases, however, during preadulthood, experienced extreme psychological stress which seemed to have pushed the genetic predisposition into the psychobiological set necessary for primary alcoholism. Alexander had earlier stated this same interpretation when he wrote, "It is probable that the genetotrophic factor alone in most cases would not lead to malignant forms of alcoholism without additional interpersonal experiences which further contribute to the development of oral fixation and a lack of internal discipline. . . ." (71: p. 140).

From the literature and my own case studies it is apparent that these early psychological stresses may take many forms. I found practically every type of inadequate parent and deprivation experience in the backgrounds of my sample of primary alcoholics. The behavioral and environmental literature on alcoholism presents an endless flow of such deprivations and it would serve no point to repeat them here. What I did find significant to primary alcoholics was that all endured preadult stresses of severe intensity. While the nature of these stresses varied, I have never met a primary alcoholic who had enjoyed an adequate childhood.

Equally significant, all the primary alcoholics whom I came to know well were deeply stamped with multiple pairs of antinomous values in the patterns of the unresolvable anxiety arrow.

The primary alcoholic lives with these contradictory clues to action all of his life and thus finds adequate and effective behavior difficult in many areas of his existence. If he acts to fulfill one value its contradiction will produce guilt or fear of failure. Therefore, he is keyed to action most of the time but is unable to act. This condition is definable as anxiety and is characterized by a high epinephrine level as well as the other biological correlates of anxiety-neurosis. I found three anxiety arrows especially prevalent in my sample. The first of these was "I must excel" vs. "I am inadequate." The second most typical of those from old-fashioned good Christian homes, was "I must be good" vs. "I am too evil to be capable of goodness." The third was "I must be popular" vs. "I am unlikeable, unlovable and no one will ever accept me." The result of these conflicts is inevitably an individual suffering from a sense of inadequacy and inferiority. He also has never learned, or is afraid to try, techniques of successful socialization. A positive feedback between the inadequate self-concept and the social reality leads to an increasing sense of unworthiness and social isolation. Although he frequently tries to please others and thus win acceptance by being *other-directed,* he always sees himself apart and rejected. The isolation in itself heightens the feelings of anxiety.

It is the primary who really knows what is meant by the statement that "Alcoholism is a lonely disease." Most of the primaries I have known felt different, apart and alone from their earliest memories. The primary is a psychological cripple and frequently does become a dependent personality long before his first drink. Several of my sample, however, had parents who would not accept them in this role. These either left home or were thrown out during their late teens. Out of the home they reacted with fairly inadequate attempts to prove their independence while displaying futile and occasionally pathological hatred of all authoritarian figures. At least three of these, once their pathological drinking began, seemed almost consciously to seek the security of being in jail where their needs were cared for, no decisions need to be made and a positive identification is found which is shared by fellow prisoners creating a temporary sense of being integrated into a community.

However, for the deprived childhood to produce the setting for future alcoholism, this stress must be translated into the physical being of the individual. The primary's genetically weak constitution is extremely susceptible to further damage by such stress. The behaviorists would disagree, but from their own evidence cannot demonstrate why identical childhood deprivation leads one case into alcoholism but not another. Menninger sought to explain the difference in terms of the relative quantity of deprivation. He wrote, ". . . the alcoholic probably does not suffer in childhood anything qualitatively different from what the rest of us suffer, but apparently there is a quantitative difference" (120: pp. 169-170). I do not believe that Menninger's argument carries any conviction. Anyone in the psychological area of research has met many individuals who suffered through childhoods as bad as or worse than any alcoholic's and yet never ended up with a drinking problem. As an example, the hideously deformed creature described by Ashley Montague as *The Elephant Man* (355) was so gross physically that he met total rejection from a hostile world until given sanctuary by a kind and caring physician. The elephant man, forced to exhibit his physical deformity as a freak to earn a bare existence, knew that he was not only different and alone, but that he repelled people. No one could have suffered a greater alienation and yet he maintained a sense of integrity and never took to drink. It is obvious that alienation and deprivation in themselves do not always automatically lead to alcoholism in Western culture. After all, values and self-concepts are not free-floating ideas but are physically recorded in the brain in as real a fashion as a song is engraved on a record. Further, the brain relates to the entire body and any modification of it must have some physical correlates. These biological facts in the alcoholic separate him from the nonalcoholic. The behaviorists, however, have ignored all biological aspects of mentality to the detriment of research and therapy. If my hypothesis is correct, psychotherapy will no more *cure* a primary alcoholic than counseling a record will correct the scratch which renders the errors in the music it plays.

The behaviorists' error stems from their reinterpretation of Freud rather than from Freud's writings. In one regard, for example, Chapple states that "Many psychoanalysts assumed that one could ignore hereditary influences. Freud, however, was by no means so dogmatic on this subject" (26: p. 128). Lowen also says

> We can be quite sure that Freud was not unaware that psycho-analysis had eventually to be grounded in biology to achieve the scientific status he desired for it. If he then limited psychoanalysis to the study of psychic phenomena it must have been because he felt that our knowledge of psychic processes was not sufficiently secure to attempt to bridge the two realms of human functioning. It is to his great merit that he did succeed in constructing a frame-work of psychic functioning which could serve as the springboard for the leap into biology (165: p. 20).

Agreeing with that interpretation, Mandell *et al.* went on to add that

> It is tempting to speculate that if Freud were alive today he would be looking for loci of his theories in neurochemical systems rather than on the couch. He would perhaps conceptualize his 'mechanisms of defense' not as repression, displacement and such but rather feedback inhibition, changes in enzyme amount or activity, increases or decreases in receptor sensitivity, and alterations in substrate supply—all in the service of keeping our neuro transmitter systems functioning to stabilize the excitability of our brains' many chemical systems (58: p. 72).

Further, as Blum (155: p. 277) points out, Freud (356), in 1940, ". . . expected that drugs would be found which cure mental illness. . . ." As far as alcoholism, and probably the whole of mental illness is concerned, I believe Freud was basically correct. His general conceptualization of mental illness is still valid if one accepts his psychic descriptions as mythological analogies for describing models of interpersonal relations and intrapsychic experiences. I therefore think it unfortunate that, as Leon Salzman says, ". . . Freud's stress on the influence of man's biological requirements on his ultimate psychological develop-ment is likewise under attack. . . ." (357: p. 8).

The exact manner by which stress permanently alters the body's homeostasis is not known, but there is little doubt that this can and does happen. It is apparent that adult homeostasis is in part inaugurated by the reception and response to certain stimuli received in preadulthood (28: p. 98). Likewise, the absence of the appropriate stimuli, the inability to respond to these appropriately, or the reception of inappropriate stimuli may produce psychological and somatic damage and the permanent imbalance of the total system. For example, Blum states, "The infant is not equipped with means to delay need-satisfactions. Tensions are not accumulated but are discharged either in crying or motor restlessness or, if help does not arrive soon enough, in pathological alterations of his body processes. . . ." (155: p. 261). However, infancy is only one of the "sensitive" or "critical" periods during the maturation process during which the adult "set" is jelled (28. p. 114; 358: p. 82). These critical periods are only roughly defined, but once the adult jell is established, it seems to be set for life no matter how inadequately the body and mind may be conditioned to cope with existence. As Selye put it, ". . . our bodily defense reactions can also fall into a groove . . . by always responding with the same exaggerated hormonal response, whether it is appropriate to the situation or not" (252: p. 257).

Many human conditions previously attributed to a purely mental or environmental causality are turning out to be due to either heredity, preadult constitutional changes or both. Depression is a case in point. Previously defined by behaviorists as purely a nonbiological mental state, depression is today being defined in physiological terms. Schildkraut *et al.,* for example, write that "Whereas specific genetic factors may be of importance in the etiology of some, and possibly all, depressions, it is quite conceivable that early experiences of the infant or child may cause enduring biochemical changes and that these may predispose some individuals to depressions in adulthood" (242: p. 28). Indications today are showing that the gene associated with depression is located in the X or female chromosome (359). The actual biochemistry of depression involves imbalances of noradrenaline, dopamine and serotonin (360). The relief of depression apparently to some degree rests on the hypothalamus producing the thyrotropin-releasing hormone (TRH) which triggers the production of TSH, the thyroid-stimulating hormone (361).

As with anxiety and depression, probably most emotional responses are products of inheritance, preadult modifications of the constitution and the immediate environment. The extent to which childhood experiences can modify the homeostasis of normal development is seen in *deprivation dwarfism.* Such dwarfs are the product of an emotionally starved infancy which results in modifications of the pituitary and hypothalamus in areas controlling growth (358, 362, 363). Likewise, early deprivation of the primary alcoholic working upon a genetic weakness produces an emotionally anxious individual set for addiction when introduced to alcohol. Further, this biological set is irreversible by the medical techniques available today.

The psychosomatic set of the primary alcoholic is especially reflected in his failure to demonstrate appropriate aggressive behavior. This correlates directly with McClelland *et al.'s* (167) definition of the alcoholic being an individual in pursuit of a sense of power. The primary alcoholic indeed feels powerless even before the onset of active alcoholism. One of my respondents summed up his youth in these words, "I felt so alone and in- effectual that I could never act from any inner conviction but the need to be accepted. My whole life seemed to be geared to pleasing others so they would tolerate me. I really felt more like a puppet whose strings others held than like a human being in my own right." The young primary never adequately develops his competitive skills and therefore comes to see himself as a *loser.* This is a feeling most of them carry for life. Even those who somehow attain high positions or honor do not overcome this inner sense of being inadequate and can rarely accept success as really their due. One of my respondents had attained an international fame in his field of endeavor and had every right to feel great satisfaction with himself. However, after we had become close friends, he one day said, "I really feel as though every success I've had has been given me by someone else or was purely accidental. I have this fear that someday everyone will recognize this fact and see me as totally inept. Rationally I know this attitude is stupid, but I can't lose the fear." More typically, the primary fails to achieve because of a low energy drive, the inability to compete, the fear of trying and the mere fact of living up to his own negative self image. Societal response to this lack of initiative and success is always negative and thereby positively reinforces his sense of inadequacy. Despite our attempt to see America as a protector of the *underdog,* we cannot tolerate underdogs that we see doomed to ultimate total failure. Above all, our respect system is based on rewarding those who successfully "fight" their way up in the dominance hierarchy (364). As Elliot Aronson has said, "As a culture, we Americans seem to thrive on competition; we reward winners and turn away from losers" (365: p. 154). This is the most destructive environment conceivable for the primary alcoholic and one in which almost inevitably he is sooner or later to seek refuge in alcohol which will usually finally destroy him.

The psychological factors in the blunting of the primary's aggressive drive are of course varied. In several of my cases, an unloving and domineering father was a major contributing factor. In another, a favorite elder brother ". . . always seemed to be rewarded for just existing and my parents seemed to ignore any small success I had. Trying just stopped being worthwhile." Several of my cases had parents who as a regular procedure belittled any accomplishment of their children. In one sad case, a young primary brought home a report card of straight A's, but as she proudly offered it to her parents she was informed that they were separating. In her mind success became associated with strife between needed protectors, a feeling of being abandoned by the father, and a sense of guilt because her report card which ". . . in my mind caused the separation." Another primary was from a family that demanded high grades and he consistently did poorly. When he was sixteen it was discovered that he suffered from both visual and auditory malfunctions. Their correction came too late for he was already self-classified as a loser and had for over a year been secretly drinking heavily on weekends.

The traumatic childhood of the primary works further damage on the genetic weaknesses of his constitution. The primary is also molded into a losing personality type. As a loser he lacks an adequate aggressive drive. The nature of this drive, however, is even more bitterly debated by specialists than is the nature of alcoholism, for it has ramifications from biology into politics and theology. To fully understand the ideological and semantic barriers in interpreting alcoholism, it will be necessary to digress into the pertinent squabble over the nature of aggression itself.

Here again, the determined opposing stands of the nature and nurture schools produce a confusing flood of contradictory statements. Biological determinists, ethologists and psychoanalysts assume the existence of a biological aggressive drive. The more dogmatic behaviorists and environmentalists define human aggression as merely the product of a constellation of learned patterns of behavior. On the ideological level the debate is even more confusing. The general American tendency is to equate aggression with violence and evil while in fact individuals are rewarded for successfully demonstrating forms of aggression in the dominance hierarchies of business, academia, science and the arts. The negative image of aggression is to a large extent rooted in our Christian tradition with its formal sanction of the nonaggressive virtues of humility and meekness. Christianity, in fact, by its concept of original sin sees aggression as part of our animal nature which is pictured as nasty, immoral and predatory. Therefore, man, according to Christian belief, can be kept within acceptable forms of behavior only by an aggressive church.

I suspect that many scientists antagonistic to the concept of a biological aggressive drive are responding to an unrecognized Christian bias deep in their make-up or to a liberal philosophy which sees goodness as irrevocably the product of an enlightened education and evil resulting only from errors in the total education process.

A need to automatically classify aggression as either good or evil would forever blind any approach to understanding it. Such *a priori* judgments will also affect any attempt to specifically define the concept of aggression. Thus, Elliot Aronson states, "I would define an act of aggression as a behavior aimed at causing harm or pain" (365: p. 143). He then goes on to say, "Thus, by this definition, the football player is not considered to be performing an act of aggression if his aim is simply to bring down his man as efficiently as possible. . . ." Aronson thus sees the main function of aggression as the satisfaction of a sadistic need. This is entirely different from the functions of aggression listed by Lorenz as '. . . balanced distribution of animals of the same species over the available environment, selection of the strongest by rival fights, and defense of the young. . . ." (36: p. 43). Likewise, Eibl-Eibesfeldt writes ". . . ethologists deal with the observed behavior patterns and label as aggressive every act that leads to spacing or subordination. . . ." (27: p. 73).

The nature-nurture debate on aggression will continue as nothing but a linguistic merry-go-round until such time as the experts realize that they are using the same term for different phenomena. A parallel is obvious in the alcohologist's treatment of alpha and gamma problem drinkers as identical and then arguing about their common genesis. In both cases the main function of the debate appears to be to allow the experts to work off their own aggressions. The current American hassle over aggression really began when some writers began applying the findings of ethological research to the human mind. Many of the students of human behavoir seemed as outraged by this insult as was the church when Darwin demonstrated that we were probably a part of the animal kingdom. Admittedly, many of the earlier attempts to show the anticipation of human behavior in the lower beasts were terribly oversimplified and generalized. However, the response of the behaviorists and culturologists was equally simple in their attempt to refute these trespassers on the territorial domain claimed by the students of human behavior. The psychocultural determinists recognized three prime trespassers on their domain: Konrad Lorenz (36), Desmond Morris (366, 367) and Robert Ardrey (368, 369, 370). John Lewis and Bernard Towers are alarmed by such writers trying to apply principles of animal behavior to a "moral" being like man. They conclude that "The theories advanced by Morris and Ardrey appear to be without scientific justification" (371: p. 101). Some anthropologists joined in this attack with gusto. Ashley Montagu (372) put together fifteen articles which furiously attacked Lorenz and Ardrey. This volume is not a very balanced or an entirely logical attack. One reviewer described it as

"Representing only one side of the issue, the volume is hardly dispassionate; lacking order, the reviews and articles are sometimes repetitive, sometimes contradictory, and of uneven value . . ." (373: p. 38). More recently Alexander Alland, Jr. (374) used all of his anthropological ammunition in an attempt to demolish the trespassers. Lewis, Towers, Montagu and Alland all assume that with the development of culture, man was somehow freed from any important genetic influence upon his behavior. Also, as noted earlier, the anthropologists have so altered the ethologists definition of aggression that they are in fact talking about something else. Eibl-Eibesfeldt has stated "Anthropologists often use 'aggressive' as a synonym for 'belligerent' and consider only warfare as an aggressive act . . ." (27: p. 73). Alland certainly goes further than this and includes violence in general. However, the concept he is trying to destroy is not what psychologists, zoologists and ethologists are talking about. This is largely but another blind battle in the linguistic jungle of the human sciences. It is further blocked from any rational conclusion by the either-or position of the psychocultural determinists who seem to feel that a synthesis would be a negotiated peace without honor.

Aggression, then, can mean many things to many people. The current either-or posture of the debaters is more emotional than rational. It should be obvious that man is more than a *naked ape* driven by immutable drives and instincts. Even apes are strongly conditioned by experience and environment. On the other side, it is ludicrous to claim that man's body is a neutral machine that can be ignored in explaining his behavior. The human body produces energy as does all living protoplasm. Energy is expended by being directed against other energies or things. One function of aggression is obviously self-preservation in the case of attack by an enemy. But man is also a social animal and much of this energy is directed toward others in the various forms of interpersonal behavior. At its opposite poles it can be manifested in either love or hate. Further, no two individuals can interact in total equality unless they are in fact exact carbon copies of each other on physical, emotional and mental levels. Humans are not as interchangeable as units of hydrogen or all fingerprints would be identical. If two individuals each desire a single indivisible goal, the most probable use of their respective energies is to compete for that goal. If they desire a shared common goal that calls for united action but are divided on the approaches to be taken, there will be an interpersonal competition in some form to decide who makes the final decision. If the loser refuses to accept the leadership of the winner he can depart and the society no longer exists. If his social needs prevent him from leaving, the two constitute a dominance hierarchy. It is not purely accidental that all paired males in fiction represent such a hierarchy. Examples would be Holmes and Watson, Laurel and Hardy and the Lone Ranger and Tonto. In one sense then, aggression can be defined as the competitive use of energy to establish a structured social unit that can effectively act toward a common problem. The competition certainly does not have to be in the form of violence. Sherlock Holmes did not achieve his dominance over Watson by brute force. The degree of difference in power between the dominant partner and the follower is of course enormous. At one extreme it can be a classic sadistic-masochistic relation. At the other it can be a near equality with the dominant barely being able to convince the other at each point of decision making. Further, in many areas the dominance may switch from one partner to the other in different situations. In a medical crisis Dr. Watson became the leader. Larger social units are but elaborations of this basic dyadic relationship. Within a single unit of society, then, aggression is a means of fulfilling one's social needs while establishing a meaningful social role in relating to others. Any social group is based upon cohesion and order. In primarily instinctive groups, such as ants and bees, the order is inherent. In vertebrates, including man, order is in large part the result of a competitive structuring for rights and responsibilities. In human societies this competition is culturally structured and takes on diverse forms in the numerous societies of the world. In some it calls for overt demonstrations of strength or knowledge. In others the cultural demand is for a suppression of any act which would belittle the rest. Thus, superiority and respect may be gained by *aggressively* suppressing hostility and observable forms of competititon. The Hopi Indian would be such an example.

While giving order to the social structure, aggressiveness also gives the individual a sense of worth. Fulfillment for instinctively controlled animals may be defined as a full manifestation of genetically determined patterns of behavior. For man, fulfillment is the achievement of culturally defined values. President Kennedy, quoting the Greeks, thus defined fulfillment as ". . . doing one's best against an accepted standard of excellence." In Adler's terms, man is characterized by a "striving for superiority." However, in the societies of lower animals and in the ideal pattern of any human society, the acquisition of a dominant position does not give one unqualified power. Power implies rights, but all societies ideally parallel rights with responsibilities. Further, in the more successful, dominant-subordinate relationships, being in the leading position does not mean depriving the follower of honor or respect. Rather, the follower feels and often openly receives respect because of his position. Thus, Watson flourished as the reporter of Holmes' activities and felt worthy because of the honor of being allowed to share in his adventures. On a large scale and in the light of a totally different value system, *good* Nazis basked in the *glory* of being followers of Hitler. Likewise, although they probably never knew their leaders personally, true disciples of Freud or Christ glory in their full submission to the ideas of their respective masters.

In human societies the same energy drive, seeking fulfillment, may be structured into artistic, scientific or sporting skills. The great painter, biologist or chess player is, in effect, competing against others using a common medium. Even artists who break from tradition are competing against their own past records or against their own standards of excellence. Thus, almost any creative activity may be seen as a reflection of an aggressive drive. Even without reference to other standards, a sculptor may be viewed as asserting his power over the piece of marble he is coercing into a statue.

All of the above uses of the term aggression may be called positive or creative in that they result in a new creation or relationship which is valued by the society. However, many psychiatrists have defined aggression primarily as the response to frustration (375). Blocked from a positive response, the energy drive in this case may be used to demand attention, solicit pity or both. The crying, hungry baby and the beggar who cuts off a hand are examples. Frustration, then, may lead to negative or destructive aggression.[14] Thus, when the individual is thwarted in his drive toward a goal, he may also try to injure or destroy the goal or whatever he thinks stands in his way. He may do so simply to prevent a competitor from gaining the goal or as a release of his pent-up hostility created by the frustration. Many cultures also provide the mechanism for devious destructive aggression through black magic or witchcraft. Also extremely common is destructive aggression aimed at a scapegoat instead of the real source of the frustration. An example would be the man who beats his wife because he feels too inadequate to defend himself against an unfair and hostile foreman. On a larger scale, Europe burned *witches* by the thousands because it was impossible to identify the real source of psychocultural discomfort produced while the continent went through the painful transition from the Middle Ages to the Renaissance. Warfare is probably also frequently a scapegoating phenomenon.

The scapegoat may be a projection of the actor's semi-awareness of his own inadequacies in creative aggressiveness. Thus, minority groups are often presented as the manifestation of the negative values of the dominant group, or a wife is accused of displaying the husband's own shortcomings. This, in effect, exorcises one's faults into another person. By assuming a dominant position over the scapegoat, one symbolically rises above the faults projected into him. More significantly, for an understanding of alcoholism and many of the neuroses of our age, frustration can lead to the directing of one's aggressive drive in a destructive pattern against one's own being. Those attacking the possibility of any biological determinants in aggression limit their definition of aggression itself to such negative and patho-

---

[14] Since writing the above, I have read Rollo May's book, *Power and Innocence: A Search for the Sources of Violence* (New York, W. W. Norton & Co., Inc., 1972). He has also distinguished between "constructive" and "destructive" aggression.

logcal manifestations. This negative definition probably began to crystallize under Christian philosophy and was completed under the direction of the psychoanalysts. As Anthony Storr has stated,

> . . . the historical development of psychoanalytic thought has been such that, although man's aggressiveness has at last been fully recognized, most writers have given the impression that it is merely a deplorable impulse which ought to be eliminated rather than a necessary part of our biological inheritance with which we have to learn to co-exist, and which has served and serves to protect us (376: p. 3).

Taking the broader view of psychology, one could define aggression as the assertive direction of energy to achieve a goal. This would apply to such diverse pursuits as eating an apple, winning a tennis game or becoming President of the United States. Such a broad approach waters down its usefulness and so, following ethology, I shall limit it to assertiveness within one's own species to determine one's rights and obligations in relationship to others. Pathological aggression could be defined as a destructive assault resulting from frustration and pursued primarily for sadistic satisfactions. We know that in monkey and ape societies operating in natural conditions such pathological aggression is extremely rare. However, years ago a baboon colony studied by Zuckerman (377) in the London Zoo seemed to be dominated by pathological aggressiveness. Looking at his study from the viewpoint of today's knowledge, we know that this pathology was due to artificial crowding and other restraints on normal baboon behavior. Likewise, humans seem capable of creating cultural frustrations conducive to pathological aggressiveness that would not appear in more ideal conditions. Man's behavior is also less genetically structured than that of the other beasts where dominance fights rarely go so far as to maim or kill. Man seems to be the only animal that has no built-in brake when aggression has reached a certain success. A baboon who has become an *overlord* of his group stops his attempts to enlarge on his power. Man frequently at that point seeks another group to bring into the dominance hierarchy. Some cultures do try to limit the felt need for power although others encourage its ever-increasing expansion. If man is to reduce violence, these restraints must be culturally instilled. It takes less training to be destructive than to be creative and cooperative and no society has been completely successful in programming against violence. Most societies, in fact, sanction violence in certain areas and carefully train their young to compete successfully and often viciously in these terrains. America is no exception. Creative or destructive means, however, are merely functional equivalents in the discharge of the energy that we call the aggressive drive. When optimally channeled, this drive creates order within a grouping reflecting our social needs and defines the individual in a meaningful and ego-satisfying relation to his fellows.

The alcoholic lacks the aggressive means to achieve a satisfying place for himself in society. I am convinced that this inadequacy is a product of the biological correlates of aggression as well as the psychocultural determinants. These biological correlates have not all been identified, but probably extend from the pineal through the hypothalamico-pituitary-adrenal axis to the gonads.[15] Testosterone is probably the major determinant of aggression according to Bryson (243: p. 14) and others. On a subhuman level, Bernstein and Rose ". . . report positive correlations between male hormone levels and aggressive behavior in rhesus monkeys. Males with highest testosterone levels were also socially dominant" (378). Likewise, Eibl-Eibesfeldt points out that young turkeys which are normally peaceful will fight each other when given testosterone (27: p. 70). At the human level, it is standard practice in America to administer the male hormone to athletes in massive amounts to increase their power and aggressiveness (379). However, the adrenals are also involved. Mazur and Robertson (28: p. 99) refer to the work of Barnett who demonstrated that "In rats and mice the weight of the adrenals is related to the number of fights they have lost, indicative of subordinate status." Further, Eibl-Eibesfeldt points

---

[15] Robert J. Trotter (Aggression: a way of life for the Qolla. *Science News, 103* No. 5:76-77, 1973) has clearly demonstrated a correlation of hypoglycemia and aggression. Individuals with slight cases of hypoglycemia tend to be explosively aggressive. Extreme cases of hypoglycemia are passive and tend to be victims.

out that there are also "... indications that catecholamine metabolism in the central nervous system plays a certain role in the build-up of readiness for aggressive action, but the details are not known" (27: p. 70). Mazur and Robertson (28: p. 100) cite Lawrence and Haynes (380) who clearly demonstrated that, at least in mice, noradrenaline increased dominance and adrenaline decreased it. Likewise, Bryson states that "The adrenals of most nonaggressive animals contain more epinephrine, whereas norepinephrine may predominate in the adrenals of aggressive animals" (243: p. 13).

High epinephrine levels and an inadequate supply of norepinephrine, then, seem to relate to anxiety, depression and a low aggressive drive. These are all correlates of primary alcoholism and apparently result from psychocultural deprivation of a genetically weak constitution. The testosterone-based aggressive syndrome within the total complex would seem to relate primarily to males. It is my totally unsubstantiated guess, however, that within the ranks of primary alcoholism males far outnumber females. What the equivalent impairment in the females would be, I could only guess. It could well be, however, an imbalance of the male and female hormonal levels. In the male, as well, a low testosterone level could reflect an elevated estrogen level. As I write, it is reported that dosing dominant male rats with estrogen causes them to lose dominant positions in rat social groupings (381). An estrogen rise may thus be accompanied by a drop in testosterone.

High estrogen levels could also account for the light body hair and lack of baldness in primary male alcoholics. As noted earlier, this condition is described by Tintera and Lovell as a product of hypoadrenocorticism which also produces the alcoholism. Wexberg (178: pp. 114-115) cites Smith's (383) description of this condition, "The average alcoholic has a good head of hair; baldness occurs in the general population eight to ten times more frequently than among alcoholics. In contrast, body hair among alcoholics is scanty and follows the female distribution." I found this to be characteristic of all primary alcoholics in my sample. Moreover, it is a widely-held popular belief that scant body hair equates to a lack of power. Thus, Wendy Cooper has

pointed to the ". . . simple equation: male hair equals virility,
equals power, equals strength. It is a very ancient belief that a
hairy man is a strong man" (382: p. 38). Male body hair may
reflect mere strength but more probably is a correlate of a high
aggressive drive. It is no accident that members of woman's
liberation groups in their quest for power stop shaving their
bodies. The male response has been to grow beards while
hoping the women will be unable to ape this male dominance
display. In ancient Egypt female rulers even duplicated this
feat by wearing false beards. This wide association of body
hair with power is no accident, for children who are dependent
and lack power, also lack heavy body hair. In many ways, the
primary alcoholic seems to carry his childhood into adulthood
with him. Along with the slight body hair, and probably also
related to hormonal dysfunction, is the maintenance, as Gottesfeld (98: p. 223) notes, of a "juvenile appearance." Coudert also
noted the many alcoholics ". . . seeming younger than their
chronological age. . . ." (127: p. 281).

Menninger noted that male alcoholics ". . . do not possess
normal sexual powers. . . ." (120: p. 180). It is also a fact that
sexual impotency is a frequent accompaniment of advanced
alcoholism (154). The impotency is probably due in large part
to the genetic weakness which, already further inhibited by
stress, is completed by the known detrimental effects on the
gonads of massive alcoholic consumption. The psychological
aspects of such impotence are also significant. The alcoholic in
an attempt to prove his manhood or womanhood frequently
pursues sex even beyond the normative American all-out effort.
Many female alcoholics are successful as for them sex does not
require a demonstrable display of sexual arousal. For the male,
the results of his sexual pursuits are increasingly belittling.
Since Americans associate alcohol and sex as closely as they do
ham and eggs, the alcoholic gladly conforms to custom which
also gives him courage for the adventure. As early as 1926,
Abraham (384) had noted the association of alcohol and sex
and the fact that manhood is confirmed by consumption in the
two areas. However, the alcoholic frequently passes out before
attaining sex or becomes so sloppy that his female partner

abandons him. If he does enter the sexual arena, he often fails in rising to the occasion. As Porter said in *Macbeth* of the perfidy of alcohol, ". . . it provokes the desire but takes away the performance." Such failures increase with age and alcoholic progression, and reinforce the alcoholic's self-image as being inadequate in all things. This has further negative results on the sex drive and aggression in general, for it is known that functioning under stress lowers testosterone levels (385). Failure is also self-reinforcing. Eibl-Eibesfeldt (27: pp. 71-72) points out that at least with mice, repeated victories increase aggressiveness while continued defeats subdue it. Failure to manifest a drive may also reflect in biological modifications. As Eibl-Eibesfeldt adds, "It is widely accepted that the repression of a drive can have degenerative effects on the physiological machinery of aggression" (27: p. 84). Under stress in every phase of his life, living with a constantly dropping self image and causing physical degeneration through a massive intake of alcohol, the primary alcoholic usually fails to demonstrate his prowess in sex. Losers are simply lousy lovers. I am convinced that it is the primary's lack of aggression and sexual adequacy that has led so many to label him as *homosexual.* It is my impression that the main damage to the aggressive-sexual mechanisms occurs during puberty. In part, this may be due to the lack of the appropriate psychocultural stimuli. Such stimuli may be one of the key functions of the initiation rites so common for the adolescent transition to manhood in so many societies throughout the world.

The primary alcoholic's inadequacy in coping with the opposite sex also frequently results in impossibly miserable marriages. Most primary alcoholics have already displayed some symptoms of pathological drinking before marriage and their spouses are aware of it. Too commonly, both alcoholic and spouse think the marriage will correct the fault and many well-meaning individuals have suffered endlessly from this error in judgment. Frequently, however, the self-defeating nature of the male alcoholic leads him into a marriage with a domineering person whose own aggressiveness increases as the alcoholic's decreases. McGenty describes a model of this type of spouse,

Controlling Catherine never thought much of men in the first place. They need managing. She picks one she can manage. She knew all about his drinking but declared it would be different when she took over. She'll manage. And she does. She became more and more dominant. He shrinks into ineptitude and escapes into alcohol. She is critical and resentful—loudly. He quavers and cowers—and escapes (386: p. 7).

The alcoholic who drew my attention to this source said that it described his wife quite well except that the label should be "Castrating Catherine." On the other hand, certain men seem to derive a perverse and near sadistic satisfaction from marrying alcoholic women. Three of the female alcoholics in my sample, following their sobriety in A.A., had divorced husbands who had been overtly sadistic throughout their marriages. Two of these men remarried and in each case the new wife was an alcoholic.

CHAPTER VIII

THE AMERICAN ALCOHOLIC: II

T HE PRIMARY ALCOHOLIC, in responding to socio-cultural pressures emerges, to use Abraham Maslow's personality dichotomy (387), as a "dependent" rather than a "dominant" type. As a part of this syndrome, the primary lacks adequate defensive mechanisms. Lisansky points out that this defenselessness has been demonstrated by a number of studies (113). The alcoholic's inability to defend himself, his general sense of inadequacy and his pervading burden of guilt make him an easy target for the aggressions of others. His fear of alienating persons on whom he is dependent or those with authority over him usually results in a Casper Milquetoast response to most situations. This inability to stand up for oneself is acknowledged by A.A.'s and one frequently hears references to having been a *doormat* in the days before sobriety produced some development of adult reactions. One A.A. told me of the day he came to realize consciously that his fear of conflict and need for acceptance had incapacitated him as a normal human. "I was on the executive board of a company that was split into two conflicting camps," he said. "I was also undergoing psychotherapy. One day with some pride I told my shrink of my ability to relate as seen in the fact that I was the only executive fully acceptable to both of the hostile camps. His reply startled me. He said, 'Christ, you must be an awfully wishy-washy personality.'"

The primary's inadequacies also increase his sensitivity and he is easily hurt by remarks or incidents that most individuals would scarcely notice. His feelings of guilt and rejection frequently lead him into an almost paranoid existence. This is at its highest after a drunk. Almost every primary I interviewed described the phenomenon of feeling that practically everyone was gossiping about him with contempt or laughing at his stupidity. One primary described his typical reactions in the office the day after a drunk: "I was sure every conversation in the office that I could observe but not hear was about my drunkenness and that every laugh I overheard was at my expense." Another jokingly said, "It was so bad with me that at football games I really thought the players in huddles were making mock of my very existence." The primary's sensitivity makes him especially susceptible to the pain of others. They anguish vicariously for suffering seen on T.V. and in the movies and on several occasions I have seen them moved to tears by a lost or wounded animal.

The primary's sensitivity combined with his inability to compete successfully does not, however, mean that he is totally lacking in aggressive drive. Speaking in general of beings with a stunted ability to be aggressive, Eibl-Eibesfeldt notes, ". . . nevertheless a certain aggressiveness remains and the longer it goes without outlet, the readier it is to prevail when opportunity offers. It is possible to reduce aggression, but certainly not to eliminate it completely" (27: p. 84). Most of the time the primary suppresses his aggressions and like a steam furnace the pressure keeps rising. He also lacks any reasonable channel to discharge the mounting tension. Catanzaro likewise comments on these alcoholic characteristics when he states "Alcoholics are in general very sensitive people. Consequently they tend to build up feelings of anger at even minor rejections or frustrations. In addition, they find it very hard to deal adequately with this great wealth of angry feelings" (74: pp. 40-41). I was also especially struck by the fact that most primaries had never really learned to play as children, and few could play as adults unless aided by alcohol. When the inner pressure is at its greatest an emotional explosion may be triggered by the smallest straw that ever fell on a camel's back, and this usually happens at the most inappropriate time and place. The primary appears, therefore, to have a low frustration level while in fact the small events which trigger emotional outbursts are the last small irritants to a daily rising burden of frustration. The probability of biological correlates is obvious. Wexberg comments on what he interprets as a low frustration level by saying, "This trait, which may be partly determined by constitutional factors, can often be traced back to the influence of childhood environment" (388: p. 230). The condition of an unbearable burden of pent-up frustration becomes the setting for a drunk which, at least for a while, allows the primary a tremendous relief. It is conceivable that a drunk acts as an emotional purge on both the psychological and physical levels in the same way that civil disorders, wars and revolutions seem to reduce anxiety and suicide in populations as a whole (389, 390). The drunk in some primaries releases a destructive aggression in fighting behavior. More typically, the drunk allows the primary to feel a sense of worth and to play the role of the person he would like to be.

While sober, the primary is never the person he would like to be. In fact, he usually sees himself as a direct contradiction of his most cherished values. Therefore, unless drunk, most of the alcoholic's anger is aimed at the least resisting target— himself. Lisansky (113: p. 7) comments on the work of Landis who had found that the more aggressive of the alcoholics were the ones most likely to recover. I would agree if this meant a creative aggression directed realistically. This may imply actual teaching of creative aggression or at least directing the anger at realistic targets. Lisansky also asked, "May not a capacity to shift this anger so that it is directed toward others be a good prognostic sign?" (113: p. 8). However, it has been my impression that this redirection of anger is most difficult for a primary alcoholic while usually a simple procedure when working with a secondary. The primary's personality is so deeply rooted that it, rather than the secondary's, fits the description by Sattler and Pflugrath who noted that the characteristics of the alcoholic are ". . . not significantly changed by chronicity" (391: p. 848).

One of the characteristics of the primary alcoholic is, as many have described, a wild series of emotional swings from elation through anxiety to total depression. The sober primary has the capacity at times to achieve ecstatic peaks when he feels, as Tiebout noted (111), that "I can do anything." This manic state, however, can quickly switch to either anxiety or the deepest of depressions when the alcoholic feels that he is hopeless in a world without justice (392). Although these emotional swings are frequently begun by a psychological fact, they often seem to emerge from within the body of the primary for no observable reason. It seems to me that the primary goes through biological cycles where an organic imbalance creates the emotion which he then rationalizes in psychological terms. Many of the elations and depressions that I have observed in primaries were not in the least explainable by the current psycho-social situation. One generalization, however, can be made with certainty. That is, the moments of happiness and elation in the primary are dwarfed by the periods spent in the psychological pain of anxiety and depression.

The emotional discomfort of the primary seems to equate to the "primal pains" described by Janov which he describes as the

> . . . central and universal pains which reside in all neurotics. I call them Primal Pains because they are the original, early hurts upon which all later neurosis is built. It is my contention that these pains exist in every neurotic each minute of his later life, irrespective of the form of his neurosis. These pains often are not consciously felt because they are diffused throughout the entire system where they affect body organs, muscles, the blood and lymph system and, finally, the distorted way we behave (393: p. 11).

However, while Janov sees most neurotics as being curable through his therapy of "the primal scream," I do not believe that any psychological experience is capable of harmonizing the dysfunctional chemistry of the primary alcoholic.

The fact that the primary's discomfort lies deeper than his alcoholism is evident from several viewpoints besides his usually miserable childhood. As Hawkins has pointed out, "One of the few medical evidences worthy of note is the appearance of psychosomatic complaints during sobriety and their remission during alcoholic phases, a fact equally pertinent to theories of constitutional defect" (172, p. 100). In my own sample of alcoholics the incidence of apparently psychosomatic complaints was enormous and appeared to typify the primaries. These ranged from "migraine" headaches, lethargy, and "tight stomachs" to itches, rashes and vague arthritic-like pains. More significantly,

I found that all of the primaries that I studied continued to show some neurotic traits regardless of their length of sobriety, extent of psychotherapy, or improvement in socioeconomic terms. The poor adjustment of sober alcoholics has been noted in a number of studies which are reviewed by Pattison and his co-authors (103: p. 623). As one example, they cite the work of Gerard, Saenger and Wile (394) who reported that in a sample of abstinent alcoholics, ". . . 43 percent were overtly disturbed, 24 percent inconspicuously inadequate, 12 percent A.A. 'addicts' and only 10 percent independently making a successful adjustment." Pattison *et al.* note similar reports by Bolman (395), Moore and Ramseur (396), Wilby and Jones (397), Pfeffer and Berger (398), Flaherty *et al.* (399) and Wellman (400). It is my belief that in all of these samples those alcoholics showing the minimum recovery from neurotic symptoms were primaries and that the central factor in their symptoms is biological. The pain begins in the body and the primary then seeks any minor irritation to rationalize and vocalize his discomfort. Alcohol apparently provides a specific though temporary relief for this somatopsychological discomfort.

Before discovering the alcoholic relief, most primaries in their predrinking days sought release from these pains through fantasies that involved either an escape into a kinder environment or the gaining of tremendous power. These fantasies were pursued in both fiction and daydreams. As an example of the former, many of the primaries I worked with listed as favorite childhood reading, *The Swiss Family Robinson* and *Twenty-Thousand Leagues Under the Sea*. The first presented an idyllic isolation from real society and in the second they could identify with Captain Nemo who held the fate of the world's shipping in his hands. Male daydreams ranged from being Robinson Crusoe to living as Superman or as some powerful outlaw or military figure. Female fantasies varied from a holy, solitary life in a religious order to wielding the sexual power of a Hollywood actress or the secular authority of a queen or a Joan of Arc. Many of these sober alcoholics whom I came to know well admitted to a continuing rich fantasy life. A number recounted their day dreams to me and the parallel to Thurber's

"The Private Life of Walter Mitty" was notable. However, fiction and daydreams never do more than temporarily relieve the primary of his discomfort. He is rarely able to consciously identify its source and is so used to it that before alcohol he was unaware that life was possible without it. All carried, in varying degrees, a sense of an impending disaster that they could not name. All were lonely and few could name more than two or three childhood friends whom they had really trusted and felt at ease with.

But in the life of every primary alcoholic there is a moment of revelation and rebirth when he loses his fears and anxieties while gaining a positive identity and a sense of power. This is the quasi-religious bliss of his discovery of the miracle of alcohol. Inevitably, alcohol dissolved the neurotic pains, resolved the conflicts and gave a self-confidence the primary had only dreamed of before his exposure to this *divine fluid*. For the first time in his life the primary thus comes to experience true happiness. He, for the first time, feels whole, at ease with himself and in a valid, positive relationship with the world. He has accomplished the human urge, described by Assagioli, to ". . . achieve a harmonious inner integration, true self-realization, and right relationships with others" (401: p. 21). The primary alcoholic, using Maslow's phrase (402, 403, 404, 405), has achieved a "peak experience." A. Hoffer, as cited by Colin Wilson (161: p. 32), is also aware that ". . . the alcoholic drinks because he wants peak experiences."

No one will understand the primary until he can understand the depth of this experience that alcohol can produce for him. The rest of his drinking career the alcoholic is trying to recapture this bliss which in fact is merely experiencing the joys of normality after an existence in another and painful existence. The normally low energy level of the alcoholic is replaced by a sense of vitality. His new ethanol-produced sense of self-worth allows him to function in society with an ease and confidence he had never before known. Primary after primary has related to me the elation of finding himself able to do what others do and thus engage with confidence and without fear of failure. Most stated that with alcohol they could do things previously denied them: dance, converse and feel at least an equal in any group. Also, as E. Y. Williams (406) has indicated, ethanol relieves the anxiety syndrome associated with sex in most alcoholics and the primary suddenly has a strong and positive sexual identity. Further, for the first time in his life the alcoholic feels free to express his own opinions and act as he chooses without the fear of losing the approval of others. He can forget the parental admonition that so many alcoholics have burned into their souls—"What will people think?" In brief, ethanol gives the primary a rebirth.

For a short interlude, ethanol physically and mentally provides the primary with a new and glorious life. However, ethanol also rapidly becomes his destroyer, for this "elixir of life" quickly becomes a deadly poison that he must keep drinking. For the primary, ethanol rapidly destroys both his ability to handle alcohol and the strength to live without it. One rather poetic primary recounted to me the agony of alcohol's duplicity: "Booze came to me as a lovely and voluptuous mistress who made all things possible and then as she seduced me she revealed her true nature as a vampire." So strong were the first rewards that, despite the agonies of alcoholic symptoms, the primary usually spends the rest of his life futilely using alcohol to recapture and hold the ecstasy he had once experienced in its embrace. With the onset of the inevitable progression of the disease, the ecstasy becomes briefer and briefer. Always, however, the first few drinks bring it back although the aftermaths becomes worse and worse. The stages of alcoholic progression, as first outlined by Jellinek (117), are a slow process for the secondary alcoholic, but for the primary they are completed like a film run at high speed. The primary, already neurotic, is constitutionally extremely susceptible to the onslaught of alcohol on his mind and body. Ethanol's temporary reward is so great, however, that he frequently follows his vampire-mistress into the grave. Throughout his life his dream is to regain and maintain the initial blissful gift that alcohol gave him without paying the inevitable consequences that come with being unable to stop. However, like Myers' rats, alcohol has created a physiological feedback so that one drink triggers the need for the next. In his experiments with controlled drinking, his thirst is never satisfied, for each drink seems to call for "just one more" (407). In a biochemical sense, each drink temporarily creates a comfortable homeostasis which quickly collapses, leaving a physical and mental demand for the temporary relief of the next drink. As alcohol continues to destroy his biological processes, the volition involved in ordering or pouring the next drink becomes less and less.

As the primary rapidly loses the ability to stop drinking he also is denied control of his drinking behavior and even of his consciousness. The power and well-being that alcohol gave him earlier in his drinking career is replaced by a new frustration as he finds that instead of giving him control, alcohol is now depriving him of it. His deep-seated conflicts now create emotional determinants of his drunken behavior. The primary's prealcoholic sense of helplessness is now increased a thousandfold and he feels that the puppet strings controlling him are being manipulated by an insane force far beyond his ability to influence it. Several alcoholics described this emotional determinant of their drunken behavior in terms of a second self bent on destroying the true identity of the sober being. References to Dr. Jekyll and Mr. Hyde were frequent. As a general principle, Edith Weigert has pointed out that "Man is afraid of losing control and being swayed by the emotions" (408: pp. 148-149). As bad experience piles on bad experience during drinking bouts, the alcoholic begins to feel total terror rather than mere fear. In time, the primary awakens the morning after each blacked-out drunk in a panic and terror that few can find the words to describe. It is always with questions screaming within him— Where am I? Who saw me? How many checks did I write? Is there blood on the car bumper? And the ultimate question is always, Why did I do it again?

The terror of the morning after frequently rests on reality, for many primaries while drunk do in fact objectify their inner fears and anxieties in behavior that outrages society. In an effort to preserve some acceptable reputation, primaries increasingly learn to head for a drinking environment where they are not known and usually are peopled by drinkers below the social class to which the primary belongs. Some primaries come to drink alone in the partial security of a rented room in a motel or hotel. However, even with these precautions, disaster is the frequent product of a drunk. Alcoholics at this point begin to manifest a variety of destructive aggressions. Some of these are relatively mild although the personal consequences for the alcoholic may be severe. Examples are telephoning one's employer to spill out one's hatred or destroying the wife's favorite cream pitcher. At the other extreme is death. Many primaries die of fire, having passed out in bed with a cigarette. Suicide among primary alcoholics is also common. Others are guilty of manslaughter while drunk driving. The A.A. repository of horror tales of such tragedies is enormous. One tells of the alcoholic looking out his window hung-over and agonized as he watched his wife go out to move his car where he'd left it in the middle of the driveway. Suddenly she fainted. He rushed out in terror and fainted beside her when he saw the three-year old child "splashed" across the grill-work of his car. Another tale concerns the young alcoholic son of a rich family who so regularly ended up in jail that he came to know each policeman by his first name. One Sunday morning, waking in a jail cell he called over the guard and said, "Guess you'd better call the old man again to bail me out." "I'm sorry, boy, I can't do that this time," said the policeman, "you killed him last night." These things do happen and their possibility should be noted by the alcohologists who are so dedicated in returning the alcoholic to the *joys* of drinking.

As the primary himself becomes increasingly aware of his own potential for destruction while drunk, he almost inevitably makes the resolve never to drink again. Many do in fact abstain for considerable periods following a drunk. The first results of sobriety are always reassuring. The primary begins to feel that he is freed of the need to drink and that he is gaining some control over his life. One alcoholic described to me the joy of going to a formal dinner party after ten days of sobriety and being able to drink soup without fear ". . . of getting the shakes and flipping a spoonful of pea soup all over myself or my hostess." However, the pleasure of sobriety soon passes. The primary finds that the stress of living with his own worst enemy, himself, increases the tension of mere existence and the need for release grows proportionately. As he gets further and further from his last drunk, the alcoholic has the unhappy facility to remember the temporary relief that alcohol offers far easier than recalling the ensuing pain. And he begins to think that ". . . next time it will be different." As he stores up frustrations that he has never learned to relieve, his body and mind increase their demand for liquor. The pain of mere existence grows but he can usually postpone the inevitable for considerable periods. Then, at some inappropriate time and place, he surrenders to his emotional needs and another binge is born. At this point the feeling permeates his being that life and his resolve of sobriety are just not worth it. The first drink is usually taken with an attitude expressible as, What the hell does it matter anyway! And with the first drink a sense of wellbeing flows into him and he *knows* that he has made the right decision. His relief is infinite but again it is but a prelude to drunkenness, terror, regret and eventually a pledge of abstinence.

To characterize the primary alcoholic as being without *willpower*, however, is erroneous, for he often displays an ability to carry on in an apparently normal fashion while suffering unbelievable physical and mental pain. This is most easily observable when he tries to present a normal appearance while in the throes of the physical malaise and psychological anxiety of a hangover. I have watched hungover primaries who should have been hospitalized appear for work and go about their regular activities with an inner strength that few nonalcoholics could muster. In one case a primary maintained his normal family relations, did his work and attended to a community commitment for over a week before he discovered that his hangover was accompanied by a severe case of pneumonia. I have watched others temporarily overcome the acute need for alcohol in what was obviously an inner battle of major proportions. I have even watched several break off a drunk to care for a family emergency when the suppression of the craving obviously called for ten times the effort needed to handle the familial crisis.

The comparative strength of the control and the craving is

the product of many causes. The primary who for various reasons
has never consistently drunk on a daily basis and who has widely
spaced his binges obviously has suffered less physical deterioration and has been able to resist total surrender to alcohol because
of a socially supported inner drive to retain an appearance of
propriety.

Generally speaking, those with highly desired goals who have
the means to attain them are the most likely to delay an
eventual alcoholic collapse. An understanding wife, family or
friend who supports his periods of abstinence in a positive way
may also help him to slow the progress of the disease. These
primaries are also usually able to hide their alcoholism for long
periods once periodic benders become inevitable. They can
also carry on normally or even with spectacular success between
drunks. One of my cases had drunk alcoholically for thirty-eight
years with no one being aware of it but his wife, his lawyer and
his physician. After trying for several years to get his patient
to abandon liquor entirely, the physician suggested the alcoholic
rent a small apartment for his binges. He did so and every five
or six months he would "take a business trip" while vanishing
into an isolated three-day drunk. His lawyer, also a close friend,
would check on his well-being several times daily. At the end
of the drunk the doctor took over and through his pharmacopoeia
restored him to health in two or three days. The alcoholic then
reappeared at work and in society looking well, calm and in
control. Others also hid their alcoholism by hiding binges in
the home or taking them out of town. Several of these had
cooperating physicians who, after each drunk, hospitalized them
under a disguised diagnosis until they were again on their feet.
Others, with less money, if adequately motivated, can time their
binges so as to fulfill them inconspicuously and so maintain social
acceptance. Such alcoholics with a social position they want
desperately to maintain will go to any lengths to avoid a revelation of their problem. As Milton Maxwell was recently quoted
as saying, "Concealment becomes great and reflects the attitude
of our society. You aren't supposed to be an alcoholic. It's an
admission of failure . . ." (409). However, between drunks these
primaries endure all of the uncertainties, self-hates and feelings

of inadequacy present in the more obviously drunk primaries. They merely hide it, often behind a superb job of acting. As one of these said to me,

I always carried a mask, in fact I had a whole collection of them. I was determined no one would ever see through them to the real me. My main job was to win the applause of an audience that I felt sure would despise me if they knew the truth. It took three years of A.A. sobriety and one of psychotherapy to give me the nerve to drop my props and costumes and start living as myself.

Many primaries have nothing that they see worth gaining or maintaining and rapidly sink into an alcoholic oblivion. These generally have no adequate social support for abstinence and either lack goals or any reasonable means to attain them. Some survive for long periods dependent on the concerned but inadequate care of distressed parents who financially support them, buy their way out of the consequences of their drunks and maintain a usually impossible dream that some day their love will sober up the alcoholic. Others survive by supporting themselves in jobs that keep them from alcohol for long periods. I have met at least three primaries who served long terms in the U.S. Navy. At sea, even when the craving set in by itself no alcohol was available as a rule to feed it. On leave, as one said, "I would burn myself out on God-awful drunks that would hold me 'till next time.'" Other primaries, those without any social backing and lacking all inner resources, rapidly sink to a skid-row existence where drunken binges alternate with dish-washing jobs, rest and recuperation in the Salvation Army or jail, and eventually end the cycle by incarceration in a mental institution, prison or death.

These totally alienated primaries merely live and die quicker and in more squalor than the more protected or motivated alcoholics. Even those who most successfully control and hide their drunks are doomed to a progressive deterioration and eventual collapse. Each is aware that in various areas his control is diminishing and that his being is constantly shrinking into a total alcoholic existence. The most dramatic case of this social shrinkage was demonstrated by an alcoholic primary whom I came to know well before his death. I shall call him Bob, for that was not his name. From a wealthy family, Bob had lived through the typical agony of a primary's childhood. He had gone through college and graduate school with few friends but without any crises except for occasional agonized drunks that he could not explain. He survived these mainly because his parents were unaware of them and he felt that without some respect from them he would be worthless. As with all primaries, there were days when Bob was suddenly drained of all energy. "It felt as though someone had pulled the plug." On other days he was almost happy and he remembered a few occasions when life was full of hope and he felt good about himself and the world. Mostly, however, he lived with an accustomed burden of anxiety and guilt. He then received his advanced degree, obtained an excellent job as an engineer and married an attractive girl his parents felt was "right" for him. He seemed, on the surface, headed for a rewarding and successful life.

Like most functioning Americans, Bob had separated most of his conflicting values by segregating them into the appropriate compartmentalized roles. Thus, like a good American business-man, he believed in equality when playing patriot but acted upon the more realistic inequalities of the competitive world of business. However, like all primaries, every one of his roles had buried within it several anxiety-arrows representing violently conflicting values. These represented in the main what he thought was ideally expected of him as opposed to his own sense of ability and self-worth. Thus, in every role he played he carried the typical alcoholic fantasy of achieving perfection coupled with the belief that he could not even attain mediocrity. In sex, his fantasies had him seducing beautiful women by the hundreds while he also accepted his prudish mother's view that sex is dirty and evil. He yearned to be popular but was convinced that no one of any value would accept him as friend. Therefore, he tended to feel most at ease with those below his educational and economic level. He wanted to conform to his father's expectations but knew he couldn't. Therefore, deep down he wanted to outdo his father and so shame him or failing that, kill the old man. But Bob "knew" that the father was a better man than himself and that he lacked the courage to murder him.

Drinking helped. Bob recalled that it took about a dozen drinking experiences before he realized how alcohol could "make life meaningful." Having twice been drunk on dates with his fiancee before marriage, he had promised her that, once married, he would always limit himself to two drinks. This worked for six months and then he got terribly drunk at a party and the next day, under her tearful assault on his honesty, Bob promised never to drink again. He didn't for five months. Then he made a business trip to Detroit and was drunk for two nights in a row. This time his resolve to maintain sobriety lasted seven months. He came home drunk and his wife spent the next week alternating between hysterics and threats of divorce. However, he so far had never missed a day at work because of drinking, fulfilled the demands of his job and received several promotions. As his drinking bouts increased, his wife now helped him conceal them, for she knew her financial future rested on avoiding a scandal. A pattern began that was to last for fifteen years. During this time he had a few happy respites when he could drink socially for a week or two, but these always passed. He also learned that when socially pressured to drink he could take one or two and stop on many occasions. It created tremendous discomfort but it was worth it to hold the respect of colleagues and avoid his wife's wrath. On occasions when such a drink created an uncontrollable urge, he found he could usually hold off until he could leave for another setting.

During these fifteen years things slowly got worse. He allowed his wife to take over all management of the home and finances. He began to miss work but was covered by rather flimsy medical excuses. He was picked up by the police who kindly drove him home instead of booking him for drunk driving. Bob also consulted seven different doctors, seeking help, but their advice was inevitable, ". . . just stop after a drink or two." His anxiety and self-hatred increased by massive leaps.

In the sixteenth year of his marriage his mother died. He got drunk after the funeral and for the first time in his life used aggression against his father. In a drunken flood Bob poured out a torrent of accusations and abuses against both the father and the dead mother. The old man, whom I once met and talked to at length, was of the type who cannot tolerate any relationship that he does not totally control. His response was to disinherit Bob and they never met again. A week later Bob showed up for work drunk. He was given a warning and with the help of a psychotherapist stayed sober for one year. At the end of that year the therapist told Bob he was now ready for a little controlled drinking. Ecstatic at the news, Bob began to experiment, and to his delight had two martinis and stopped. Now he began to drink almost ritually once a week at a regular gathering he and his wife attended, but never had more than two drinks. Six months of this convinced him he was cured. He called his psychotherapist and in a prolonged eulogy sang his praises. The next week he was arrested for drunk driving.

His drinking now increased almost in proportion to the shrinkage in his social roles. Having lost the role of son, he now lost the role of driver for a second driving-while-intoxicated charge occurred even before the hearing on the prior arrest. His periods of sobriety shrank until he was drunk at least twice a week. His wife divorced him and he was expelled from his club "for conduct unbecoming a gentleman." Then he was fired for gross misbehavior while drunk at the office. Two weeks later his bank account was overdrawn.

Bob now entered upon the biggest drunk of his career. It lasted for four days and three nights. He awoke in a cheap motel room not remembering anything of the night before. He stumbled into the bathroom hoping to find a bottle and suddenly looked into the mirror. "And you know," he told me, "there was nothing looking back." One could dismiss this lack of a reflection as a mere hallucination. I think it went much deeper. Stripped of his social roles, Bob saw himself as not even existing. He had no central sense of being to sustain him when all else was gone. In the terms of Viktor Frankl (410, 411), Bob's core of being was an *existential vacuum*. Other primaries have experienced similar feelings of emptiness and I have heard A.A.'s refer to it as *the peeled zero*. Several alcoholics, in describing their dread of psychotherapy to me, have stated in almost identical terms, the fear that ". . . if all that outer garbage is ripped off my soul, what if they find there's nothing underneath?"

The reflectionless mirror signalized Bob's psychological and social death. However, he had a second chance when, after further drinking, he was committed to a state mental institution. Here, he said, "I got a steady dose of tranquilizers instead of therapy but I was contacted by A.A." On being released he joined A.A., got a job at manual labor and maintained seven months sobriety. Then he applied for a job at his old profession and was hired "pending clearance in a security check." He actually began work and did well. A week later he was called in and told that regrettably the job was not his. The security check had turned up his stay in the mental hospital and this finding disqualified him. He bought a bottle and went to his room. His body was found the next morning in the chair where he had killed himself.

In short, primaries like Bob lack the self-respect and power to cope with reality. As Rollo May has pointed out, "The word 'power' comes from the Latin 'posse,' meaning 'to be able!' " (412: p. 19). The primary from infancy on is unable to fill the roles that he sees thrust upon himself. He seeks the power to be able to do so in alcohol. Unfortunately, the alcohol which temporarily relieves his physical and mental stress inevitably drastically reduces his power to control either his drinking or his behavior. This is in marked contrast to the secondary alcoholic who usually is able to fulfill his roles adequately or superlatively until the onset of alcoholism.

The secondary is born with a healthy and resistant constitution and usually enjoys an adequate childhood. Those who suffer stressful childhoods are constitutionally strong enough to survive the experience without experiencing physical or mental damage. A few do have marked neurotic traits but they show no common psychological pathology. Most significantly, their bodies lack the primaries' vulnerability to collapse when exposed to alcohol. In their prealcoholic lives many secondaries are highly productive and creative. Most of them, therefore, display a well-directed and constructive aggressive drive. The one thing all secondary alcoholics share is a long and heavy drinking history. This overindulgence may be the product of a heavy-drinking subculture, an *occupational hazard* or an individual response to a stressful existence. However, the heavy intake of alcohol slowly but surely is destroying the secondary's physical mechanism for handling alcohol while serving him well both psychologically and socially. Eventually the first signs of alcoholism do appear, but these may be from ten to forty years after the beginning of excessive drinking.

The onset of secondary alcoholism is generally so slow that the drinker suffers no great trauma from its appearance. If he is part of a heavy-drinking group he may assume that blackouts and the shakes are merely normal traits for a heavy drinker. In several of my cases of secondary alcoholism extremely long periods existed between symptoms of alcoholism. One secondary, a successful senior executive of an enormous business complex, had his first remembered blackout at seventeen and his second shortly after his forty-eight birthday. He was fifty-six before pathological drinking began seriously to affect his life. There does appear to be a very generalized pattern, however, for the secondary's biology to break down in the late forties and fifties when the endocrine systems are apparently undergoing rapid change and deterioration. Female secondaries are prone to demonstrate alcoholism during the menopause. Abraham (384) had also noted that, at least for men, this is also a period when drinking increases. It is apparently a common practice for males to compensate for a dwindling sexual drive with an increased alcoholic consumption in the need to prove manliness and power. A large number of female secondaries told me that drinking helped perpetuate the self-image that they were still young, desirable and wielded a sexual power over the opposite sex. This theme is also the subplot of Mary Laswell's lovely novel, *Tio Pepe*. Alcohol of course, is a magnificent releaser of the psychological trauma that comes with the realization that youth is gone and death is ahead. The American idealization of youth and horror of death increase these anxieties enormously.

When alcoholism does appear, the secondary's drinking alone has paralleled the biological damage the primary experienced through a genetic predisposition, a traumatic childhood and alcohol itself. However, the increasing loss of control is rarely accompanied by the range of destructive aggressions seen in the primary. The secondary usually has an integrated personality with a successful compartmentalization of most of his conflicting values. He also usually has a very positive self-image. He, therefore, usually goes through a blackout demonstrating behavior that others see as amusing rather than obnoxious. However, an increasing number of blackouts and hangovers with a resentment at playing the clown begin to compound anxieties within the secondary. Like the primary, he will usually at this point decide to abstain. However, also like the primary, he usually returns eventually to drinking and thus becomes a periodic drinker. Having far more control of his life than the primary, the secondary usually finds it difficult to admit he cannot control what one called ". . . a small thing like booze." He will rarely admit a problem until a crisis develops. Six of the secondaries I met in A.A. entered that organization after convictions for drunk driving. One surgeon came in when ". . . a sudden case of the shakes seriously interfered with major surgery." A housewife sought A.A. after accidentally burning down her home during a drunk. Three stated that their drunks were finally just too incompatible with their usual sense of order and control. When the secondary sobers up, he falls back on a solid and integrated prealcoholic personality. When the primary sobers up he is left with the original neurotic personality that preceded his drinking. The difference is clearly visible in any group of A.A.'s who have respectable lengths of sobriety behind them. Many primaries are anxious, smoke continually, gulp cup after cup of coffee and are hung up on some insignificant problem. Secondaries use fewer cigarettes and less coffee and generally present a rather calm and controlled appearance.

Jellinek's delta alcoholic differs from the primary and secondary in suffering from true addiction rather than from what might be called *cyclical addiction*. As Jellinek points out, unlike the gammas, with the delta ". . . there is no ability to go 'on the water wagon' for even a day or two without the manifestation of withdrawal symptoms . . ." (4: p. 38). There is no behavioral problem and the alcoholism may not even be noted unless the daily ration of alcohol is cut off. As Jellinek points out, this is the predominant species of alcoholism ". . . in France and some other countries with a large wine consumption" (4: p. 38). He also points out that "There is in the French literature on alcoholism frequent mention of 'l'alcoolisme sans ivresse' (alcoholism without drunkenness)—that is, it is asserted that a drinker can become an alcoholic without showing signs of intoxication" (413: p. 384). French tolerance for massive wine consumption would make it difficult to actually identify a delta alcoholic in this setting. As Inspector Maigret states of the victim in his case of "the headless corpse": ". . . The condition of the liver suggests a steady drinker, but I wouldn't say he was an alcoholic. More probably the sort who likes a glass of something, white wine mostly, every hour or even every half-hour" (414: p. 39). The French pattern is unmistakable. Joe Allen, an American who recently had the gaul to open a hamburger stand in Paris, is quoted as observing that "The French drink mildly but on a continuous basis. They're never really drunk but never really sober either" (415).

The delta or addicted alcoholic also exists in America, although here he is a minority in the alcoholic ranks. Unlike his European counterpart, the American delta usually drinks distilled beverages although a few are beer drinkers. He is also difficult to distinguish in heavy-drinking subcultures. The primary factor in such addictive alcoholism must be biochemical although what processes are involved we cannot say with any certainty. One possible explanation of addictive alcoholism is a metabolic aberration which produces an alkaloid which is the *hooking mechanism*. Bryson (243: p. 18) points out that ". . . catecholamines condense with aldehydes at body temperatures to form . . ." various alkaloids. Bryson then continues citing the work of Davis and Walsh (416) to state that ". . . the derivative from dopamine is tetrahydropapaveroline, an intermediate in the synthesis of opium by the poppy. . . . A plausable neuropharmacologic basis for alcohol addiction thus emerges." In another publication Davis and Walsh review their research by again stating "These data support the concept that alcoholism is a true addiction which may involve specific biochemical events leading to the formation of the morphine-type alkaloids" (417, p. 1006). Cohen (418) has expressed the same possibility. Geller

(256) has demonstrated that darkness-induced melatonin increases drinking in rats. He postulates that the melatonin increase with acetaldehyde could produce an alkaloid which would account for the ethanol preference. This chemical addictive factor, whatever its nature, is powerful and I have never seen a delta successfully attain sobriety without hospitalization during his withdrawal.

If this hypothesis should prove to be true, it may prove that true addictive alcoholism and the two gammas rest on different biochemical bases. On the other hand, it is conceivable that primary and secondary alcoholism somehow represent periodic appearances of the same alkaloids which are destroyed by a binge.

In any case, it is my firm belief that the primary and secondary gammas and the deltas represent true alcoholism in the sense that there is a basic underlying biochemical pathology. These represent an entirely different set of problems from those who are problem drinkers mainly because of psychocultural reasons. Further, I find most of our experiments in alcoholism totally invalid because of the failure to definitely separate problem drinkers from true alcoholics in the research populations. Statistical tools are extremely useful, but only if you know what you're counting. Even within the valid alcoholic samples, I know of no study that makes an adequate distinction between primary and secondary alcoholics and separates those in various stages of the disease.

The nonalcoholic problem drinkers also need valid research on the nature of their problem before a reliable therapy can be developed for them. Again, they are not all identical and specialized approaches will be needed for their subvarieties. These variations have not all been identified, but at least two clearly emerge The first of these is the *symptomatic problem drinker*. This individual overdrinks to relieve an underlying physical or psychological pain. Symptomatics may be neurotic or psychotic, but they lack any biochemical basis for either cyclical or continual addiction. The *situational problem drinker* has learned to use alcohol for the chemical relief of tension or stress. He also lacks an addictive physiological mechanism and can stop drinking at any time without true withdrawal symptoms.

It should be remembered that models of drinking are not absolutes and that individual variation within each category is enormous. Primaries share a basic neuroticism and a cyclical addiction but otherwise demonstrate an extremely wide range of behavioral and mental characteristics. Secondaries share nothing but the alcohol-produced cyclical addiction. The delta alcoholics all are dependent on a daily alcohol intake to function but range from extroverts to introverts, economic successes to failures and a personality ranging from normal to pyschotic. Likewise the lines of demarcation between the types of alcoholics may be vague for the primary and the secondary depending upon the extent of genetic preconditioning, childhood trauma and exposure to alcohol. Even the line between alcoholic and non-addicted problem drinkers may be difficult to draw. Both symptomatic and situational problem drinkers may in time through massive alcohol intake produce the damage that underlies secondary alcoholism. In any therapy, the individual's characteristics and needs should overrule any scientific classification. All too frequently a dogmatic theory has stood between any understanding and empathy between patient and therapist.

CHAPTER IX:

A.A.: BIRDS OF A FEATHER

THE ALIENATED ALCOHOLIC is a confused and frightened person. Above all, he is lonely. This is especially true of the primary. His loneliness in itself is so stress-producing that he rarely makes it to sobriety on his own. When he does sober up by himself, the effort frequently produces an extremely bitter and hostile person. Our folklore is full of references to the grouchy and nasty ex-drunk. Others go to strange and macabre lengths to maintain their sobriety. An extreme and pathetic example is seen in the case of Matt Talbot. A hopeless drunkard from youth, Talbot found and maintained sobriety by fulfilling the masochistic rites of a Christian penitent. His methods became known upon his death when his body was examined at Jervis Street Hospital in Dublin on June 7, 1925. The examiners of the corpse wrote,

> . . . and when we the undersigned undressed the remains we found chains, ropes and beads on the said body. Around the middle of his waist were two chains and a knotted rope. One chain we took to be an ordinary chain used as a horse trace, and the other a little thinner. Both were entwined by a knotted rope, and medals were attached to the chain by cords. Both were deeply embedded in the flesh and rusted. Also on the left arm was found a light chain tightly wound above the elbow; and on the right arm above the elbow, a knotted cord. On his left leg a chain was bound round with a cord below the knee, and on the right leg, in the same position, was some heavy and knotted cord. Around his neck was a very big beads (sic), and attached to some were a great many religious medals . . . (419: p. 7).

How does one judge Matt Talbot? Orthodox psychiatry would see him as a confirmation of the hypothesis that alcoholism is a form of masochism. The American public would view him as a freak. However, the Catholic Church is considering him for beatification and perhaps canonization (419: pp. 123-125).

Talbot's lonely and painful solution to his alcoholism represents the opposite pole from the social cooperative known as
Alcoholics Anonymous. A.A. has been tremendously successful
and yet both human beings and social scientists have found its
success a mystery. As Milton Maxwell has said, ". . . the 'A.A.
recovery program' remains an unknown quantity to many, and
at least something of an enigma to most" (16: pp. 211-212). I
really do not think it is so great a mystery. In fact, from
an anthropological viewpoint, it is in America the most probable
psychocultural response to a scientifically untreatable disease.
Alcoholics Anonymous above all fulfills the social need for which
Talbot was driven to substitute chains. A.A. is no more a mystery
than the American "colony" in Mexico City or Chinatown in San
Francisco. Birds of a feather do indeed flock together. A.A.
represents a bonding of alcoholics for the same basic reason that
stamp collectors enjoy other philatilists and that physicians
belong to the A.M.A. The main difference is that the bonds of
A.A., which are forged in a common history of suffering and
alienation, are far stronger than those between Rotarians or labor
union members. As Joseph Kessel said of the A.A. members he
came to know,

> They all had one thing in common; a stronger link bound them
> than social environment, nationality, family or even love . . . they
> were united by a bond of fellowship, they were brothers till death,
> just because they had all suffered from the same devouring
> disease. . . . They had all been down into the depths of the abyss,
> and if they had managed to return to the light of day among
> their fellow men, they owed it entirely to this solidarity, this
> fraternal feeling (420: p. 4).

As a voluntary association, A.A. is simply following a traditional American pattern. Barnouw (421: p. 171) points to the
fact that Alexis de Tocqueville observed the prevalence of such
associations during his American visit when he wrote:

> As soon as several of the inhabitants of the United States have
> taken up an opinoin or a feeling which they wish to promote in
> the world, they look for mutual assistance; and as soon as they
> have found one another, they combine. From that moment on
> they are no longer isolated men, but a power seen from afar, whose
> actions serve for an example and whose language is listened to (422).

Later, Barnouw describes the extent to which this pattern continues. He states, "The United States is a nation in which all kinds of voluntary associations flourish—clubs, including women's clubs (unheard of in some nations), learned societies, Rotarians, Lions, Moose, Elk, nudist groups, bird watching societies, veterans associations, alumni, chess players, societies for helping the American Indian or Negro Americans, associations for aiding museums, conserving nature and many other causes" (421: p. 171). I have already noted that one function of such groupings is to find others sharing a common value system in the quest for the psychocultural security of a folk society. As a voluntary association, then, A.A. is as American as our fear of body odor.

A.A. also follows the American pattern of forming self-help groups in areas where no remedial social means exist. Philip Bock has remarked on this pattern: "Task-oriented voluntary groups become more permanent when continuing social demands cannot be met by the regular groupings in a society" (423: p. 153). A.A. is a specifically American response to a problem that has proven to be beyond the solution of the family, police, church, medicine and psychotherapy. It is as typically American as the vigilante groups that spring up when local law enforcement agencies are unable to control crime. A.A. is by no means the first voluntary group associated with the rehabilitation of alcoholics. The Washingtonian Movement is a notable predecessor, but one that failed for reasons ably resuméd by Milton Maxwell (424). However, A.A. is the only continuing and successful group dealing with alcoholism.

A.A.'s philosophy and structure, however, are American and its foreign successes are most notable in related cultures such as Canada, Ireland, England, Scandinavia, New Zealand and Australia. A.A. has also failed to make any notable inroads into the alcoholism of Mexican-American and Negro groups within this nation. In part this is due to the fact that white alcoholics share the prejudices of the larger white society. However, from my own observations, I would say that there is a greater effort to repress racial and ethnic hostility within A.A. than any other typically American association that I have encountered. The main block to minority success in A.A. is probably the core of Protestant middle-class values that unconsciously form the central philosophy of A.A. I have watched Mexican-American alcoholics encounter this ethic and retreat back to alcohol. For a traditional Mexican-American to seek aid from an Anglo-dominated group is, in the first place, a nearly traitorous act. It implies that the alcoholic's family, church and community are unable to care for their own. Once in A.A., most Mexican-Americans find the unspoken, but felt, reformed-sinner syndrome difficult to take. Further, A.A. offends the *Mexicano* sense of dignity and especially the masculine value of *machismo*. I asked one sober Mexican-American alcoholic, whom I knew well enough to joke with, how he handled his machismo within the context of A.A.'s philosophy. I found his reply quite appealing: "It is better," he said, "to be a live chicken than a dead rooster." We badly need a study of A.A. in those Latin American cultures where modifications have made it compatible. The most significant of these is San Salvador, where A.A. has flourished for decades. Another is Mexico City, where after years of bare survival, A.A. is now growing rapidly. It is of course possible that the current A.A. success in the Mexican capital is as much a product of the alienation of accelerated urban growth as of accommodation to Mexican patterns. I suspect that a successful Mexican-American version of A.A. however would need to emphasize the alcoholic's *strength* in overcoming the disease rather than the concept of *surrender*. It would also have to go much further than A.A. in freeing the individual from assuming any responsibility for past alcoholic misbehavior. Possibly it would have to abandon the concept of anonymity and replace it with a public image of *recovered alcoholic* that the community must be conditioned to see as brave, commendable and noble.

A.A. is probably best viewed as a minority movement that in many ways sets the basic pattern for all the ethnic movements of contemporary America. The active alcoholic has frequently suffered every discrimination any Black or Mexicano has endured. The effects of alcohol are as solid a base for discrimination as is skin color or language. Many of the advanced alcoholics in my sample had been fired, denied security clearance, banned from restaurants and bars, and physically assaulted because of alcohol-based behavior that they had only slightly more control over than a Black does his skin color. Quite a few knew the ego-shattering effect of being jailed. A few had lived through nearly unbelievable man-handling by sadistic police officers. Two, however, stated that their first exposure to Alcoholics Anonymous was through A.A. members of the police force whom they met in jail. With a shared history of socially administered abuse, alcoholics in A.A. have banded together to seek to improve their condition and to educate the public. As a part of their group movement they produced the philosophy that no one can understand an alcoholic but another alcoholic. This preceded by far the current Black parallel in the concept of *soul*.

Like all the minority movements, A.A. has created an integrated set of core values that all good members must accept without reservation. The shared deprivations of the past and the commonly held values of the group combine to give A.A.'s a sense of togetherness which is accentuated by their sense of apartness from the rest of society. This dichotomy of we-they separates alcoholic from nonalcoholic in the same way that Black Power groups identify themselves on the basis of a white-black opposition. However, the A.A. does not look upon the nonalcoholic with hostility but sees him as different and in many ways alien to the idealized A.A. way of life. The difference is clearly visible in the A.A. terms for nonalcoholics such as *normies* (i.e. normals), *civilians*, and most charmingly, *earth people*. Active alcoholics are seen as individuals suffering by their apartness from A.A. truth but as individuals who may be salvageable.

A.A., along with the other minority movements, thus emerges as a folk culture. In all of these movements there is an attempt to recapture the love and security of a family group. Unlike the Blacks, A.A. members do not refer to each other as brother and sister, but a feeling of kinship runs deep. Many A.A.'s have said to me, "A.A. is the only family I have." In nearly every way, except actual kinship, then, A.A. fits Kroeber's definition of a folk society as a

. . . small, isolated, close-knit society, in which person-to-person relations are prevalent, kinship is a dominant factor, and organization, both societal and cultural, is therefore largely on a basis of kinship—sometimes including fictitious kinship, as in many clans and moieties. By contrast, political institutions are weakly developed: primitive democracy is the characteristic form; but this denotes only a maximum of equality coexisting with a minimum of authority or control (19, p. 281).

The primitive democracy is indeed one of the facts of A.A. that has been noted by many observers who wondered at its effectiveness. In fact, as a folk society, no other form could function. Likewise, A.A. participation in their group activities parallels Kroeber's definition of folk interaction:

Folk cultures afford their individual members full participation in their functioning—they invite and encourage such participation; their functioning, however limited and inadequate, is therefore personalized and saturated. The relatively small range of their culture content, the close-knitness of the participation in it, the very limitation of scope, all make for a sharpness of patterns in the culture, which are well characterized, consistent and interrelated. Narrowness, depth and intensity are the qualities of folk cultures (19: p. 282).

Anthropologists use the term "folk" to refer to either primitive or peasant societies. The primitive generally lives in some isolation from civilization while peasants are adjuncts of city life. As a part of a larger totality, Kroeber refers to peasants as "part-societies." As A.A.'s also are a part of the larger more sophisticated society of America, in one sense A.A. could be defined as a part-society. A.A. fits Kroeber's definition of peasants insofar as ". . . they form a . . . segment of a larger population . . . They form part-societies with part cultures . . ." (19: p. 284). A.A.'s who are most deeply imbedded within the sociocultural framework of A.A. when speaking of the "other world" frequently remind me of the peasant referring to the way of life of the market-town of the larger society which he must enter on occasion. One of these totally enculturated A.A.'s said to me, "Most of my life I operate out there with the normies. I'm not really comfortable there. I know the rules and can abide by them but they're not my rules any longer. I can play their game but I'm always up-tight about it. I don't think I ever really relax in a group unless they're all A.A.'s."

Another folk-like aspect of A.A. is the mystical or pseudo-religious tone of much of its philosophy and history. Primitives and folk-peoples do not dichotomize the natural and supernatural into separate realities as we do. Rather, they see these two aspects as being totally intertwined into the one reality of being. Even the genesis of A.A. was in a mystical experience that paralleled many of the religious movements of primitive and folk peoples which rose as desperate reactions to the onslaught of the more civilized nations. As Bronislaw Malinowski (425, 426, 427) so clearly demonstrated, one of the functions of the supernatural is to give man the feeling that he can predict the unpredictable and control the uncontrollable. As less developed people see themselves and their cultures rapidly collapsing before more technically advanced societies, they frequently seek help from the supernatural. Likewise, the culturally deprived and alienated within the more powerful civilizations have at times been offered a solution by *saviors* such as Christ or the Buddha. Anthropologists have used a variety of terms for these religions of the deprived. These include "nativistic movements" (428), "revitalization movements" (429), "crisis cults" (430) and "Messianic movements" (431). At the primitive and folk levels many of these movements began when a leader received a sanction for his creation of a cult through a vision or dream of a protective supernatural being. Examples are numerous such as the American Indian Ghost Dance (432), and the Cargo Cults of Melanesia (433, 434).

Alcoholics Anonymous also began with a vision. It is possible that the preconditioning for that event was Bill's awareness of Carl G. Jung's beliefs about apparently hopeless cases of alcoholism. Admitting his inability to help these, Jung had said that in this type of "incurable" alcoholism a few recoveries had been observed of individuals who had had a transcending religious experience. During my visit with him, Bill gratefully acknowledged this probable indebtedness to Jung for his later peak experience which was to culminate eventually in Alcoholics

Anonymous. Bill was also strongly influenced by a fellow alcoholic, Ebby, who had found a temporary sobriety in the Oxford Movement. Because of this exposure, some of the basic tenets of that movement later were incorporated in A.A. (435). The actual vision occurred in 1934 while Bill was in Towns Hospital in New York City because of his alcoholism. In the depths of despair, Bill was experiencing what Assagioli, in words duplicating those of A.A., calls the "crisis preceding a spiritual awakening." This is a feeling of utter hopelessness and, as Assagioli says, ". . . a sense of unreality and emptiness of ordinary life" (401, p. 41). Bill has described his vision in writing:

> My depression deepened unbearably and finally it seemed to me as though I were at the very bottom of the pit. I still gagged badly on the notion of a Power greater than myself, but finally, just for the moment, the last vestige of my proud obstinancy was crushed. All at once I found myself crying out, 'If there is a God let Him show Himself! I am ready to do anything, anything.'
> Suddenly the room lit up with a great white light. I was caught up into an ecstasy which there are no words to describe. It seemed to me, in the mind's eye, that I was on a mountain and that a wind not of air but of spirit was blowing. And then it burst upon me that I was a free man. Slowly the ecstasy subsided. I lay on the bed, but now for a time I was in another world, a new world of consciousness. All about me and through me there was a wonderful feeling of Presence, and I thought to myself, 'So this is the God of the preachers!' A great peace stole over me and I thought, 'No matter how wrong things seem to be, they are still right. Things are all right with God and His world.
> Then, little by little, I began to be frightened. My modern education crawled back and said to me, 'You are hallucinating. You had better get the doctor.' Dr. Silkworth asked me a lot of questions. After a while he said, 'No, Bill, you are not crazy. There has been some basic psychological or spiritual event here. I've read about these things in the books. Sometimes spiritual experiences do release people from alcoholism' (436: p. 63).

At that brief moment the genesis of A.A. probably hung in the balance. Had Dr. Silkworth informed Bill that he had experienced an alcoholic hallucination it is probable that he would never have sobered up. Later, Bill received further sanction for the validity of his vision from a careful study of William James'

Varieties of Religious Experience.

Anthropologists would see Bill's quest and discovery of God as falling into the same pattern as the *vision quest* of American Indians by which power and sanction was obtained from the supernatural to attain particular goals (437). It could also be defined in terms of a fairly typical conversion phenomenon. Whatever psychological dynamics were involved, Bill was given a belief in a source of power other than alcohol. He also experienced a psychological readjustment of his value system which made concrete and meaningful five core values in place of an existential vacuum. These were: (1) Life is meant to be meaningful rather than chaotic and senseless; (2) Sobriety is the key to alcoholic success; (3) A *power greater than oneself* can enable one to overcome a craving; (4) The alcoholic is a person of worth or God would not have bothered Himself with Bill; and (5) the alcoholic is not really alone for Someone up there knows and cares. Bill then saw the prophetic need to share this message and to bring other alcoholics out of their alienation and despair. As Bill wrote, "My thoughts began to race as I envisioned a chain reaction among alcoholics, one carrying this message and these principles to the next. More than I could ever want anything else, I now knew that I wanted to work with other alcoholics" (436: p. 64). He took his message to Oxford Groups but they felt that he ". . . had better forget about alcoholics" (436: p. 65). Then he met another alcoholic, Dr. Bob, in Akron, Ohio, and the interaction between them based on Bill's *message* produced what was to be the first group of Alcoholics Anonymous.

The "power" to resist alcohol which Bill at first thought he obtained from God now was translated into the power of a group dedicated to the goal of a shared sobriety. This is a curious reversal of the principles formulated by Emile Durkheim (438) who saw faith in a social group leading to the creation of a god. The idea of group solidarity permeates A.A. and members speak of sharing "their experience, strength and hope." Following basic Christian principles, A.A.'s see themselves united by their own choice in a cause that transcends the personal needs of any individual member. Edith Weigert sees this relationship as basic to any successful relationship between a therapist and a patient. She has said, "Both must have a faith to some degree in freedom of choice, alteration of decisions, commitment and responsibility in relation to values that have a super-personal meaning" (408: p. 155). This transcending meaning is at the base of any successful movement. Lacking an instinctive fulfillment, man needs faith in a goal that will make any sacrifice in that direction significant and meaningful. In an extreme form this was once expressed by someone as "Life is worth living only when one is willing to lose it for a cause." I know of no one who has died for A.A. but I do know several who would literally rather die than violate its principles by drinking.

Success in A.A. is directly proportional to the ability to identify with its ranks and to feel as an integral part of its being. One A.A. told me he finally knew that he was "in the program" when he altered the pronoun used to describe its meetings to his wife. After his first four meetings, he described the A.A. activities by using the term "they" to describe the membership. On his return from his fifth meeting he told his wife, "Tonight we talked about gratitude." To me he said, "A moment later I realized I'd said 'we' and that I no longer felt about A.A. as an outside agency but as a group to which I was committed to the very depths of my soul." The ability to become committed depends largely on being able to identify other A.A.'s as duplications of one's own problems rather than merely as teetotaling strangers. A positive identification with A.A. is frequently directly proportional to the alcoholic suffering that the individual has experienced in relationship to that of the A.A. members he encounters on first contacting the fellowship. An alcoholic who has suffered no more than the anxiety of a few blackouts will be unable to identify if he attends a meeting of A.A.'s whose common history includes bankruptcy, broken marriages, arrests and hospitalizations with D.T.'s and convulsions. By analogy, a rooster who has lost three tailfeathers would not relate well to a flock of chickens that had been plucked bare. Such was apparently the case with the fictional alcoholic Katie Crane in Robert Ruark's *Uhuru*. She said, ". . . I tried psychiatry and hypnosis and, God forgive us all, had a small riffle at Alcoholics Anonymous which drove me back to drink faster than drink ever drove me to A.A." (439: p. 259).

In the early years of A.A. most of its membership consisted of those who had *gone all the way* down the alcoholic chute. In today's A.A. terminology, they were *low-bottom drunks,* alcoholics whose suffering has reached its final limit. The low-bottom drunk usually has a long record of social rejection, job failures, arrests and commitments to mental hospitals. Some of the old-timers in A.A. have told me that until the very late forties it was assumed that only this type of advanced alcoholic was really eligible for the fellowship. One of my respondents had attended his first A.A. meeting in 1945 at the age of seventeen and been flatly told that he was "too young to get anything out of the program." He was urged, however, to return when he was really "into the disease." He did so after his third attack of alcoholic convulsions and has been sober ever since.

Today the image of who can be helped by the program has radically altered and the A.A. ranks have enough alcoholics under thirty, including many teenagers, to hold an annual young people's convention. Although low-bottom drunks still abound in A.A., they are today outnumbered by the *high-bottom drunks.* These are the alcoholics who have suffered practically no socio-economic conseqences from their alcoholism. Many of these still have the material rewards of pursuing the Protestant ethic but see these threatened by their increasingly compulsive drinking patterns. Among their ranks are a sizeable number of *silk-sheet drunks,* the very, very rich who have been protected from the full consequences of their alcoholism through the care of hired servants, bodyguards and physicians. These designations, however, do not necessarily indicate any difference in the experienced psychological stress of the disease. One can experience psychic agony under silk sheets as acutely as in the drunk-tank of the local jail. The fear of losing a license to practice medicine can be more stress-producing than losing the job of ditch-digger. The degree of suffering is not proportional to the alcoholic's socioeconomic level although the upper class alcoholics are probably more prone to try to hide their disease.

The high-bottom drunks on contacting A.A. generally need more than a common alcoholism to facilitate identification with the fellowship. Although A.A. rigidly insists on rejecting any recognition of class differences, a high-bottom alcoholic in his first A.A. contact will rarely affiliate unless he meets someone with whom he shares more than a drinking problem. One alcoholic I interviewed had literally been scared away from A.A. for six years because the first meeting he attended had been composed of people totally alien to any he had known before. The alcoholic was a tiny and timid individual in his early forties who had led, in his words, "the pampered, protected life of one who lives on inherited riches rather than by honest toil." Although terrified of people in groups, he was a distinguished amateur pianist, fully appreciated his magnificent collection of modern German art and was widely read in the literature of European and Asiatic porcelains. When his solitary drinking had reduced him to a fear of insanity and three psychiatrists had failed to help him, he called the A.A. central office and asked where he could find a meeting. He went to the address given him just before meeting time and went ". . . through a fright as bad as my last alcoholic hallucination." The meeting was on skid row and in my respondent's terms, ". . . the smell of sweat and pee was overwhelming, one bum threw up and the speaker calmly described how, on a drunk he'd nearly beaten a woman to death." The little alcoholic fled to the safety of his magnificent apartment and some fine imported Scotch.

However, A.A. is today diversified and despite its denial, groups do exist in large numbers that are unofficially defined by education and class as well as by alcoholism. My rich and dilettante artistic alcoholic went back to A.A. in desperation six years later and found a group that he "fell in love with" from the time of his first exposure. By then he had been through an expensive drying-out establishment nine times and exhausted four more psychiatrists. Guided to his second meeting by a physician who was also in A.A., my respondent "finally found a home." This group met in a private room of an exclusive club and its membership included "two well-known artists, one famous but undistinguished author, three physicians and some dozen other individuals who speak my language." Such a group would not think of excluding any alcoholic who came to its doors and really does not think of itself as exclusive. Rather, it defines itself as bringing together alcoholics who share similar interests. Others simply do not know of its existence or, if they do, are not sure where it meets. Likewise, there are groups made up exclusively of physicians, lawyers, policemen and newspaper writers. There is also, in any large city, an *anonymous anonymous group* composed of individuals in such sensitive positions that their careers would be jeopardized if their A.A. affiliation were even suspected.

Most A.A. groups, however, are overwhelmingly middle class with a sprinkling of alcoholics from the lower and upper classes. Within this setting, the newcomer who finds someone with a similar background and a parallel drinking history is the most likely to immediately relate to the group and the program. His prospects are also immeasurably improved if the group membership includes someone he can strongly admire. One of my respondents, a lawyer, told me of the elation he felt on attending his first A.A. meeting to find that the alcoholic speaker was a high court judge whom he had always respected. Several commented that affiliation was made almost glamorous by the presence of one or more attractive female members. One A.A. described his first meeting by saying,

> Before going I'd resigned myself to a life of sobriety in a sterile, drab existence without beauty or happiness. I was cheered up by the first members I met before the meeting for they seemed genuinely happy. And then this vision walked in, one of the sex symbols I've seen on TV a dozen times. Sobriety took on a new dimension—and it hasn't let me down.

If the alcoholic's inner suffering and sense of alienation has been severe and his first contact with A.A. conducive to affiliation, he may be primed for the second peak experience of his life. This one may surpass his first which accompanied the discovery of the miracle of alcohol. This is a sensation that may actually take hold during the meeting or come upon the alcoholic after several A.A. sessions when he is by himself. The descriptions of these closely parallel Maslow's description of peak experiences of "healthy people." Colin Wilson quotes from Maslow's paper which was read in La Jolla in 1961:

> I found that these individuals tended to report having had something like mystic experiences, moments of great awe, moments of the most intensive happiness, or even rapture, ecstasy or bliss. . . . These moments were of pure, positive happiness, when all doubts, all fears, all inhibitions, all tensions, all weaknesses, were left behind. Now self-consciousness was lost. All separateness and distance from the world disappeared as they felt one with the world, fused with it, really belonging to it, instead of being outside, looking in. (One subject said, for instance, 'I felt like a member of a family, not like an orphan')" (161: p. 16).

Such an experience works for the new A.A. with the same effectiveness that the vision had on Bill Wilson. It frequently launches him into a period of euphoria that may last for a few days or many months. A.A.'s refer to this period of delight as "being on a pink cloud."

The pink cloud is produced by several interrelated processes. The first of these is the sheer joy of belonging to a caring group. As Daniel Callahan has written,

> Human beings also need a sense of community, the possibility of living in peace and mutual enrichment with others. For community to exist, truth is fundamental, springing from shared values, an interdependent life in common, and a sustaining belief that in the ordinary course of events one's neighbor is not one's enemy (440: p. 6).

This trusting affiliation is something the primary alcoholic has searched for all his life. The secondary and delta alcoholics see A.A. as a group that will help them regain what they are losing or have already lost. Within the confines of A.A., alcoholics find their own kind, and with this, as one primary said, ". . . the joy of coming home to a family I didn't know I had." Another expressed his own discovery of A.A. by saying, "I felt as though I were a Hopi Indian who had wandered all my life among the Sioux. Then, when things were blackest, I found my own people. I finally knew who I was."

With the group affiliation, the alcoholic gets an identity to build on. For the primary this is usually the first solid self-concept he has ever had. For the secondary, it is a basis to rebuild what he had lost. To the rest of us, alcoholism may seem like a shoddy and unstable foundation from which to seek normalcy. However, it is a realistic one and it works. For the alcoholic, it explains the enigma of his past. One said to me,

> For years I thought I was going crazy. Nothing I did made sense and I was afraid of every person I met. I worried and worried. Why was I so different and why did I do the looney things I did? I fretted about being unhappy and worried about being happy. And then A.A. explained it to me. I wasn't crazy, I wasn't different, I was just an alcoholic doing what alcoholics do!

While the alcoholic is a deviant in the larger world, within the boundaries of A.A. he is normal. To feel normal for a primary is a deeply joyous and inspiring event unparalleled in the past except when drunk among drunks. For the secondary alcoholic it is a rediscovery of the feeling he once had, as one said, ". . . of being a part of the human race." In A.A. the alcoholic learns to put his alcoholism at the very center of his being and it becomes a hub from which all else in his life radiates.

Working from the basic concept that *I am an alcoholic*, the A.A. member begins to create a positive image of himself. In the words of Daniel Callahan, he begins to fulfill the very human ". . . drive for integrity, for a unified self, one certain of its own worth, at ease with itself" (440: p. 7). The alcoholic's worth is demonstrated by the warmth and affection showered upon him when he enters A.A. His alcoholism, which had alienated others from him in the greater world, brings him love, acceptance and respect. As Charles McCabe has observed about life in general, "To be assured of your worth, in a lonely and uncaring world, is maybe what it's all about" (441). One newcomer on the program described the effect of her first meeting to me,

> I snuck in like a terrified fugitive from God and society knowing I deserved the awful punishments they had in store for me. I walked out of that meeting with a sense of total freedom with my chin high and a warmth of love I'd never known. And for the very first time in my life I knew I wasn't alone. At long last I was going to have a chance to be me and I knew I would be acceptable."

When the first contact with A.A. is this effective, the alcoholic,

like any convert, sees his life as divided into the period before
and after enlightenment. It is the basic saved-sinner syndrome
of Christianity. A.A.'s inevitably in meetings speak of the horror
and despair of their drinking existence as opposed to the controlled joys of their present sobriety. However, A.A. does offer
them a reprieve from guilt for the sinner period. By the disease
concept, the alcoholic's failures and shortcomings are explained
as a product of the disease and not of his own inherent wicked-
ness. For many alcoholics, the acceptance of the disease concept
removes a burden of guilt and shame that they have carried
for years. As one A.A. said to me, "It was like getting rid of a
ton of garbage I'd carried on my shoulders as long as I can
remember. I realized that the crap in my past was piled on me
by the disease. It was not my will."

The concept of will is a critical one in A.A. By the disease
concept it is assumed the alcoholic could not have avoided his
pathological drinking. If the disease is seen as a force beyond
his control, it must be countered by a stronger force. That force,
of course, is Alcoholics Anonymous. However, the alcoholic is
not seen as a hopeless, paralyzed object snatched from destruction
as the White Knight rescues the bound virgin from the fire-
breathing dragon. The responsibility of recovery is put on the
alcoholic and A.A. is described as merely a "tool" to aid him in
his recovery. He must, of his own volition, be willing to pick
up and use the tool. A favorite A.A. expression is, "We will walk
with you but we cannot walk for you." A.A., then, identifies the
alcoholic's misery before affiliation as due to ignorance of the
disease and of the steps necessary to arrest it. Once he is made
aware of the disease concept of alcoholism, he is offered the
defense of the fellowship and the program. No strenuous attempt
is made to stop his leaving if he rejects these. If he accepts
them along with a desire for sobriety, he is told that like those
already sober in A.A., he will succeed. The desire for sobriety
and the decision to affiliate must be his alone, but the means
to success is through group effort. I asked one A.A. how he saw
the role of will power in his recovery: "I've got some of that,
but not much," he said. "It's like traveling. A.A. is like a train
that can take me where I want to go. But I get on of my own

free will and I can jump off any time I want. However, as long as I stay in that train and follow instructions, I'm okay."

The instructors are the other members of A.A. Every member of the organization is a folk-curer, one who administers therapy outside the formal disciplines of medicine. The more religious would qualify as shamans, an anthropological term borrowed from Siberia to label folk-curers who receive their curative powers from a supernatural source (442). Bill's vision which gave sanction to his later role as curer comes close to the classic sanctioning of Siberia shamans in many respects. Several of the more devout A.A.'s openly state that A.A. members were "chosen by God" for their role as healers of alcoholism. Others see their power derived simply from their own recovery from the disease. This parallels the many curing groups in primitive and folk societies where it is believed that to recover from a disease conveys the power to cure that disease. This argument follows the principle of imitative magic that like can cure like. The majority of A.A.'s however, see their gift as simply the ability to share their experience and knowledge.

Whatever the sanction to treat, A.A.'s view alcoholism as deriving from and influencing every aspect of the alcoholic's life. This is in sharp contrast to the monocausal approaches of most scientific therapies and more closely resembles the folk Mexican-American definition of all disease. Of the latter, Ari Kiev says, ". . . for the Mexican-American, illness relates to an individual's life, his community, his interpersonal relationships and, above all, to his God. In such a culture, illness is a social as well as a biological fact" (443: p. 117). By treating the whole person, folk psychotherapy is frequently far more effective than modern medical and psychiatric approaches (444). Likewise, Alcoholics Anonymous has achieved a success in treating alcoholics that dwarfs the combined efforts of medicine, psychology and psychiatry.

A.A.'s success rests largely on its assumption that alcoholism has both psychocultural and biological aspects. Alcoholics Anonymous admits that it can neither explain nor treat the biological correlate of alcoholism. A newcomer is urged to have a regular medical examination and seek treatment for any detected malfunction or physical ailment. He is also given such practical health rules as "Don't get too hungry, too tired or too thirsty." The key to the A.A. handling of the physical side of alcoholism, however, rests in classifying it as an allergy. Alcohol is stated to create a physical craving for more of the same along with the resultant psychological suffering and social consequences. The simplest solution, therefore, is to avoid the alcohol. As one A.A. put it to me,

> For me to drink would be as reasonable as stripping and rolling in poison ivy. Both booze and the ivy make me dreadfully ill. Before A.A., I continually poisoned myself on booze which I could no more handle than my skin could resist the consequences of contact with poison ivy. My drinking can only be explained as insanity.

An A.A. recovery, therefore, rests on total abstinence. The one piece of advice hammered into the newcomer again and again is "Don't take the first drink." The best defense against the temptation to take that first drink is seen as massive exposure to A.A. contacts, literature and meetings. The meetings are seen as especially important and the beginner is urged to keep coming back. The alcoholic is also told to practice *dime therapy* when alone and feeling an urge to drink. This refers to the practice of calling another A.A. on the phone when despondent or feeling like imbibing. Each newcomer usually quickly collects many telephone numbers for such emergencies.

To take that first drink is to slip, the great fear of every A.A. With one drink, the alcoholic automatically resigns from Alcoholics Anonymous. He also, as one A.A. told me, ". . . throws out the window his accumulated sobriety, his self-respect and the trust others have shown him." This is such an ego-shattering shock that the slipper usually goes into a full-fledged drunk even if a total physical compulsion is not upon him. The reasons for slips are probably infinite. Frequently, acute anxiety or depression launches one. I watched several A.A.'s slip following severe frustrations. Many have a slip in a last desperate attempt to prove themselves to be social drinkers.

A common cause of slips, especially in high-bottom drunks, is the fear of rejection by civilians or at the least, of not living up to an imaginary image of sophistication and control. Pete's slip was typical. He had three months on the program and still held an excellent job as a stock broker. Going to lunch one day in his favorite restaurant, he found all the tables taken. He decided to eat at the bar. As he sat down an old and respected friend joined him. At the same moment the bartender came up and asked, "The usual?" The friend and then Pete both nodded yes. By ten o'clock that night Pete had blacked out, wrecked his car and ended up asleep in the hallway of his home. I later asked Pete why he hadn't said no to the bartender. "I don't know," he answered. "I think I was ashamed." Jim's slip in many ways paralleled Pete's except that he had nine months of sobriety when he took his next drink. Jim had carefully avoided bars during that time. However, attending a professional convention in Los Angeles, he suddenly decided to enter a night club and watch the show. He did so, drank ginger ale and enjoyed it. Then a B-girl suddenly joined him and asked if he'd buy her some wine. He ordered the bottle of champagne and joined her in drinking it as well as two others. However, he didn't black out, did sleep with the girl and awoke the next day convinced he was cured. He drank successfully for four more days but on the fifth he blacked out. "I woke the next day with the horrors," he said. He was too ill to get up all day but the following morning he called A.A. for help. I asked why he had taken the champagne. "I don't know," he said, using the same response as Pete. "I do know I wanted that bitch to think well of me." He paused and added, "Besides that, how the hell do you make a girl while drinking ginger ale?" Both Pete and Jim came back on the program. Both had resigned with the first drink. However, as they both knew when they walked out of A.A., "the door swings both ways" and they were welcomed back.

These two slips represent some of the psychocultural pitfalls of American culture that cause many abstinent alcoholics to fall back into once-abandoned drinking patterns. In a strange way Americans associate maturity and sophistication with the violation of some of our historical and puritanical taboos. Thus, for years adolescents have sought to prove their worth by committing those *naughty* adult acts of smoking, drinking and pursuing sex. Physically mature, the American teenager is denied any demonstration of responsibility aside from the puberty rite of getting a driving license. The adolescent primary alcoholic suffers from an acute lack of self-worth and profits from these mature *sins* even more than his fellows. As the early use of the sin syndrome gave him some sense of social ability, ever afterward he tends to associate these acts with social acceptance, self-worth and maturity. Further, until recently with the youth, the pursuit of sex without alcohol was unthinkable. The alcohol dulls the taboo side of the sexual anxiety-arrow and later provides an excuse for the act. The female rationalization for committing it is almost hackneyed, "It wasn't my fault. He got me drunk." Further, until the recent *sexual revolution,* American male culture assumed the girls so valued their purity that the only way to *score* was to lower their defenses with alcohol.

The carry-over of this adolescent value structure into American life is reflected in the sophisticated circles the alcoholic would like to identify with. The Playboy syndrome does indeed assume that the teetotaler is almost sexless. By extension, the nondrinker is also characterized as powerless and dull. Most alcoholics would agree and therein lies one of their main stumbling blocks. As one A.A. said to me, "We need our Big Book, but by God I wish someone would add a chapter to it on 'How to Sin Without Booze!'" The sober alcoholic must, in fact, abandon many of the standard American fun-and-games or somehow learn to play them without recourse to the courage-builder—alcohol. If he does enter the American Dionysian playground, he must acquire a defense against the common American intolerance of alcoholic abstinence. I doubt if the society itself will rapidly accommodate itself to a broader view of individual worth. Years ago a Frenchman said to me,

> You Americans are so immature. You demand the love that is only given infants while trying to prove your worth by displaying your genitals and destroying your minds with bourbon. The best man is really not the one with the biggest drinking capacity, the longest list of seductions, the largest bank account and the most

powerful bombs. The mature individual is one who seeks happiness by living up to his own adequate value system and not the other who has to prove himself by being loved and applauded or by dominating others.

Very few Frenchmen, of course, live up to this version of Enlightenment philosophy. Parts of it, however, are important to alcoholic recovery. The alcoholic must either control or purge his being of those American values which lead him to attempt to prove himself by the American fascination with excess. He must learn an ecclecticism in his reliance on the overflowing barrel of U.S. values. Once in A.A., the alcoholic is expected to begin the rebuilding of his psyche. A few attain an almost instant reconstitution of an integrated value system that reinforces their sobriety. These are invariably low-bottom drunks from small religious communities in the Middle West or the South who had moved to the big city. I have seen several of these who experienced a religious experience upon exposure to A.A. and almost instantaneously were purged of all secondary values derived from the larger society. They are left with an integrated God-fearing and sin-hating folk adherence to fundamentalist Christian faith. Instead of thumping Bibles, however, they now thump the Big Book. They are most frequently dogmatists and seek to resolve every argument by asking, ". . . What does the Big Book say about it?" These are the true disciples and are thereafter usually as free of the painful tasks of decision-making and original thinking as any other religious or scientific disciple.

Most A.A.'s, however, do not experience this type of instant salvation. Following affiliation, most alcoholics, especially the high-bottom drunks, begin the long process of A.A. folk psychotherapy. Its goals are to allow the alcoholic to know himself, define reasonable goals, simplify and integrate the jungle of conflicting values within him and develop the precious quality of self-respect. In the A.A. approach, the newcomer is urged to "Keep it simple." This is in sharp contrast to the involved and complex approaches to life that the alcoholic had practiced in his drinking days. The active alcoholic plays many conflicting roles and tries to maintain his social integrity through a massive system of deception and lies. In contrast, once he is in A.A., he is told he has only one identity—that of alcoholic. The principal consideration in any act for the alcoholic now becomes: Will this strengthen or weaken my sobriety? In making this judgment he learns that he must practice total honesty. In part, this refers to honesty in dealing with others at meaningful levels where its opposite would cause stress or further complications in life. Primarily, it refers to self-honesty, a difficult feat for anyone, and an especially painful process for the alcoholic. For the primary alcoholic it can be agonizing. The first honest step is the admission of alcoholism rather than the earlier attempts to hide that fact from himself and others.

The alcoholic is now told that his *ego* is an enemy of his sobriety and must be cut down to size. This causes confusion in the mind of any alcoholic who has a smattering of psychology. In view of psychological theory, anyone suffering from a sense of inferiority needs to build up his ego. In fact, this is but another case of linguistic confusion. By ego, A.A. refers to the false and flattering mask that the alcoholic tries to wear in an attempt to favorably influence others as well as himself. It parallels very closely the false shield of "machismo" that Samuel Ramos (445) and Octavio Paz claim the Mexican mestizo male uses to hide his deep sense of inferiority. The ego of A.A. is the phoney egotism of popular speech. In an attempt to hide a sense of inadequacy, the alcoholic has frequently acquired a self-confident manner and enlarged on his accomplishments and worth to fantastic proportions. Many have worn this mask so long that they find it difficult to remove. Many alcoholics actually come to regard this disguise as a reality in the same way that Octavio Paz (446) claims the Mexican male comes to dupe himself into believing his mask of machismo is really not a mask but himself. In part, this ego is reflected in the totally unrealistic goals that he has set for himself. In opposition to a sense of failure, his rich fantasy life has created a scene of his future outstanding success. This is especially notable in primary alcoholics. Few of these see themselves becoming merely adequate businessmen. Rather, they fantasize a future as captains of industry. Few who want to write visualize a small success. Rather, they are the future Pulitzer Prize winners. When the newcomer is told to smash his ego, he is being instructed to pull down the irrational edifice of his self-proclaimed worth and promise. He is informed that despite his illusion, rewards are deserved only after the accomplishment. In short, he is to cut himself down to a realistic size and lower his goals. In the jargon of A.A., this is to realize the value of "humility."

To remove this fantasy from his being is traumatic for the alcoholic. However, it is counterbalanced by his acceptance as a valued person in A.A. Further, each time a chip of his pretended exterior is removed, he receives increased demonstrations of love and understanding. The positive value of affiliation thus offsets the jar of, as one A.A. put it, "stripping my soul naked and looking in the mirror." A meaningful self-esteem is rarely realistic or satisfying when it is the product of a play acted merely to an audience of self. Adler (447) was keenly aware that the best remedy for a sense of inferiority is the feeling obtained by becoming a functioning member of a social group. Within A.A. the alcoholic learns that without elaborations or disguises it is his real self that is accepted. Through group acceptance, self-acceptance begins to take place. With self-acceptance comes confidence. With confidence comes the alcoholic dream of a sense of worth. By destroying what A.A. calls "ego," the alcoholic begins to develop the "ego strength" of psychology.

With an increasing sense of ability and worth, the primary alcoholic begins to learn what one A.A. described as ". . . the simple facts of life that Mom forgot to teach me." The first of these are the virtues of patience and persistence. Primaries especially are impatient for rewards and are frustrated at the tedium of any long task. In their lives they have usually begun innumerable projects with enthusiasm, only to abandon them when the actual unexciting steps begin to bore and annoy them. Their usual sense of inadequacy then returns to convince them that they will fail anyway or that the project itself is a waste of time. Within A.A., they first learn patience and persistence in the maintenance of sobriety. If they remain in close contact with their fellows, each weak moment when the newcomer finds abstinence just isn't worth it, he encounters the full supportive

strength of A.A. He also learns the valid lesson that one can only
... live "one day at a time." If the moment is painful, "it will pass."
If it is pleasant, enjoy it. The alcoholic is encouraged in every
way to forget the two time periods his mind tends to dwell in—
the past and the future. Most alcoholics carry a burden of guilt
from past misadventures that is most difficult to bear. They also,
alternately, see the future as glorious or catastrophic. I listened
to one A.A. counsel an anxious newcomer who was bemoaning
the futility of today's sobriety in light of a horrendous past and
an uncontrollable future. The supporting A.A. said,

> You can't change one damn thing in the past, but what does
> it matter? It's past, gone, dead. It doesn't exist anymore. You are
> not your past. You are now. You can't control the past, but you are
> in full control right now. This is the first day of the rest of your
> life. Take care of the now and you don't have to worry about the
> future. Today may be bad, but, baby, you play it right and it gets
> better. But the only control you will ever have is what you have
> over this very second.

The newcomer is urged to "let go" of the burden of the past and
the expectations of tomorrow's consequences. His life is now.

Focusing on the now, A.A. is primarily concerned with techniques to deal with frustration and pain. The newcomer is
first brought face-to-face with the fact that his Christian-
American dream of a coming utopia when everyone will live
happily ever after is a lie, or at least not to happen in his
lifetime. He learns that pain and pleasure are both eternal and
he must learn to live with both. How to survive when things
go badly is, after all, a major part of the message of any religion
or system of therapy. As Edith Weigert has said, "The great
philosophies of world history have recommended various techniques to learn the endurance of suffering" (408: p. 157). She
also observes that "one value which comes out of the therapeutic
process is the development of the ability to endure frustration"
(408: p. 156). When things get rough, the A.A. is taught to
react constructively, or, if no appropriate action exists, he learns
to hang in until the unpleasantness passes. He also learns what
not to do.

The A.A. hears again and again, "No matter how bad things

are, one drink will make them worse." From past experience, he knows this to be true, for the problems remain and to drink is to add the consequence of a bender to the situation. The A.A. also learns that he is not to seek other chemical alternatives for alcohol. As one A.A. said, " 'Better living through chemistry' is fine for the earth people, but when I try it, the 'better' goes bitter very quickly." In this age of pharmaceutical marvels, few alcoholics reach A.A. who have not already experimented with drugs as alcohol substitutes. For many, drugs could not produce an equivalent result. Others became addicted to either tranquilizers or amphetamines. From massive experience with the alcoholic propensity to become addicted to any chemical, A.A. condemns the use of any mind-altering drug unless it is administered under the care of a doctor who understands alcoholism. Some of the more dogmatic A.A.'s go so far as to condemn the use of any medication, including aspirin. However, although they do not advertise the fact, I know several alcoholics who have maintained sobriety with low doses of tranquilizers along with A.A. These are mostly secondary alcoholics, although a few primaries claim that without some chemical aid, they would never have been able to make it on the A.A. program. On the other hand, I have twenty-two case histories of alcoholics who sobered up only to become addicted to pills. Two of these died when they also returned to drinking. My A.A. correspondents have informed me of a number of A.A.'s who have of late attempted to use marijuana as an alcohol substitute. With three it seems to be working well and has produced no complications. Nine, however, stated that pot so relaxed their guard that they began to drink again with extremely unfortunate results.

Denied any chemical means of tension reduction, the A.A. relies in large part upon interaction with fellow alcoholics in innumerable settings, but especially in the fellowship and sharing found in the meetings. The vast variation in meetings ultimately falls under two main headings: speaker and discussion. Speaker meetings are enjoyed for the dramatic content usually present in the speaker's story and for insights into how another alcoholic utilized the program to gain and maintain sobriety. Like all A.A. functions, a speaker meeting is also a social occasion with interaction before, and especially after the talk. Like any A.A. meeting, many alcoholics have said of it, "The main message is to remind us who we are and what we have to do about it." However, most of the alcoholics I worked with preferred discussion meetings. These are usually loosely structured and each participant has the opportunity to speak. Frequently, they are centered on a topic but many are open-ended. It is here that the alcoholic has an opportunity to vocalize his frustrations and tensions, or as frequently said, ". . . to share my problems." No matter how apparently trivial or childish, the alcoholic's problem is heard out and in return he receives advice, understanding and support. Here he also hears the problems of others and the dimensions of his own fall into a more reasonable perspective. The alcoholic also learns to laugh at himself and his problems. Humor and laughter can function magnificently as tension reducers and A.A.'s make heavy use of them. Any outsider visiting an A.A. meeting is usually struck by the frequent explosions of laughter that rock the group. Each wave of humor appears to leave the individual members in a more positive mood. Practically every alcoholic I know reports a sense of relaxation and control following the attendance at a meeting. To share with one's own kind is reassuring and seems to leave the alcoholic in better shape to cope with his life in the "outside world." Several A.A.'s described meetings as "charging my storage battery" or "depositing in my savings account" as a defense against future crisis.

Along with attending meetings, the alcoholic is expected to utilize the A.A. program. This involves careful study of the Big Book and other A.A. literature. It also calls for carrying out the Twelve Steps. These are simply recommendations for a "program of growth" and are listed in the Big Book (124: pp. 59-60) as follows:

1. We admitted we were powerless over alcohol—that our lives had become unmanageable.
2. Came to believe that a Power greater than ourselves could restore us to sanity.
3. Made a decision to turn our will and our lives over to the care of God *as we understood him.*
4. Made a searching and fearless moral inventory of ourselves.

5. Admitted to God, to ourselves, and to another human being the exact nature of our wrongs.
6. Were entirely ready to have God remove all these defects of character.
7. Humbly asked Him to remove our shortcomings.
8. Made a list of all persons we had harmed, and became willing to make amends to them all.
9. Made direct amends to such people wherever possible, except when to do so would injure them or others.
10. Continued to take personal inventory and when we were wrong promptly admitted it.
11. Sought through prayer and meditation to improve our conscious contact with God *as we understood Him*, praying only for knowledge of His will for us and the power to carry that out.
12. Having had a spiritual awakening as the result of these steps, we tried to carry this message to alcoholics, and to practice these principles in all our affairs.

Although the dogmatists believe that these steps should be followed to the letter, most newcomers are told that the whole program ". . . is like a cafeteria. You take what you can use and leave the rest." Out of a sample of 100 A.A.'s, I found only 41 had made a point of going through all the steps. In talking informally to the others, I found that they had, in fact, through meetings and other A.A. interactions, carried out the spirit of most of them. However, how these steps are interpreted is subject to almost infinite variation. Roughly, two main camps can be defined within the A.A. membership. These are the dogmatists who "go by the book." The other is composed of liberals who are far more open to variations in approach. Most, but not all, of the liberals are high-bottom drunks and their educational level tends to be considerably higher than that of the dogmatists. The liberal-dogmatic distinction rarely represents a formal split and both types interact easily and with amazing tolerance of each others' views. Occasionally, a particular meeting will come to be primarily favored by one or the other, but I have never seen any serious questioning of either approach at any meeting. The view for each person is that "It takes what it takes," and toleration is held up as a prime virtue. It is only where an A.A. clubhouse becomes the sole focus of activity that the split clearly shows. In many parts of the southwest and Texas, elaborate A.A.

clubhouses, held legally by dummy corporations, dominate the local alcoholic scene. Even here, the relationship is usually one of tolerant friendliness. But when major issues arise and votes must be taken, the split emerges and occasionally with bad feeling. Following the crisis, however, every effort is made to patch up the split and regain the sense of unity. The A.A.'s are keenly aware of the dangers of rupture and one said, "With us, the meaning is very real and literal of 'united we stand, divided we drink.'"

Both dogmatists and liberals use the same language, so their differences are not obvious to an observer. A nearly ritual uniformity in the use of certain key words or phrases is observable at most meetings. However, the same word may have an entirely different meaning for the speaker and each of the listeners. An example is the word "God" used in the steps. The writers of the Big Book wisely introduce Him in Step 2 simply as "a Power greater than ourselves." His nature is left open in Steps 3 and 11 by the modifier "as we understood Him." To most dogmatists, God is the paternal patriarch of Judeo-Christian tradition. At the other extreme are the militant atheists who at first refuse to mention His name. Later, these use the word freely merely to conform, but do not visualize anything like the Biblical God. One of these in private mocks the entire religious tone of A.A. When he uses the word, he told me, "I try to visualize something pleasant—like Raquel Welch's navel." More commonly, the liberal sees himself as a religiously-inclined agnostic who uses God for an undefinable something that makes life meaningful rather than seeing it as a dirty joke. Many of the liberals define a Higher Power as the A.A. group. As one said, ". . . separately we're just so many drunks. When we get together, our relationship produces a spirit I can't define. But it's a spirit that keeps us sober. I call it God."

On the first step, however, A.A.'s have practically no division in meaning. Further, they see in it far more than the mere words. When an A.A. says he has "taken the first step," it means he has "surrendered" in his long battle to use alcohol constructively. He has resolved the anxiety-arrow that pointed to drink-don't drink. It is total surrender and he admits alcohol is stronger than he is.

Instead of fighting, he retreats and refuses to enter into combat. By implication, it also means a willingness to give up many of the old ideas and fantasies of the period of active alcoholism. This would create an openness to new and more constructive ideas.

Steps 2, 3, 6 and 7 are interpreted as the acceptance of the A.A. program and a faith in its ability to work. The devout, including the dogmatists, see A.A. as divinely inspired and therefore are accepting God's will. The liberals take a more secular approach and interpret these steps as the embracing of the A.A. program. Step 4 is a self-analysis. Step 5 is a verbalization of the weak points in one's character that need repair. The religious may make this "confession" to a priest. A liberal may do it with a psychiatrist, with a close friend in A.A. or by himself. Step 6 admits a willingness to try to purge oneself of these negative traits in the quest of sobriety. Steps 8 and 9, the restitution steps, are designed to relieve the conscience and to regularize one's relations with others. Steps 10 and 11 imply that the whole program is a continuous one and that the alcoholic must stay with it. Step 12 is the missionary step, the pledge to help other alcoholics onto the road to sobriety.

Twelfth-stepping gives a sense of purpose and serves as a constant reminder to the alcoholic of "where he's been." In most communities an A.A. switchboard is maintained and advertisements run in the local paper stating that by calling that number, help is available for the alcoholic. A.A. volunteers are contacted by the switchboard following a call for help or information. A.A.'s in pairs then visit the person who called. They are urged never to go alone for such 12-step calls can prove dangerous. I know of several A.A.'s who were attacked by drunks who had called for help and then gone into temporary drunken psychosis by the time it arrived. For many, 12-step calls prove to be Dionysian experiences of the highest order. If the caller is a woman, it is believed preferable for at least one of the A.A.'s calling on her to be female. Many female drunks who call turn aggressively amorous when help arrives in the form of a male A.A. One of my male respondents described the day he thus visited a woman who had called. He was unable to find anyone to accompany him, so he went alone. "She was kind of pretty in a drunken, slovenly way," he said. "I entered her apartment and she asked, 'What the hell can you do for me?' I replied, 'I can bring you help.' At this point, she flung off her robe and charged me screaming, 'I don't want help! I want a man!'" The A.A. fled. The use of pairs is also designed to protect the alcoholic from accepting proffered sex by the one who called for help. To do so is seen as taking advantage of one who is still "sick." More importantly, if the one called on is drinking, sex can lead to a sharing of bottles as well as bodies.

The caller is urged to attend a meeting after an empathy on shared alcoholism has been established. Frequently, the A.A.'s who called take the newcomer to his first meeting. As soon as possible, the newcomer is expected to pick out an A.A. sponsor. The newcomer thereby becomes the sponsor's *baby* or *pigeon*. If the relationship does not prove effective, the pigeon is free to change sponsors or to ask several A.A.'s to serve in that capacity. The close tie between sponsor and pigeon may be brief or last for a lifetime, varying with the dependency needs of the pigeon. Generally, the most effective sponsor is one who has been on the program for only a short time, for he and the newcomer are closer to the drunken experience than the old-timer. The story is told of an alcoholic who listened with indifference as he met various old-timers and was told that this one had twenty years of sobriety, another ten and a few five or six. Then he was introduced to Jimmy who had been sober eight days. The newcomer gasped, "Eight days! How did you do it?" For the newcomer, a model is sought with a goal within his immediate reach. If identification is made with A.A. and a sponsor, the newcomer is on the program and his chances for a sober life are excellent.

The new member's success in the program is measured in terms of his days of continuous sobriety. In any project, some index of progress is reassuring. The commonest A.A. technique for noting advancement is by counting the days without alcohol. The importance put on this numerical measure of sobriety varies. In Texas, I am told, every alcoholic at a meeting introduces himself by saying, "My name is (so-and-so) and I haven't had

a drink or mind-altering drug for (so many) days (or years)."
In that state, the beginner also goes through the ritual of
receiving a *chip* to mark his first three weeks of sobriety. This
chip is usually of metal and is modelled after the poker chips
used by the group that invented the technique. On one side is
stamped A.A. and on the other 21 to represent the days of
sobriety. The recipient makes a short talk and receives tremendous applause. After the meeting, everyone present personally
congratulates him. The same rite is repeated at the third and
sixth month of sobriety. In California, on the other hand, many
groups consider it bad form to mention the length of one's
sobriety so openly. Here, more usually, a member opens his
"pitch" at a meeting by merely saying, "My name is (so-and-so)
and I'm an alcoholic." He is then greeted by a loud "Hi (so-
and-so)" from the others, a practice openly borrowed from the
Rotarians. Several California A.A.'s have disparaged to me the
Texas custom of mentioning specific days of sobriety. One likened
it to bragging and the opposite of the humility to be expected
of an A.A. "It's just typical Texan braggadocio," he said. Another
California alcoholic said, "It's sick to count days. It's like counting the days one has served in prison. It's unhealthy. It could
only lead to plans for a jail-break and I don't want any out
from A.A." However, A.A.'s in California, Texas and every
other state do count years and one's first birthday on the program
is a momentous affair. At the end of his first year of sobriety,
the A.A. receives a birthday cake with one candle at a regular
meeting. It is always the high point of the A.A.'s career in the
fellowship and a time for massive congratulations and expressions
of love. From now on, unless he slips, he is no longer a newcomer. He will receive a cake at each succeeding birthday, but
all A.A.'s agree that the thrill of that first cake is never equalled.
I watched a beautiful actress receive her first cake and with
tears in her eyes she said, "It's ridiculous. I've drunk the best
champagne in France, worn Tiffany pearls, and collected fine
art—but that lousy cake is the most beautiful thing I've ever
seen." Emotionalism is typical of "rites of passage" (448) in
any closely-knit group whether one is talking about the Arunta,
the Igorot, the Masons or A.A. The one difference between the

standard rites of A.A. and other groups is in the absence of any form of physical torment in an initiation rite (421: Chap. 13: pp. 164-172). As A.A.'s explain, they suffer the pain of initiation separately before induction into A.A. They also joke about the initiation *fee*. It is commonly said, "A.A. is the costliest club in the world to join. Each of us has had to spend 25 to 30,000 dollars on booze to qualify for admission." Such rites are not only a mechanism for gaining respect, but create an endowment the alcoholic would hate to throw away by taking a drink. They also reinforce the sense of belonging and therefore the need to conform to others' expectations. One A.A. said to me,

> When I tried to abstain in my 'drinking' days, it was painful to refuse a drink at a party. I was afraid to refuse for fear of what the others would think. Now when I'm offered a drink and feel tempted, I visualize every A.A. I know watching me. And I say 'no.' I'm now seeking the applause of a different audience.

While length of sobriety is the principal criterion for measuring success in A.A., it is not the only one. The membership distinguishes between a *good* and a *bad* sobriety. However, although an A.A. may be frequently told if he has a good sobriety, he is warned of a bad sobriety only in private by a sponsor or a good friend. A poor sobriety is accompanied by *stinking thinking*. This refers to an attitude that could be conducive to taking a drink. One A.A. described it to me: " 'Stinking thinking' leads to 'drinking thinking' which leads to drinking without thinking." On the other hand, a good sobriety is the product of "growth," a continual development of emotional maturity. It is seen as the inevitable reward of *working the program*. Growth, of course, means different things to different people. Many of the low-bottom drunks who are especially emotionally disturbed see the fact of merely staying sober as growth. This is also true of some of the more affluent silk-sheet drunks who feel no need to prove themselves in the outside world. These tend to make A.A. their entire way of life. For them it is, I believe, an eminently successful adjustment and they seem to find the fulfillment they need. One of these whom I came to know well, was indeed as nearly happy as any human can be. He described his contentment,

> I was a total and hopeless drunk for 30 years and had resigned myself to death in a gutter or a straight jacket. I wanted sobriety so badly that it was an absolute hell to find I couldn't achieve it. Then, with A.A., I did. Every night when I climb into bed, I thank God for another day's sobriety. I know I've had a completely successful day. I also know that very few people on this green earth can ever end a day knowing that it's been perfect.

Few A.A.'s in fact attain the serenity and sense of fulfillment expressed by this happy alcoholic. Many of them, however, do attain an inner sense of worth and a confidence and direction that they have never before enjoyed. This accomplishment rests in large part in a positive identification as an alcoholic. I listened to one of my respondents lecture to a service club on his recovery. Afterwards, in conversation, one of the audience said, "It must be tough to find you're an alcoholic." The A.A. replied, "I don't think you see the point. I know what my problem is and what to do about it. Do you even know your problem?" Working on this identity, the A.A. hopefully develops a realistic world-view and a defined sense of good and evil that will allow him to resolve many of the conflicts within himself. Upon the resolution of the to-drink—not-to-drink conflict by joining A.A., the alcoholic sets a pattern to resolve many of the other anxiety-arrows in his make-up. Their resolution rests upon two premises. The first is that sobriety is the keystone to any success for the alcoholic. The second is that A.A. ". . . is a selfish program." By this is meant that the individual's sobriety comes above everything else. It is also assumed that the most reliable sobriety is a *comfortable* sobriety. The good for the A.A. member includes those things which contribute to a comfortable sobriety. Evil is any threat to sober living. Further, the ultimate concept of good and evil must be a matter of individual concern.

Although A.A.'s do not consciously think in terms of good and evil, these premises determine their every action. Although the individual definitions of these opposites vary from A.A. to A.A., certain rough generalizations seem to emerge. These, at a folk level, duplicate in a very rough way the thinking of some of the early philosophers. A.A.'s usually see an integrated psyche and a meaningful relationship to society as good. Therefore, like

St. Augustine (449) they view evil as disharmony and disorder. This also conforms to the world-view of innumerable societies, including that of the Zuni Indians (348). On the other hand, like Hume (450), the good is that which creates harmony, peace and security. The A.A. also comes to realize that the disharmony is really a product of his own stinking thinking, most of which involves conflicting value constellations. He comes to view himself as Hans Strupp defines the unhappy condition of the neurotic: "Since, like Hamlet, he pursues contradictory goals, he continues to suffer" (85: p. 37). He seeks a resolution of these conflicts in the A.A. program although today increasingly many liberal high-level drunks are also seeking the aid of understanding psychotherapists. Most A.A. groups in a city environment can suggest some therapists who will work in conjunction with the program of Alcoholics Anonymous. Although the dogmatists disparage any recourse to help outside of A.A., all agree that if such help is sought, it should be only after the alcoholic has built up a respectable sobriety. As one A.A. explained,

> Alcoholics are great con artists. Any alcoholic worth his salt can run rings around any psychiatrist to the point where he is leading the shrink rather than the other way around. But the 'alky' especially cons himself. No amount of psychotherapy is going to help an alcoholic until he has been sober long enough to acquire a little self-honesty.

Some of the anxiety-arrows are ideally visualized as consisting of the opposition of absolute good to absolute evil. The commitment here is made as completely as the good Christian pledges for God and rejects Satan. As an example, I have already cited the acceptance of alcoholic abstinence over drinking. However, in vast areas of life, most alcoholics come to realize that absolutes simply do not exist, and a compromise is essential if one is to act at all. This comes with difficulty, especially for the primary alcoholic who has usually seen choices as only between such absolutes as being either Dr. Jekyll or Mr. Hyde. Some, in their drinking days, alternated from one to the other. One A.A. described his past by saying,

> I was always one of two people who hated each other. At times I played the role of Billy Good Guy. In those periods, I was the

epitome of virtue and love. I sought acceptance by gracefully
dedicating myself to pleasing everyone in sight. Then, the reaction
set in and I became Billy Bad Guy. This was usually an imaginary
game as I lacked the guts to carry it out. As the Bad Guy, I
tortured my enemies, blew up cities, and spit on every social
propriety. I flipped back and forth between these for years, and it
wasn't a very happy existence.

Billy's two lives represent one version of the common alcoholic
conflict between dependent and dominant needs. This basic
opposition was also described to me by another A.A., a woman
in her thirties,

I had an awful time trying to visualize a happy marriage.
When I felt sad and depressed, I thought a husband should be
someone who sheltered and protected me while providing for all
my needs. I wanted to be babied and freed from making decisions
for myself. At other times I saw a perfect husband as a kind of
slave who took care of those needs I told him to fulfill and who did
so by my schedule. In this role I wanted a man who by my will
would increase my freedom to do what I wanted.

She laughed a bit painfully and added, "It's little wonder that
three different husbands divorced me before I found A.A." Most
primary alcoholics have equally contradictory feelings toward
someone on whom they are dependent, usually a parent or spouse.
One A.A. described his earlier attitudes toward his father with
whom he lived as a total dependent until he joined A.A. at the
age of 44:

I wanted him dead and out of the way. I thought I'd kill him,
but lacked the nerve. I hated him for the way he ordered me
around and for the contempt he showed for me. And then I'd
remember. Once he was gone, who would support me, bail me
out of jail, and care if I got sick? My God, I used to think, I can't
live without him and with him life isn't worth a damn. I thought
he was responsible for my drinking, but I also knew that without
his support I couldn't afford to drink. When I felt manic, I fantasized
becoming a millionaire and, by clever stock manipulation, bank-
rupting him. When I felt low, I knew I didn't have the ability to
even get a ditch-digging job.

The anxiety-arrow of seeing himself as a total success or a
total failure is one absolute the alcoholic must rid himself of if

he is to grow. It is here that a compromise allowing a realistic self-image comes hard. A success with sobriety can lead the alcoholic to feel an omnipotence that can threaten his very being. It is specifically to counter this trend that A.A. puts such a heavy emphasis on humility. Without it, the alcoholic extremism may lead him into situations he cannot handle. As many A.A.'s said to me, "Prosperity is as big a threat as hardship." I watched several A.A.'s crash into drunkenness after allowing a success to lead them to reach for impossible goals. Pat's story is but one example:

> After I got that first birthday. cake, I realized I could do anything I wanted to do. The old ego came back and grabbed me and I, like a fool, ran with it. I was sure I didn't have to let others boss me around any more. I quit my job managing a prosperous restaurant of a large chain, conned a bank into a big loan and opened my own bistro. It was beautiful and on opening night we filled up. I felt so on top of it, I just had to celebrate and had some wine. The next day I had a little more. This went on for three weeks. Then, it all came back and I went on a drunk that surpassed any I'd had before. It lasted three weeks and I came to in another city. My restaurant folded and I realized what a total failure I was. I drank for my failure's sake for another six months. Then I came back to the 'tribe.' I'm doing all right now and I'm sure I've learned a little humility.

For a successful recovery, the alcoholic must develop a sense of self-worth and optimism, but his runaway perfectionism must be tempered. Without using that terminology, the growing alcoholic comes to realize that he will never live in a utopia and that evil is a constant. The recovering alcoholic learns that he can maintain his sobriety, but it is not always accompanied by serenity or joy. He is also made aware that he himself is far from perfect. The alcoholic authors of the Big Book made the point clearly that "We are not saints" (124: p. 60). Finally, realizing the shortcomings of one's fellow A.A.'s comes as a shock to the alcoholic who entered A.A. with a peak experience and floated for awhile on a pink cloud. All of these clouds eventually dissolve when, as one A.A. said, "That inevitable day arrives when you find that there are bastards in A.A., that your sponsor can't walk on water, and that sobriety hasn't given you everything you ever wanted." This, in their own parlance, is the end of the "honeymoon with A.A." It is also a critical time for the individual's continuing affiliation. A.A. has by then tried to condition the alcoholic for the inevitable disillusionment. Newcomers hear again and again the fact that the ultimate perfection of A.A. is an ideal that no one ever attains. He has heard repeatedly that he should put ". . . principles above personalities." And he, optimistically, by that point has come to realize that sobriety in A.A., although it does not equate to Nirvana, is a better life than he would have alone in a drinking world. One A.A. who had experienced the collapse of his pink cloud explained his own compromise with reality:

> I somehow came to see myself as a very capable person but as a person who is a far lesser type than the competent and sophisticated cookie I used to think I was after a couple of martinis. I'm certainly no longer the incompetent bastard who used to wake up in his own vomit the next morning. I know that I've risen above that mess only because of A.A. My tribal members in that group are a bunch of nuts and as fragile as clay pots. But they're my kind of pot and although they're full of flaws, they're a hell of a lot better than the normies. I will never be totally happy, but I know if I stick with A.A., I'll have a lot of happiness. If I leave it, I'm either dead drunk or just dead.

Once this compromise with reality has been made, it sets a pattern so that all decision-making is made on the concept that nothing is perfect but some things are better than others. Although most A.A.'s would not put it in the same terms, Lewis Meyer describes what is in essence the A.A. pattern of decision-making in his book *Off The Sauce* (451). Having assumed that nothing is perfect, says Meyer, one should compare the bad with the good in any decision. If the bad is 49 percent and the good 51 percent, take it. I have watched A.A.'s using this basic technique again and again. One, for example, was offered a new job with double the salary and twice the responsibility of his current position. He thought about it at length and then refused the new post. He explained why:

> I wanted that money awfully bad. I think I wanted the prestige too. But to be honest, I doubt if I could handle any more responsi-

bility than I've got right now. It could threaten my sobriety and without that I've got nothing. Maybe in a year or two I'll be strong enough to think about moving up if the chance comes again.

This particular alcoholic had attained a realistic evaluation of his own worth in relation to his desired goals. Although humility was needed to temper the occasional extreme over-confidence of a runaway ego, as he lowered his goals he was also learning a constructive channeling of his aggressive drive. A.A. rarely refers to this drive, but in fact a large part of the growth in A.A. rests upon its most effective utilization. Demonstrations of meaningful aggression by recovering alcoholics on the A.A. program are common. It would seem probable that the inability to act because of an anxiety-arrow weighted 50-50 at its opposite poles produces an unbearable anxiety with all of the physical correlates, including a high level of epinephrine. Before A.A., the alcoholic had practiced "displacement," that is, acted in an entirely unrelated field of behavior. The same reaction has been noted in most primate studies (452). A gorilla confronted by an enemy and unable to decide between fighting or fleeing may "displace" and eat instead. The active alcoholic drinks. When trying to maintain sobriety on his own, he may substitute irrational shopping sprees. During the early days on A.A., he learns to attend an A.A. meeting instead. As he grows on the program he learns to resolve his dilemma, make a decision and act constructively. When he acts, aggression is involved and the physical aspects of anxiety from high epinephrine are corrected by the utilization of norepinephrine and the other biological mechanisms of aggression. Emotionally, the actor feels enormous relief.

The helplessness of an anxiety-arrow weighted at 50-50 is primarily a product of conflicting internalized values. Once these are resolved by the acceptance of the prime value of A.A. (sobriety), the alcoholic is primed to attempt to act in a constructively aggressive way on the external situations reflecting his dilemma. These social situations accompanying conflicting values can take many forms. The alcoholic who is afraid to move out of his father's house is but one example. Likewise, wives fear to divorce their husbands, aspiring authors dare not write and romantically inclined individuals fear to approach the opposite sex. Once the dilemma blocking action is resolved, the actor has a goal. If in A.A. the alcoholic has also gained some self-confidence, he acts. He has gained the ability to use power.

A.A. strongly urges the alcoholic to avoid all situations which cause him tension and other discomforts. The successful ones follow this advice. Some, for example, avoid meeting close friends who rendezvous in bars. This in itself involves the use of power, the ability to resist an urge to socialize in accustomed environments. Others, with a little sobriety, begin to try to regulate a home environment. The active alcoholic has generally relinquished most of the traditional roles in the home which the spouse gradually takes over as the alcoholism progresses. With a returning sobriety, the alcoholic yearns, as one male alcoholic said, ". . . to put my own pants on again." If the nonalcoholic spouse has enjoyed the dominant position assumed as the partner went into alcoholism, a power fight results. Many of these are never resolved amicably, but rather result in divorce. As one lady A.A. told me,

> I'd lived under that bastard's domination for 32 years. I hated every minute of it, but never had the guts to leave him. When I got sober I realized I didn't have to put up with it and actually had the ability to take care of myself. I divorced him, got a job and it's been beautiful. All those years I'd carried two God-awful burdens: booze and him. And now I'm free of both.

I watched other alcoholics in A.A. change jobs, demand and get pay raises and tell unbearable friends that the relationship is over. In all these breaks with old relationships, however, the alcoholics acted with a consideration and a lack of expressed hatred that would be exceptional in earth-people.

The recovering alcoholic also begins to assert himself in all the desired avenues he'd only previously dreamed of entering or had stumbled into drunkenly and ineffectively. One of my male respondents rushed to see me joyously one morning and almost breathlessly related, "I dd it. I went out with a lovely gal last night and made love to her." He sighed and added, "I didn't think you could do that sober. It's the first time in my life I've had sex sober. The very first time!" Other alcoholics fulfill artistic drives that they had let atrophy for fear of failure or being laughed at. Several that I knew became very competent amateur artists. One, who had never painted before in her life, had a professional exhibit two years after her last drink. Another took up metal sculpture and now supports himself by his art. Many started writing either on their own or following instruction in school. Two of these sober writers claim they only write for their own pleasure, although they admit the hope to one day submit a manuscript for publication. Four of the A.A.'s I met published for the first time after attaining sobriety. The acute sensitivity in alcoholics undoubtedly creates a fine field for artistic and literary cultivation. The rate of alcoholism among writers and artists is extremely high. Upton Sinclair in his diatribe against the liquor industry, *The Cup of Fury* (453), points to the alcoholism of such authors as Jack London, Dylan Thomas, Sinclair Lewis, Stephen Crane, O. Henry, William Seabrook and many others. The question arises, Could they have been as equally creative if sober? I think so. I believe it was their sensitivity that produced both the writing and the alcoholism. I have met several eminent authors in A.A., and if anything, their writing has risen in both quality and quantity with sobriety. However, I do know one sober author who quit writing with his last drink. He sadly said, "My pen dried up when I did."

Following the American pattern, however, most recovered alcoholics seek to prove themselves in the more orthodox fields of business and labor. Some of my respondents learned new skills and entered various trades. Many entered business ventures with a new determination and a few became outstanding successes. Some who had earlier failed in business returned and now profited. One recovered alcoholic, who is well known in the lecture circuit of A.A. throughout the country, returned with a vengeance. As an active alcoholic his position in a well-established and powerful business sank lower and lower. Finally the inevitable happened and he was fired. He drank desperately for a few years and joined A.A. It took from the first meeting and he found sobriety. Then he began the task of regaining what he had lost. After proving himself in several other enterprises he was hired back by the business establishment that had fired him. Starting in a lowly position, he worked his way upward. Today he owns the corporation that fired him for drunkenness.

The economic success of most A.A.'s is far less spectacular. A recovered alcoholic is by that fact alone, however, a success, even if he never advances in wealth or fame. Although an exact estimate is admittedly impossible, probably some half-million alcoholics are today sober on the A.A. program. There is absolutely no way of knowing how many alcoholics fail to achieve sobriety with A.A. It is my very unqualified opinion that of every ten who attend an A.A. meeting for the first time, only three stay with the program. However, as the A.A.'s say, it is possible that at that first meeting ". . . the seed is planted," even if it takes a long time to sprout. I did indeed meet alcoholics who attended one meeting and returned to drinking only to affiliate finally with A.A. months or even decades later. Of those who stay with the program from the first, I would estimate that 50 percent stay sober for life, although about 60 percent of these may take up to six months before really getting on the program and have one or many slips before giving up alcohol for good. Every A.A. group has a few slippers—alcoholics who keep trying but never manage to achieve a lasting sobriety. They are treated kindly and encouraged in their efforts. Every A.A. group also has its *graduates*. These are the alcoholics who decide they never had the disease or are free of it. They leave A.A. to be social drinkers. I know quite a few of these and none have as yet disproved their alcoholism. Others also graduate in another sense. They stop attending A.A. meetings but remain sober.

Generally speaking, after about a year of sobriety, most A.A.'s cut down dramatically their dependence on meetings. However, I knew a few hard-core members who for twenty years or more had regularly attended five or more meetings a week. Many of these were dogmatists and had been very low-bottom drunks. Others were silk-sheet alcoholics who had no need to labor to exist and were thereby able to devote their lives more wholeheartedly to A.A. as a means of attaining a positive identity. Many of my respondents had attended five to ten A.A. meetings a week during their first year on the program. They averaged one or two meetings a week in the following year. Those with five years' sobriety averaged a meeting or two a month. Some return only once a year for their annual cake. There are also A.A.'s who have never attended a meeting. These are the *loners*. Mostly they are individuals living in remote areas where meetings are not available. Some maintain a regular correspondence with A.A.'s elsewhere as their main contact and a few do it solely with the aid of A.A. literature.

Alcoholics Anonymous obviously, as one member said, ". . . is not for every alcoholic." Many simply cannot relate to it and some who do are still not capable of recovery. Yet in comparison with other therapies, its success rate is nearly miraculous. It is no wonder, then, that so many studies have been made of the fellowship. It has also been subject to innumerable interpretations to explain its origin, growth and success. This is not the place to attempt to resumé these, but the literature in itself reflects the variations in A.A. and the theories of its nature. There are books by A.A.'s (124, 128, 436, 454, 455), by journalists (420), by sociologists (435) and novelists (456, 457). The list of popular and scientific articles on A.A. is almost infinite and include general descriptions (458), A.A.'s relationship to the church (459) and to Protestantism (460), in prisons (461) and in hospitals (462). There are articles defining the role of A.A. in times of national emergency (463) and in foreign settings (464). Others analyze the A.A. therapy from a sociological viewpoint (465) or compare its worth to other therapies (466). Writers have seen A.A. as a form of group therapy (467, 468), as logotherapy (469) or as "no therapy" (470). The group dynamics of A.A. have been scrutinized from many viewpoints ranging from its cooperative nature (471) to the role of charismatic leadership (472).

Most of these authors would agree that in large part, A.A.'s success can be attributed to its being a primary group that has provided an adequate substitute for alcohol. Other therapists could learn much of value from A.A. if adequate communication between A.A. and the scientists could be established. This will not be easy for as is true of any quasi-religious group, A.A. has its dogmas and its hostilities. In its early days, A.A. thought it had the sole answer to alcoholism and most of its members saw all of psychotherapy as mere superstition. This exclusiveness is today breaking down as the liberals in A.A. increase. Hard-core old-timers, the so-called "bleeding deacons," rant in outrage as Alcoholics Anonymous becomes more open-minded. Their fears may be based on reality, for if A.A. ever loses its tightly-knit folk aspect, I believe it will lose its efficacy. However, A.A. is today nearly wide open to dialogue if science will listen. In return, the dogmatists in science must be willing to consider other interpretations than their own. Especially they must be willing to re-evaluate the absolutism that alcoholism is entirely physical or entirely psychological, according to their stance. The psychotherapists especially should heed the words of Wolfgang Köhler who decades ago noted that ". . . it seems highly improbable that our young science is right in holding conservative views, when these views are constantly contradicted by actual experience. . . ." (473: p. 60). They must also come to recognize that man is a social animal with social needs. The emulation of A.A. in other problem areas should indicate that a positive identification with one's own kind facilitates recovery in a multitude of areas. As A.A. is a response to scientific inadequacy, so are its imitators: Narcotics Anonymous, Gluttons Anonymous, Gamblers Anonymous, Smokers Anonymous, Schizophrenics Anonymous and Neurotics Anonymous. Even the highly efficient Synanon is but a form of A.A. with a Marine Corps type discipline. Its founder was not a narcotic addict, but an alcoholic who had learned the therapeutic value of banding together.

My exposure to the culture of Alcoholics Anonymous left me with a quiet hope for mankind. We live in an age when we have transferred our guidance from leadership by God to a faith in scientific infallibility. But science has proved to be all too inadequate to solve the world's needs. We still have warfare, poverty, insanity and massive anxiety. As science blocked the threat of infantile paralysis, it also left us with the terror of a nuclear doomsday. I think we are slowly finding that science is not in fact a deity out there guiding us, but rather a man-made tool. And like all human products it is not perfect. However, throughout history man has come up with alternate answers and survived despite the death of gods or the failure of scientific techniques. Science has failed to cure alcoholism, and the alcoholics, despite their seeming inadequacy, came up with an answer. It is not a perfect answer, but nothing on this earth ever is. A.A. has demonstrated that man has within himself the resources to survive handicap and disaster. A major part of that resource is the ability to cooperate with others to solve a common problem. A.A., to me, is a demonstration of the words of Camus, as quoted by Colin Wilson (161: pp. 28-29), ". . . Man's greatness . . . lies in his decision to be stronger than his condition."

REFERENCES

1. Moderation for drunks. *Time*, p. 67, Sept. 18, 1972.
2. A genetic theory of alcoholism. *San Francisco Chronicle*, p. 47, Sept. 14, 1972.
3. Fox, R. (Ed.): *Alcoholism: Behavioral Research, Therapeutic Approaches.* New York, Springer, 1967.
4. Jellinek, E. M.: *The Disease Concept of Alcoholism.* New Haven, College & University Press, 1960.
5. Mann, M.: *New Primer on Alcoholism.* New York, Holt, Rinehart & Winston, 1958.
6. Doyle, A. C.: *The Valley of Fear.* New York, Berkeley Medalion Books, 1964.
7. Madsen, W.: *Christo-Paganism: A Study of Mexican Religious Syncretism.* New Orleans, Tulane University, 1957.
8. Madsen, W.: *The Virgin's Children; Life in an Aztec Village Today.* Austin, University of Texas Press, 1960.
9. Madsen, W., and Madsen, C.: The cultural structure of Mexican drinking behavior. *Q J Stud Alcohol, 30:*701-718, 1969.
10. Madsen, W.: *Mexican-Americans of South Texas.* New York, Holt, Rinehart & Winston, 1964.
11. Madsen, W.: Value conflicts and folk psychotherapy in south Texas. In Kiev, A. (Ed.): *Magic, Faith and Healing,* Glencoe, Ill., The Free Press, 1964, pp. 420-440.
12. Madsen, W.: Value conflicts in cultural transfer. In Worchel, P. and Byrne, D. (Eds.): *Personality Change,* New York, Wiley, 1964, pp. 470-488.
13. Madsen, W.: The alcoholic agringado. *American Anthropologist, 66:*355-361, 1964.
14. Madsen, W.: Report on the Serano Project. MS [mimeographed], 1963.
15. Steiner, C.: *Games Alcoholics Play; The Analysis of Life Scripts.* New York, Grove Press, 1971.
16. Maxwell, M. A.: Alcoholics Anonymous, an interpretation. In Pittman, D. J. (Ed.): *Alcoholism.* New York, Harper & Row, 1967, pp. 211-222.
17. Eysenck, H. J.: *The Biological Basis of Personality.* Springfield, Ill., Thomas, 1970.
18. Kroeber, A. L.: *Anthropology.* New York, Harcourt, Brace, 1923.

19. Kroeber, A. L.: *Anthropology*, Rev. Ed. New York, Harcourt, Brace, 1948.
20. Goldschmidt, W.: *Comparative Functionalism*. Berkeley, University of California Press, 1966.
21. White, L. A.: *The Science of Culture*. New York, Farrar, Strauss, 1949.
22. White, L. A.: *The Evolution of Culture*. New York, McGraw-Hill, 1959.
23. Freedman, D. G.: A biological view of man's social behavior. In Etkin, W. (Ed.): *Social Behavior from Fish to Man*. Chicago, University of Chicago Press, 1967. pp. 152-188.
24. Dixon, W. M.: *The Human Situation*. London, Edward Arnold, 1937.
25. Delgado, J. M. R.: *Physical Control of the Mind*. New York, Harper Colophon Books, 1969.
26. Chapple, E. D.: *Culture and Biological Man; Explorations in Behavioral Anthropology*. New York, Holt, Rinehart & Winston, 1970.
27. Eibl-Eibesfeldt, I.: *Love and Hate: The Natural History of Behavior Patterns*. New York, Holt, Rinehart & Winston, 1972.
28. Mazur, A., and Robertson, L. S.: *Biology and Social Behavior*. New York, The Free Press, 1972.
29. Hsu, F. L. K.: *Psychological Anthropology*. Homewood, Illinois, The Dorsey Press, 1961.
30. Martin, M.: The scientist as shaman. *Harper's*, pp. 54-61, March, 1972.
31. Chomsky, N.: The case against B. F. Skinner. *The New York Review of Books*, pp. 18-24, Dec. 30, 1971.
32. Myers, R. D., and Veale, W. L.: The determinants of alcohol preference in animals. In Bissin, B., and Begleiter, H. (Eds.): *The Biology of Alcoholism*. New York, Plenum, 1971, Vol. II, pp. 131-168.
33. Watson, J. B.: *Behaviorism*. New York, Norton, 1925.
34. Skinner, B. F.: *Walden II*. New York, Macmillan, 1948.
35. Skinner, B. F.: *Beyond Freedom and Dignity*. New York, Knopf, 1971.
36. Lorenz, K.: *On Aggression*. New York, Harcourt, Brace & World, 1966.
37. Lorenz, K.: *Studies in Animal and Human Behavior*. Cambridge, Harvard University Press, 1970-1971.
38. Watson, G.: *Nutrition and Your Mind: The Psychochemical Response*. New York, Harper & Row, 1972.
39. Daniels, J., and Houghton, V.: Jensen, Eysenck and the eclipse of the Galton Paradigm. In Richardson, K., and Spears, D. (Eds.): *Race and Intelligence; The Fallacies Behind the Race I.Q. Controversy*. Baltimore, Penguin, 1972, pp. 68-83.

40. Opler, M. K.: Anthropological aspects of psychiatry. In Masserman, J., and Moreno, J. L. (Eds.): *Progress in Psychotherapy*. New York, Grune and Stratton, 1959, Vol. IV, pp. 125-130.
41. Chein, I.: *The Science of Behavior and the Image of Man*. New York, Basic Books, 1972.
42. Asimov, I.: *Guide to the Biological Sciences*. New York, Cardinal, 1964.
43. Heim, A.: Intelligence and personality, their relationship and appraisal. *Impact of Science on Society, 21*:347-355, 1971.
44. Berelson, B., and Steiner, G. A.: *Human Behavior; An Inventory of Scientific Findings*. New York, Harcourt, Brace & World, 1964.
45. Eysenck, H. J.: The effects of psychotherapy; an evaluation. *J Consult Psychol, 16*:319-324, 1952.
46. *Behavior Today, 3* (No. 2):2, 1972.
47. Wechsler, J. A.: *In a Darkness*. New York, Norton, 1972.
48. *Human Behavior, 13* (No. 3):69, 1972.
49. Pitts, F. N., Jr.: The biochemistry of anxiety. *Sci Am, 220* (No. 2): 69-75, 1969.
50. Sarbin, T. R.: Schizophrenia is a myth, born of metaphor, meaningless. *Psychology Today, 6* (No. 1):16-27, 1972.
51. Schizo correlate claim raises hope, skepticism. *Behavior Today, 3* (No. 20):2, 1972.
52. Goldfarb, A. J., and Berman, S.: Alcoholism as a psychosomatic disorder. *Q J Stud Alcohol, 10*:415-429, 1949.
53. Hoffer, A., and Osmond, H.: *How to Live with Schizophrenia*. New York, University Books, 1971.
54. Cheraskin, E., Ringsdorf, W. M., Jr., and Clark, J. W.: *Diet and Disease*. Emmaus, Penn., Rodale Books, 1971.
55. Clausen, J. A.: Mental disorders. In Merton, R. K., and Nisbet, R. A. (Eds.): *Contemporary Social Problems*. New York, Harcourt, Brace & World, 1961, pp. 127-180.
56. *Intellectual Digest, 1* (No. 11): 55, 1972.
57. Klinefelter's syndrome and schizophrenia. *Science News, 101* (No. 24): 376, 1972.
58. Mandell, A. J., Segal, D. S., Kuczenski, R. T., and Knapp, S.: The search for the schizococcus. *Psychology Today, 6* (No. 5): 68-72, 1972.
59. Man in a stress society; an interview with Joseph J. Schwab. *Center Report, 5* (No. 3):15-17, 1972.
60. McCabe, C.: The fearless spectator. *San Francisco Chronicle*, p. 57, Oct. 4, 1972.
61. Saghir, M. T., and Robbins, E.: Male and female homosexuality: natural history. *Comprehensive Psychiatry, 12* (No. 6):503-510, 1971. [Reviewed in *Human Behavior, 1* (No. 3):45, 1972.]

62. Bergler, E.: Contributions to the psychogenesis of alcohol addiction. *Q J Stud Alcohol,* 5:434-449, 1944.
63. Eisinger, A. J., Huntsman, R. G., Lord, J., Merry, J., Polani, P., Tanner, J. M., Whitehouse, R. H., and Griffiths, P. D.: Female homosexuality. *Nature,* 238:106, 1972.
64. *San Francisco Chronicle,* p. 3, Oct. 2, 1972.
65. Cure. *Behavior Today,* 2 (No. 47): 4, 1971.
66. Sex-behavior switchover. *Behavior Today,* 3 (No. 6): 2, 1972.
67. Schopler, E.: Parents of psychotic children as scapegoats. *J Contemporary Psychotherapy,* 4 (No. 1): 17-22, 1971. [Reviewed in *Human Behavior, 1* (No. 3):29, 1972.]
68. Von Wartburg, J. P.: Alcohol dehydrogenase distribution in tissues of different species. In Popham, R. E. (Ed.): *Alcohol and Alcoholism.* Toronto, University of Toronto Press, 1970, pp. 13-21.
69. Thomas, J. M.: Alcoholism and mental disorder. *Q J Stud Alcohol,* 3:65-78, 1942.
70. Landis, C., and Bolles, M. M.: *Textbook of Abnormal Psychology.* New York, Macmillan, 1950.
71. Alexander, F.: Alcohol and behavior disorder; alcoholism. In Lucia, S. P. (Ed.): *Alcohol and Civilization.* New York, McGraw-Hill, 1963, pp. 130-141.
72. Moore, A.: The conception of alcoholism as a mental illness: implications for treatment and research. *Q J Stud Alcohol,* 29:172-175, 1960.
73. Berreman, J. V.: The escape motive in alcoholic addiction. *Res Stud St Coll Wash,* 18:139-143, 1950. (Abstract) *Q J Stud Alcohol,* 12:624, 1951.
74. Catanzaro, D. J.: Psychiatric aspects of alcoholism. In Pittman, D. J. (Ed.): *Alcoholism.* New York, Harper & Row, 1967, pp. 31-45.
75. Fox, R.: Conclusions and outlook. In Fox, R. (Ed.): *Alcoholism: Behavioral Research, Therapeutic Approaches.* New York, Springer, 1967, pp. 328-334.
76. Carroll, J. B. (Ed.): *Language, Thought and Reality: Selected Writings of Benjamin Lee Whorf.* Boston, Technological Press of the Massachusetts Institute of Technology, 1956.
77. Hoijer, H.: The Sapir-Whorf hypothesis. In Hoijer, H. (Ed.): *Language in Culture.* Proc. of a Conference on the Interrelations of Language and other Aspects of Culture. American Anthropological Association, 56 (No. 6). Part 2, Memoir 79, 102-104, 1954.
78. Romney, A. K., and D'Andrade, R. G. (Eds.): Transcultural studies in cognition. *American Anthropologist, 66* (No. 3), Part 2, 1964 (Special Publication).
79. Tyler, S. A. (Ed.): *Cognitive Anthropology.* New York, Holt, Rinehart & Winston, 1969.

80. Christopher D. Smithers Foundation, Inc.: *Understanding Alcoholism.* New York, Scribner, 1968.
81. Tringo, J. L.: The hierarchy of preference toward disability groups. *Journal of Special Education, 4* (No. 3): 295-306, 1970.
82. Linsky, A. S.: The changing public views of alcoholism. *Q J Stud Alcohol, 31:*692-704, 1970.
83. Glock, C. Y.: Images of man and public opinion. *Public Opinion Q, 28:*539-546, 1964.
84. Björk, S.: Psykologiska synpunkter pa alkoholismen (Alcoholism from a psychological viewpoint.) *Svenska Läkartidn, 47:*1018-1026, 1950. (Abstract) *Q J Stud Alcohol, 12:*526, 1951.
85. Strupp, H. H.: Freudian analysis today. *Psychology Today, 6* (No. 2):33-40, 1972.
86. Verden, P., and Shatterly, D.: Alcoholism research and resistance to understanding the compulsive drinker. *Ment Hyg, 55* (No. 3): 331-336, 1971.
87. World Health Organization. Expert Committee on Mental Health, Alcoholism subcommittee. Second report. World Health Organization, Technical Report Series No. 48, 1952.
88. Keller, M.: Definition of alcoholism. *Q J Stud Alcohol, 21:*125-134, 1960.
89. Osborn, L. A.: New attitudes toward alcoholism. *Q J Stud Alcohol, 12:*58-60, 1971.
90. Tiebout, H. M.: The role of psychiatry in the field of alcoholism. *Q J Stud Alcohol, 12:*52-57, 1951.
91. Bjurulf, P., Sternby, N. H., and Wistedt, B.: Definitions of alcoholism: relevance of liver disease and temperance board registration in Sweden. *Q J Stud Alcohol, 32:*393-405, 1971.
92. Mayer, J., and Myerson, D. J.: Outpatient treatment of alcoholics: effects of status, stability and nature of treatment. *Q J Stud Alcohol, 32:*620-627, 1971.
93. Popham, R. E., and Schmidt, W.: *A Decade of Alcoholism Research: A Review of the Research Activities of the Alcoholism and Drug Addiction Research Foundation of Ontario, 1951-1961.* (Brookside Monograph No. 3.) Toronto, University of Toronto Press, 1962.
94. Pokorny, A. D., Miller, B. A., Kanas, T. E., and Valles, J.: Dimensions of alcoholism. *Q J Stud Alcohol, 32:*699-705, 1971.
95. Miller, B. A., Pokorny, A. D., Valles, J., and Cleveland, S. E.: Biased sampling in alcoholism treatment research. *Q J Stud Alcohol, 31:*97-107, 1970.
96. Srole, L., Langer, T. S., Michael, S. T., Opler, M. K., and Rennie, T. A. C.: *Mental Health in the Metropolis: The Midtown Manhattan Study.* (Thomas A. C. Rennie Series in Social Psychiatry, Vol. I.) New York, McGraw-Hill, 1962.

97. Curlee, J.: Sex differences in patient attitudes toward alcoholism treatment. *Q J Stud Alcohol, 32*:643-650, 1971.
98. Gottesfeld, B. H., and Yager, H. L.: Psychotherapy of the problem drinker. *Q J Stud Alcohol, 11*:222-229, 1950.
99. Horn, J. L., and Wanberg, K. W.: Dimensions of perception of background and current situation of alcoholic patients. *Q J Stud Alcohol, 31*:633-658, 1970.
100. Goffman, E.: *Asylums.* New York, Anchor, 1961.
101. Chafetz, M. E.: The alcoholic symptom and its therapeutic relevance. *Q J Stud Alcohol, 31*:444-445, 1970.
102. Kaplan, R., Blume, S., Rosenberg, S., Pitrelli, J., and Turner, W. J.: Phenytoin, metronidazole, and multivitamins in the treatment of alcoholism. *Q J Stud Alcohol, 33*:97-104, 1972.
103. Pattison, E. M., Headley, E. B., Gleser, C. C., and Gottschalk, L. A.: Abstinence and normal drinking: an assessment of changes in drinking patterns in alcoholics after treatment. *Q J Stud Alcohol, 29*:610-633, 1968.
104. Ward, R. F., and Faillace, L. A.: The alcoholic and his helpers: a systems view. *Q J Stud Alcohol, 31*:684-691, 1970.
105. Todd, J. E.: *Drunkenness a Vice, Not a Disease.* Hartford, Case, Lockwood & Brainard, 1882. [Quoted in Jellinek, E. M.: *The Disease Concept of Alcoholism.* New Haven, College & University Press, 1960, pp. 207-210.]
106. Paley, A.: Hypnotherapy in the treatment of alcoholism. In Podolsky, E. (Ed.): *Management of Addictions.* New York, Philosophical Library, 1955, pp. 279-288.
107. Edwards, G.: Hypnosis in treatment of alcohol addiction: controlled trial, with analysis of factors affecting outcome. *Q J Stud Alcohol, 27*:221-241, 1966.
108. Abramson, H. A. (Ed.): *The Use of LSD in Psychotherapy and Alcoholism.* New York, Bobbs-Merrill, 1967.
109. Lolli, G.: *Social Drinking: The Effects of Alcohol.* New York, Collier Books, 1961.
110. Lawlis, G. F., and Rubin, S. E.: 16-PF study of personality patterns in alcoholics. *Q J Stud Alcohol, 32*:318-327, 1971.
111. Tiebout, H. M.: Psychology and treatment of alcoholism. *Q J Stud Alcohol, 7*:214-227, 1946.
112. Wexberg, L. E.: Psychodynamics of patients with chronic alcoholism. *J Clin Psychopath, 10*:147-157, 1949.
113. Lisansky, E. S.: Clinical research in alcoholism and the use of psychological tests: a reevaluation. In Fox, R. (Ed.): *Alcoholism: Behavioral Research, Therapeutic Approaches.* New York, Springer, 1967, pp. 3-15.
114. Trice, H. M.: *Alcoholism in America.* New York, McGraw-Hill, 1966.

115. McCord, W., and McCord, J.: A longitudinal study of the personality of alcoholics. In Pittman, D. J., and Snyder, C. R. (Eds.): *Society, Culture and Drinking Patterns.* New York, Wiley, 1962, pp. 413-430.

116. Sutherland, E. H., Schroeder, H. G., and Tordella, C. L.: Personality traits and the alcoholic: a critique of existing studies. *Q J Stud Alcohol, 11*:547-561, 1950.

117. Jellinek, E. M.: Phases of alcohol addiction. *Q J Stud Alcohol, 13*:673-684, 1952.

118. McCabe, C.: The fearless spectator. *San Francisco Chronicle,* p. 51, Aug. 25, 1972.

119. Schulman, A. J.: Alcohol addiction. *Univ Toronto Med J,* 28:219-229, 1951. (Abst.) *Q J Stud Alcohol, 12*:625-626, 1951.

120. Menninger, K. A.: *Man Against Himself.* New York, Harcourt, Brace & World, 1938.

121. Schopler, E.: Parents of psychotic children as scapegoats. *J Contemp Psychother, 4* (No. 1):1722, 1971.

122. Szasz, T. S.: *The Myth of Mental Illness.* Scranton, Harper & Row, 1961.

123. Szasz, T. S.: *Psychiatric Justice.* New York, Macmillan, 1965.

124. *Alcoholics Anonymous* (Rev. Ed.). New York, Alcoholics Anonymous World Services, 1955.

125. Ludwig, A. W.: On and off the wagon: reasons for drinking and abstaining in alcoholics. *Q J Stud Alcohol, 33*:91-96, 1972.

126. Bacon, S. D.: Alcoholics do not drink. In Sellin, T., and Lambert, R. D. (Eds.): *Understanding Alcoholism. Annals of the American Academy of Political and Social Science,* Vol. 315, 1958, pp. 55-64.

127. Coudert, J.: *The Alcoholic in Your Life.* New York, Stein & Day, 1972.

128. Roth, L.: *I'll Cry Tomorrow.* New York, Frederick Fell, 1954.

129. Keatringe, W. R., and Evans, M.: Effect of food, alcohol and hyoscine on body temperature and reflex responses of man immersed in cold water. *Lancet 2*:176-178, 1960.

130. Kalant, H.: Some recent physiological and biochemical investigations on alcohol and alcoholism: a review. *Q J Stud Alcohol, 23*:52-93, 1962.

131. Cicero, T. J., and Black, W. C.: Increase in volitional ethanol consumption following interference with a learned avoidance response. *Physiol Behav, 3*:657-660, 1968.

132. Myers, R. D., and Holman, R. B.: Failure of stress of electric shock to increase ethanol intake in rats. *Q J Stud Alcohol, 28*:132-137, 1967.

133. Myers, R. D., and Cicero, T. J.: Effects of serotonin depletion on the volitional alcohol intake of rats during a condition of

psychological stress. *Psychopharmacologia, Berlin,* 15:373-381, 1969.

134. Masserman, J. H., and Yum, K. S.: An analysis of the influence of alcohol on experimental neurosis in cats. *Psychosom Med,* 8:36-52, 1946.

135. Masserman, J. H.: *Principles of Dynamic Psychiatry,* 2nd ed. Philadelpha, Saunders, 1961.

136. Anisman, H.: Fear reduction and active avoidance learning after alcohol administration during prior CS-shock exposure. *Q J Stud Alcohol,* 33:783-793, 1972.

137. Gillespie, R., and Lucas, C.: An unexpected factor affecting the alcohol intake of rats. *Can J Biochem,* 36:37, 1958.

138. Myers, R. D.: Voluntary alcohol consumption in animals: peripheral and intracerebral factors. *Psychosom Med,* 28:484-497, 1966.

139. Cappell, H., and Herman, C. P.: Alcohol and tension reduction: a review. *Q J Stud Alcohol,* 33:33-64, 1972.

140. Huxley, J.: Forward. In Lorenz, K. (Ed.): *King Solomon's Ring: New Lights on Animal Ways.* New York, Crowell, 1961, pp. vii-xi.

141. Gottheil, E., Corbett, L. O., Grasberger, J. C., and Cornelison, F. S., Jr.: Fixed interval drinking decisions. I. A research and treatment model. *Q J Stud Alcohol,* 33:311-324, 1972.

142. Vannicelli, M. L.: Mood and self-perception of alcoholics when sober and intoxicated. I. Mood change. II. Accuracy of self-prediction. *Q J Stud Alcohol,* 33:341-357, 1972.

143. Vanderpool, J. A.: Alcoholism and self-concept. *Q J Stud Alcohol,* 30:59-77, 1969.

144. Gottheil, E., Murphy, B. F., Skoloda, T. E., and Corbett, L. O.: Fixed interval drinking decisions. II. Drinking and discomfort in 25 alcoholics. *Q J Stud Alcohol,* 33:325-340, 1972.

145. Lolli, G.: Alcoholism as a disorder of the love disposition. *Q J Stud Alcohol,* 17:96-107, 1956.

146. Radó, S.: Narcotic bondage. *Am J Psychiatry,* 114:165-170, 1957.

147. Fenichel, O.: *The Psychoanalytic Theory of Neurosis.* New York, Norton, 1945.

148. Button, A. D.: The genesis and development of alcoholism: an empirically based schema. *Q J Stud Alcohol,* 17:671-675, 1956.

149. Wortis, H., Sillman, L. R., and Halpern, F.: *Studies of Compulsive Drinkers.* New Haven, Hillhouse Press, 1946.

150. Cloete, S.: *The Curve and the Tusk.* New York, Pyramid Books, 1961.

151. Prout, C. T., Strongin, E. I., and White, M. A.: A study of results in hospital treatment of alcoholism in males. *Am J Psychiatry,* 107:14-19, 1950.

152. Botwinick, J.: A psychometric examination of latent homosexuality in alcoholism. *Q J Stud Alcohol,* 12:268-272, 1951.

153. McCord, W., and McCord, J.: *Origins of Alcoholism*. Stanford, Calif., Stanford University Press, 1960.
154. Alcohol, drugs and sex. (Roundtable.) Moderator, John M. Ewing; panel, Ruth Fox, G. Morris Carstairs, Michael H. Beaubrun. *Medical Aspects of Human Sexuality, 4* (No. 2):18-34, 1970.
155. Blum, E. M.: Psychoanalytic views of alcoholism: a review. *Q J Stud Alcohol, 27*:259-299, 1966.
156. Tremper, M.: Dependency in alcoholics: a sociological view. *Q J Stud Alcohol, 33*:186-190, 1972.
157. Evans-Pritchard, E. E.: *Theories on Primitive Religion*. Oxford, Eng., Clarendon Press, 1965.
158. Emerson, R. W.: Self reliance. In Atkinson, B. (Ed.): *The Selected Writings of Ralph Waldo Emerson*. New York, Modern Library, 1950, pp. 145-169.
159. McCabe, C.: The fearless spectator. *San Francisco Chronicle*, p. 39, Sept. 18, 1972.
160. Freud, S.: Letter No. 79 (1897). In Bonaparte, M., Freud, A., and Kris, E. (Eds.): *The Origins of Psychoanalysis: Letters to W. Fliess*. New York, Basic Books, 1954.
161. Wilson, C.: *New Pathways in Psychology: Maslow and the Post-Freudian Revolution*. New York, Taplinger, 1972.
162. Maugham, W. S.: The vessel of wrath. In W. S. Maugham: *Ah King*. Garden City, N.Y., Doubleday Doran, 1935, pp. 94-146.
163. Ryback, R. S.: The continuum and specificity of the effects of alcohol on memory: a review. *Q J Stud Alcohol, 32*:995-1016, 1971.
164. Cutter, F., Cantor, J., and Potter, M. M.: Suicidal intent, alcoholism and syndrome-related concepts. *Q J Stud Alcohol, 31*:861-867, 1970.
165. Lowen, A.: *The Language of the Body*. New York, Collier Books, 1971.
166. Adler, A.: *The Pattern of Life*. New York, Cosmopolitan Book Co., 1931.
167. McClelland, D. C., Davis, W. N., Kalin, R., and Wanner, E.: *The Drinking Man*. New York, The Free Press. 1972.
168. Wodehouse, P. G.: *Jeeves and the Feudal Spirit*. London, Herbert Jenkins, 1962.
169. A power theory for why people drink. *Science News, 101* (No. 24): 375, 1972.
170. Claeson, L. E., and Carlsson, C.: Cerebral dysfunction in alcoholics: a psychometric investigation. *Q J Stud Alcohol, 31*:317-323, 1970.
171. Olson, R. E., Gursey, D., and Vester, J. W.: Evidence for a defect in tryptophan metabolism in chronic alcoholism. *New Eng J Med, 263*:1169-1174, 1960.

172. Hawkins, N. G.: *Medical Sociology: Theory, Scope and Method.* Springfield, Ill., Thomas, 1958.

173. Charcot, J. M.: *Leçons sur les Maladies des Vieillards et les Maladies Chroniques.* Paris, A. Delahaye, 1867.

174. Cruz-Coke, R.: Genetic aspects of alcoholism. In Israel, Y., and Mardones, J.: *Biological Basis of Alcoholism.* New York, Wiley-Interscience, 1971, pp. 335-363.

175. Legrain, M.: *Hérédité et Alcoolisme.* Paris, 1889.

176. Keller, M.: The 1st American medical work on the effects of alcohol: Benjamin Rush's "An inquiry into the effects of ardent spirits upon the human body and mind." *Q J Stud Alcohol,* 4:321-341, 1943.

177. Partanen, J., Bruun, K., and Markkanen, T.: *Inheritance of Drinking Behavior: A Study of Intelligence, Personality and the Use of Alcohol in Adult Twins.* Helsinki, The Finnish Foundation for Alcohol Studies, 1966.

178. Wexberg, L. E.: A critique of physiopathological theories of the etiology of alcoholism. *Q J Stud Alcohol,* 11:113-118, 1950.

179. Roe, A., and Burks, B.: Adult adjustment of foster children of alcoholic and psychotic parentage and the influence of the foster home. Memoirs of the Section on Alcohol Studies, Yale University, No. 3. *Q J Stud Alcohol,* New Haven, 1945.

180. Mardones, J., Segovia-Riquelme, N., Hederra, A., and Alcaino, F.: Effect of some self-selection conditions on the voluntary alcohol intake of rats. *Q J Stud Alcohol,* 16:425-437, 1955.

181. Eriksson, K.: Genetic selection for voluntary alcohol consumption in the albino rat. *Science,* 159:739-741, 1968.

182. Segovia-Riquelme, N., Hederra, A., Anex, M., Barnier, O., Figuerola-Camps, I., Campos-Hoppe, I., Jara, N., and Mardones, J.: Nutritional and genetic factors in the appetite for alcohol. In Popham, R. E. (Ed.): *Alcohol and Alcoholism.* Toronto, University of Toronto Press, 1970, pp. 86-96.

183. Smith, J. W., and Brinton, G. A.: Color-vision defects in alcoholism. *Q J Stud Alcohol,* 32:41-44, 1971.

184. Schuckit, M. A., Goodwin, D. A., and Winokur, G.: A study of alcoholism in half siblings. *Am J Psychiatry,* 128:1132-1136, 1972.

185. *Behavior Today, 1* (No. 20): 21, 1970.

186. de Torok, D.: Chromosomal irregularities in alcoholics. *Ann NY Acad Sci, 197*:90-100, 1972.

187. Nature-nurture debate. *Behavior Today, 36* (No. 10): 2, 1972.

188. Sheldon, W. H., Stevens, S. S., and Tucker, W. B.: *The Varieties of Human Physique.* New York, Harper, 1940.

189. Sheldon, W. H., and Stevens, S. S.: *The Varieties of Temperament.* New York, Harper, 1942.

190. Sheldon, W. H., Hartl, E. M., and McDermott, E.: *The Varieties of Delinquent Youth.* New York, Harper, 1949.
191. Lecomte, M.: Eléments d'hérédopathologie (Elements of heredopathology.) *Scalpel, Brux., 103*:1133-1145, 1950. (Abst.) *Q J Stud Alcohol, 12*:528, 1951.
192. Ryback, R. S.: State-dependent or 'dissociated' learning with alcohol in goldfish. *Q J Stud Alcohol, 30*:598-608, 1969.
193. Ryback, R. S.: Alcohol amnesia: observations in seven drinking inpatient alcoholics. *Q J Stud Alcohol, 31*:616-632, 1970.
194. Silkworth, W. D.: Alcoholism as a manifestation of allergy. *Med Rec, 145*:249-251, 1937.
195. Robinson, M. W.: The immunological properties of alcohol. A survey of the literature. *Ann Allergy, 8*:468-487, 1950. (Abst.) *Q J Stud Alcohol, 12*:132, 1951.
196. Karolus, H. E.: Alcoholism and food allergy. *Ill Med J, 119* (No. 3): 151-152, 1952.
197. Block, M. A.: *Alcohol and Alcoholism: Drinking and Dependence.* Belmont, California., Wadsworth, 1970.
198. Randolf, T. G.: The descriptive features of food addiction; addictive eating and drinking. *Q J Stud Alcohol, 17*:198-224, 1956.
199. Williams, R. J.: The etiology of alcoholism: a working hypothesis involving the interplay of heredity and environmental factors. *Q J Stud Alcohol, 7*:567-587, 1947.
200. Williams, R. J.: *Nutrition and Alcoholism.* Norman, University of Oklahoma Press, 1951.
201. Williams, R. J.: The genetotrophic concept—nutritional deficiencies and alcoholism. *Ann NY Acad Sci, 57*:794-811, 1954.
202. Williams, R. J.: *Alcoholism: The Nutritional Approach.* Austin, University of Texas Press, 1959.
203. Williams, R. J.: *Nutrition Against Disease: Environmental Prevention.* New York, Pitman, 1971.
204. Smith, J. A., Dardin, P. A., and Brown, W. T.: The treatment of alcoholism by nutritional supplement. *Q J Stud Alcohol, 12*:381-385, 1951.
205. O'Malley, E., Heggie, V., Trulson, M., Fleming, R., and Stare, E. J.: Nutrition and alcoholism. *Fed Proc, 10* (Pt. 1):390, 1951. (Abstract) *Q J Stud Alcohol, 12*:528, 1951.
206. Cheraskin, E., and Ringsdorf, W. M.: *New Hope for Incurable Diseases.* New York, Exposition Press, 1971.
207. Dahl, S.: Morbus alcoholicus. *Dtsch Med J, 19*:73-76, 1968. (Abstract) *Q J Stud Alcohol, 31*:508, 1970.
208. O'Brien, C. C.: Calcium therapy in the treatment of alcoholism. In Podolsky, E. (Ed.): *Management of Addictions.* New York, Philosophical Library, 1955, pp. 187-193.

209. O'Brien, C. C.: Hospital and ambulatory cases of alcoholism: intensive calcium therapy. In Podolsky, E. (Ed.): *Management of Addictions.* New York, Philosophical Library, 1955, pp. 194-198.
210. Voegtlin, W. L., O'Hollaren, P., and O'Hollaren, N.: The glucose tolerance of alcohol addicts: a study of 303 cases. *Q J Stud Alcohol,* 4:163-182, 1943.
211. Tennent, D. M.: The influence of alcohol on the emptying time of the stomach and the absorption of glucose. *Q J Stud Alcohol,* 2:271-276, 1941.
212. Pansini, R., and Casaula, A.: Sui rapporti tra alcolemia e metabolismo glicidico. La glicemia dopo carico di alcool per via orale. (The relationship between blood alcohol and glycide metabolism. Blood sugar after administration of alcohol by mouth.) *Boll Soc Ital Biol Sper,* 27:910-913, 1951. (Abstract) *Q J Stud Alcohol,* 13:517, 1952.
213. Lovell, W. L., and Tintera, J. W.: Hypoadrenocorticism in alcoholism and drug addiction. *Geriatrics, 6* (No. 1):1-11, 1951.
214. Nitzuleczu, D., Zosin, C., and Ionescu, M.: Variations de la glicémie chez les pneumoniques sous l'action des injections intraveineuses d'alcool (Blood sugar variations in pneumonia due to intravenous injections of alcohol.) *Rev. méd-chir., Paris,* 59:68-71, 1948. (Abst.) *Q J Stud Alcohol, 13*:131, 1952.
215. Isolation and brain glucose. *Behavior Today, 23* (No. 27):2, 1972.
216. Zarrow, M. X., Aduss, H., and Denison, M. E.: Failure of the endocrine system to influence alcohol choice in rats. *Q J Stud Alcohol, 21*:400-413, 1960.
217. Rodgers, D. A., and McClearn, G.: Sucrose versus ethanol appetite in inbred strains of mice. *Q J Stud Alcohol,* 25:26-35, 1964.
218. Abramson, E. M., and Pezet, A. W.: *Body, Mind and Sugar.* New York, Holt, Rinehart & Winston, 1951.
219. A metabolic clue to Indian endurance and intolerance for alcohol. *Psychology Today, 6* (No. 2): 16, 1972.
220. Kretchmer, N.: Lactose and lactase. *Sci Am,* 227 (No. 4):71-78, 1972.
221. Of man and milk. *Time,* p. 59, July 13, 1970.
222. The fat bottle babies. *San Francisco Chronicle,* p. 2, Sept. 9, 1972.
223. Voltz, J.: Fat warning given on the bottle. *Los Angeles Times,* Part IV, p. 1, Sept. 8, 1972.
224. McLaughlin, M.: *The Neurotic's Notebook.* New York, Signet Books, 1970.
225. Stuhlfauth, F., and Neumaier, H.: Die Wirkung der Laevulose auf Alkohol-intoxikationen (The effect of levulose on alcohol intoxication.) *Med Klinik,* 46:591-593, 1951. (Abst.) *Q J Stud Alcohol, 12*:621-622, 1951.
226. Smith, J. J.: The endocrine basis for hormonal therapy of alcoholism. *NY St J Med,* 50:1704-1706, 1711-1715, 1950.

227. Tintera, J. W.: *Hypoadrenocorticism.* New York, The Hypoglycemia Foundation, Inc., n.d.

228. Goldberg, M.: The occurrence and treatment of hypothyroidism among alcoholics. *J Clin Endocrinol, 20*:609-621, 1960.

229. Smith, J. J.: The blood eosinophol responses of the alcoholic to epinephrine and to ACTH, with a note on the treatment of chronic alcoholism with ACTH. *Proc 2nd Clin ACTH Conf, 2*:161-171, 1951.

230. Segal, B. M., Kushnarev, V. M., Urakov, I. G., and Misionzhnik, E. U.: Alcoholism and disruption of the activity of deep cerebral structures: clinical-laboratory research. *Q J Stud Alcohol, 31*:587-601, 1970.

231. Valles, J.: *From Social Drinking to Alcoholism.* Dallas, Tane Press, 1969.

232. Myers, R. D.: Alcohol consumption in rats: effects of intracranial injections of ethanol. *Science, 142*:240-241, 1963.

233. Myers, R. D.: Modification of drinking patterns by chronic intracranial chemical infusion. In *Thirst.* Proc. 1st International Symposium on Thirst in the Regulation of Body Water, pp. 533-549, 1963.

234. Myers. R. D., and Veale, W. L.: Alterations in volitional alcohol intake produced in rats by chronic intraventricular infusions of acetaldehyde, paraldehyde or methanol. *Arch Int Pharmacodyn, Brussels, 180* (No. 1):100-113, 1969.

235. Redmond, G. P., and Cohen, G.: Sex difference in acetaldehyde exhalation following ethanol administration in C57BL mice. *Nature,* 236 (No. 5342):117-119, 1972.

236. Myers, R. D., Veale, W. L., and Yaksh, T. L.: Preference for ethanol in the rhesus monkey following chronic infusion of ethanol in the cerebral ventricles. *Physiology and Behavior, Gt Brit, 8*:431-435, 1972.

237. Myers, R. D., and Veale, W. L.: Alcohol preference in the rat: reduction following depletion of brain serotonin. *Science, 160*:1469-1471, 1968.

238. Veale, W. L., and Myers, R. D.: Decrease in ethanol intake in rats following administration of p-chlorophenylalanine. *Neuropharmacology, 9* (No. 4):317-326, 1970.

239. Myers, R. D., and Tytell, M.: Volitional consumption of flavored ethanol solution by rats: the effects of p-CPA and the absence of tolerance. *Physiology and Behavior, Gt Brit, 8*:403-408, 1972.

240. Blum, K., Wallace, J. E., and Gellar, I.: Synergy of ethanol and putative neurotransmitters: glycine and serine. *Science, 176*:292-294, 1972.

241. Davis, V. E., and Walsh, M. J.: Effect of ethanol on neuroamine metabolism. In Israel, Y., and Mardones, J. (Eds.): *Biological*

212

The American Alcoholic

Basis of Alcoholism. New York, Wiley-Interscience, 1971, pp. 73-102.

242. Schildkraut, J. J., and Kety, S. S.: Biogenic amines and emotions. Science, 156:21-30, 1967.

243. Bryson, G.: Biogenic amines in normal and abnormal behavioral states. Clin Chem, 17 (No. 1):5-26, 1971.

244. MacDonnell, M. F., and Fessock, L.: Aggression and associated neural events in cats: effects of p- Chlorophenylalanine compared with alcohol. Q J Stud Alcohol, 32:748-763, 1971.

245. Knapp, S., and Mandell, A. J.: Narcotic drugs: effects on the serotonin biosynthetic systems of the brain. Science, 177:1209-1211, September 29, 1972.

246. Janov, A.: The Anatomy of Mental Illness: The Scientific Basis of Primal Therapy. New York, Putnam, 1971.

247. Funkenstein, D. H., King, S., and Drolette, M.: Mastery of Stress. Cambridge, Harvard University Press, 1957.

248. Hoffer, A., and Osmond, H.: Concerning an etiological factor in alcoholism. The possible role of adrenochrome metabolism. Q J Stud Alcohol, 20:750-756, 1959.

249. Lingeman, R. R.: Drugs from A to Z: A Dictionary. New York, McGraw-Hill, 1969.

250. Hobson, G. N.: Anxiety and the alcoholic: as measured by eye-blink conditioning. Q J Stud Alcohol, 32:976-981, 1971.

251. Cannon, W. B.: Bodily Changes in Fear, Hunger, Pain and Rage. 2nd ed., Boston, Branford, 1953.

252. Selye, H.: The Stress of Life. New York, McGraw-Hill, 1956.

253. Cannon, W. B.: 'Voodoo' death. American Anthropologist, 44:169-181, 1942.

254. Jung, C. J.: Preface. In Custance, J. (Ed.): Wisdom, Madness and Folly: The Philosophy of a Lunatic. New York, Pellegrini & Cudahy, 1952, pp. 1-4.

255. Fabre, L. F., Farmer, R. W., Pellizzari, E. D., and Farrell, G.: Alderstone secretion in pentobarbital-anesthetized ethanol-infused dogs. Q J Stud Alcohol, 33:476-484, 1972.

256. Geller, I.: Ethanol preference in the rat as a function of photoperiod. Science, 173:456-459, 1971.

257. Axelrod, J.: The pineal gland: a neurochemical transducer. 5th Int Congr Pharmacol, Abstracts of Invited Presentations, pp. 3-4, 1972.

258. Wallerstein, R. S., Chotlos, W., et al.: Hospital Treatment of Alcoholism; A Comparative Experimental Study. New York, Basic Books, 1957.

259. Mardones, R. J.: 'Craving' for alcohol. Q J Stud Alcohol, 16:51-53, 1955.

260. Summers, T.: Validity of alcoholics' self-reported drinking history. *Q J Stud Alcohol, 31*:972-974, 1970.
261. Sobell, L. C., Sobell, M. B., and Christelman, W. C.: The myth of one drink. *Behav Res & Therapy,* Summer, 1972 (reprint, Pergamon Press, Eng., 1-5)
262. Merry, J.: The 'loss of control' myth. *Lancet 1*:1257-1268, 1966.
263. Mello, N. K., McNamee, H. B., and Mendelson, J. H.: Drinking patterns of chronic alcoholics; gambling and motivation for alcohol. *Psychiatr Res Rep, 24*:83-118, 1968.
264. Mello, N. K.: Some aspects of the behavioral pharmacology of alcohol. In Efron, D. (Ed.): *Psychopharmacology; A Review of Progress, 1957-1967* (Public Health Service Publication No. 1836.) Washington, D.C., U.S. Govt. Print. Off., 1968, pp. 787-809.
265. Paredes, A., Ludwig, K. D., Hassenfeld, I. N., and Cornelison, F. S., Jr.: A clinical study of alcoholics using audiovisual self-image feedback. *J Nerv Ment Dis, 148*:449-456, 1969.
266. Mendelson, J. H.: Experimentally induced chronic intoxication and withdrawal in alcoholics. *Q J Stud Alcohol,* Suppl. No. 2, 1964.
267. Cutter, H. S. G., Schwaab, E. L., Jr., and Nathan, P. E.: Effects of alcohol on its utility for alcoholics and nonalcoholics. *Q J Stud Alcohol, 31*:369-378, 1970.
268. Faillace, L. A., Flamer, R. N., Imber, S. D., and Ward, R.: Giving alcohol to alcoholics: an evaluation. *Q J Stud Alcohol, 33*:85-90, 1972.
269. A matter of morality. *Time,* 54, Aug. 7, 1972.
270. Davies, D. L.: Normal drinking in recovered alcohol addicts. *Q J Stud Alcohol, 23*:94-104, 1962.
271. Davies, D. L.: Normal drinking in recovered alcoholics. Comment by various correspondents. *Q J Stud Alcohol, 24*:109-121, 321-332, 1963.
272. Cain, A. H.: Alcoholics Anonymous: Cult or Cure? *Harpers,* p. 48-52, Feb. 1963.
273. Cain, A. H.: *The Cured Alcoholic: New Concepts in Alcoholism Treatment and Research.* New York, John Day, 1964.
274. Steiner, C. M.: The alcoholic game. *Q J Stud Alcohol, 30*:920-938, 1969.
275. Therapy for the nondiseased: comment on 'The alcoholic game.' *Q J Stud Alcohol, 30*:939-956, 1969.
276. Sobell, M. B., and Sobell, L. C.: *Individualized Behavior Therapy for Alcoholics: Rationale, Procedures, Preliminary Results and Appendix.* [In press.]
277. Sobell, M. B., and Sobell, L. C.: Individualized behavior therapy for alcoholics. *Behavior Therapy.* [In press.]

278. Mills, K. C., Sobell, M. B., and Schaefer, H. H.: Training social drinking as an alternative to abstinence for alcoholics. *Behavior Therapy*, 2:18-27, 1971.
279. Baker, T. B., and Sobell, M. B.: Re-education for the alcoholic. *Journal of Alcohol Education.* [In press.]
280. Shocking habits. *Human Behavior, 1* (No. 2):57-58, 1972.
281. *Santa Barbara News-Press* (AP), p. A-5, July 27, 1971.
282. Alcoholics learn to drink. *San Francisco Chronicle*, p. B-6, Aug. 22, 1971.
283. Keller, M.: Alcoholism: nature and extent of the problem. In Bacon, S. D. (Ed.): *Understanding Alcoholism. Ann Am Acad Pol Soc Sci*, Vol. 315, 1958.
284. Bloomberg, W.: Treatment of chronic alcoholism with amphetamine (benzedrine) sulfate. *N Engl J Med*, 220:129-135, 1939.
285. Little, W. G.: Alcoholism. *Pt II.* Etiology and therapy. *J Osteopathy*, Vol. LXX (No. 8) 1963. (Reprint without numbered pagination).
286. Feldmann, H.: Introduction aux traitements modernes de l'alcoolisme chronique. Considérations biologiques, psychologiques et social (Introduction to the present day treatments of chronic alcoholism. Biological, psychological and social considerations.) *Méd Hyg, Geneva*, 8:383-385, 1950 (Abstract) *Q J Stud Alcohol*, 12:528-529, 1951.
287. De Morsier, G.: Le traitement de l'alcoolisme chronique (Treatment of chronic alcoholism.) *Méd Hyg Geneva*, 8:425. (Abst.) *Q J Stud Alcohol, 12*:528-529, 1951.
288. Feldmann, H.: Contribution à la thérapeutique biologique de l'alcoolisme chronique. Le traitement par l'apomorphine (Contribution to the biological therapy of chronic alcoholism. Treatment with apomorphine.) Paris, Expansion scientifique française, 1951. (Abstract) *Q J Stud Alcohol, 12*:649-650, 1951.
289. De Morsier, G., and Feldmann, H.: Le traitement de l'alcoolisme par l'apomorphine; étude de 500 cas (The treatment of alcoholism with apomorphine; a study of 500 cases.) *Schweiz Neurol Psychiatry, 70*:434-440, 1952.
290. Schlatter, E. K. E., and Lal, S.: Treatment of alcoholism with Dent's oral apomorphine method. *Q J Stud Alcohol, 33*:430-436, 1972.
291. Lemere, F.: Comment on "Normal drinking in recovered alcohol addicts." *Q J Stud Alcohol, 24*:727-728, 1963.
292. Moore, R. A.: Alcoholism in Japan. *Q J Stud Alcohol, 25*:142-150, 1964.
293. Taylor, J. A.: Metronidazole—a new agent for combined somatic and psychic therapy of alcoholism. *Bull Los Angeles Neurol Soc, 29*:158-162, 1964.

294. Semer, J. M., Friedland, P., Vaisberg, M., and Greenberg, A.: The use of metronidazole in the treatment of alcoholism: a pilot study. *Am J Psychiatry, 123*:722-724, 1966.
295. Goodwin, D. W.: Metronidazole in the treatment of alcoholism: a negative report. *Am J Psychiatry, 123*:10, 1276-1278, 1967.
296. Fried, R.: Biochemical studies of a new anti-alcoholic drug, metronidazole. In Popham, R. E. (Ed.): *Alcohol and Alcoholism*. Toronto, University of Toronto Press, 1970, pp. 63-72.
297. Strassman, H. D., Adams, B., and Pearson, A. W.: Metronidazole effect on social drinkers. *Q J Stud Alcohol, 31*:394-398, 1970.
298. Rothstein, E., and Clancy, D. D.: Combined use of disulfiram and metronidazole in treatment of alcoholism. *Q J Stud Alcohol, 31*:446-447, 1970.
299. Accidental help for alcoholics. *Time*, p. 67, Nov. 12, 1965.
300. Geller, I., Campbell, N. D., and Blum, K.: Protection against acute alcoholic intoxication with Diethanolamine-Rutin. *Research Communications in Chemical Pathology and Pharmacology, 1*: (No. 3):383-394, 1970.
301. Bacon, T.: D-R: new hope for the alcoholic. *The Rotarian*, pp. 40-43, 57-61, April, 1970.
302. Mendelson, J. H., Rossi, A. M., and Bernstein, J.: Effects of propranolol on behavior of alcoholics following acute alcohol intake. *5th Int Congr Pharmacol*, Abstracts of Volunteer Papers, p. 157, 1972.
303. An alcohol antagonist. *Science News, 102*:88, 1972.
304. Psyching the alcoholic. *Newsweek*, p. 62, Aug. 21, 1972.
305. Wallace, R. K., and Benson, H.: The physiology of meditation. *Sci Am, 226* (No. 2):84-90, 1972.
306. Karlins, M., and Andrews, L. M.: *Biofeedback: Turning on the Powers of Your Mind*. Philadelphia and New York, Lippincott, 1972.
307. Goodwin, D. W., Crane, J. B., and Gruze, S. B.: Felons who drink: an 8-year follow up. *Q J Stud Alcohol, 32*:136-147, 1971.
308. Criteria Committee, National Council on Alcoholism: Criteria for the diagnosis of alcoholism. *Ann Intern Med, 77*:249-258, 1972.
309. Seixas, F. A.: Criteria for the diagnosis of alcoholism. *JAMA, 222*, No. 2:207-208, 1972.
310. Jellinek, E. M.: Phases of alcohol addiction. In Pittman, D. J., and Snyder, C. R. (Eds.): *Society, Culture and Drinking Patterns*. New York & London, Wiley, 1962, pp. 356-368.
311. Noble, E. P., Butte, J. C., and Kakihana, R. A.: A test for alcoholism? *Lancet, 2*:107, 1969. (Abst.) *Q J Stud Alcohol, 31*:741, 1970.
312. Merry, J., and Marks, V. A.: A test for alcoholism? *Lancet, 2*:107-108, 1969. (Abst.) *Q J Stud Alcohol, 31*:741, 1970.

313. The Einstein of child psychology. *San Francisco Chronicle*, p. 31, Oct. 28, 1972.
314. Perls, F. S.: *In and Out of the Garbage Pail.* New York, Bantam Books, 1972.
315. Berne, E.: *Games People Play.* New York, Grove, 1964.
316. Drinking cop sues to regain disability pay. *San Francisco Chronicle*, p. 1, Sept. 21, 1972.
317. Disabled officer is found dead. *Santa Barbara News Press*, p. B-7, Sept. 29, 1972.
318. Drinking cop 'killed by alcohol.' *San Francisco Chronicle*, p. 5, Oct. 12, 1972.
319. Cop to face hearing on alcoholism charge. *San Francisco Chronicle*, p. 2, Oct. 13, 1972.
320. Broadhurst, P. L.: *The Science of Animal Behavior.* Baltimore, Penguin Books, 1963.
321. Toffler, A.: *Future Shock.* New York, Random House, 1970.
322. Rousseau, J. J.: *The Political Writings of Jean Jacques Rousseau.* Cambridge, The University Press, 1915.
323. Israel, J.: *Alienation from Marx to Modern Sociology: A Macrosociological Analysis.* Boston, Allyn & Bacon, 1971.
324. Merton, R.: *Social Theory and Social Structure.* Glencoe, Ill., The Free Press, 1957.
325. Josephson, E., and Josephson, M.: *Man Alone: Alienation in Modern Society.* New York, Dell, 1962.
326. Lemert, M.: *Social Pathology.* New York, McGraw-Hill, 1951.
327. Becker, H. S.: *Outsiders: Studies in the Sociology of Deviance.* New York, The Free Press, 1963.
328. Packard, V.: *A Nation of Strangers.* New York, David McKay, 1972.
329. Riesman, D., Denney, R., and Glazer, N.: *The Lonely Crowd: A Study of the Changing American Character.* New Haven, Yale University Press, 1950.
330. Linton, R.: *The Study of Man.* New York, Appleton-Century-Crofts, 1964.
331. Fromm, E.: *Escape from Freedom.* New York, Holt, Rinehart & Winston, 1941.
332. An immense proposal. *Intellectual Digest*, 2 (No. 6):50-51, 1972.
333. Holmes, L. D.: *Anthropology: An Introduction.* New York, Ronald Press, 1971.
334. McCabe, C.: The fearless spectator. *San Francisco Chronicle*, p. 39, Oct. 3, 1972.
335. Festinger, L.: *A Theory of Cognitive Dissonance.* Stanford, Calif., Stanford University Press, 1957.
336. Myerson, A.: Alcohol: a study of social ambivalence. *Q J Stud Alcohol*, 1:13-20, 1940.

337. Washburne, C.: *Primitive Drinking: A Study of the Uses and Functions of Alcohol in Preliterate Societies.* New York & New Haven, College & University Press, 1961.

338. MacAndrew, C., and Edgerton, R. B.: *Drunken Comportment: A Social Explanation.* Chicago, Aldine, 1969.

339. Horton, D.: The functions of alcohol in primitive societies: a cross-cultural study. *Q J Stud Alcohol, 4*:199-320, 1943.

340. Singer, K.: Drinking patterns and alcoholism in the Chinese. *B J Addict, 67*:3-14, 1972. [Reviewed in *Human Behavior, 1* (No. 5): 34-35, 1972.]

341. Snyder, C. R.: *Alcohol and the Jews: A Cultural Study of Drinking and Sobriety.* Glencoe, Ill., The Free Press, 1958.

342. Cheinisse, L.: La race juive, jouit-elle d'une immunité à l'égard de l'alcoolisme? (Does the Jewish race enjoy an immunity to alcoholism?) *Sem Med, 28*:613-615, 1908.

343. Lolli, G., Serianni, E., Golder, G. M., and Luzzatto-Fegiz, P.: *Alcohol in Italian Culture: Food and Wine in Relation to Sobriety Among Italians and Italian-Americans.* Glencoe, Ill., The Free Press, 1958.

344. Castaneda, C.: *The Teaching of Don Juan: A Yaqui Way of Knowledge.* Berkeley, University of California Press, 1968.

345. Castaneda, C.: *A Separate Reality: Further Conversations with Don Juan.* New York, Simon & Schuster, 1971.

346. Castaneda, C.: *Journey to Ixtlan: the Lessons of Don Juan.* New York, Simon & Schuster, 1972.

347. Weil, A.: *The Natural Mind.* Boston, Houghton Mifflin, 1972.

348. Benedict, R.: *Patterns of Culture.* Boston, Houghton Mifflin, 1934.

349. Segovia-Riquelme, N., Varela, A., and Mardones, J.: Appetite for alcohol. In Israel, Y. and Mardones, J. (Eds.): *Biological Basis of Alcoholism.* New York, Wiley-Interscience, 1971, pp. 299-334.

350. Fox, R.: Treatment of alcoholism. In Himwich, H. E. (Ed.): *Alcoholism: Basic Aspects and Treatment.* American Association for the Advancement of Science, Publication No. 47, pp. 163-172, 1957.

351. Tintera, J. W., and Lovell, H. W.: Endocrine treatment of alcoholism. *Geriatrics, 4*:274-280, 1949.

352. Knight, R. P.: The psychodynamics of chronic alcoholism. *J Nerv Ment Dis, 86*:538-548, 1937.

353. Diethelm, O.: The alcohol problem. In Podolsky, E. (Ed.): *Management of Addictions.* New York, Philosophical Library, 1955, pp. 289-300.

354. Kalow, W.: Genes controlling drug action in man. *5th Int Congr Pharmacol, Abstracts of Invited Presentations,* pp. 10-11, 1972.

355. Montagu, A.: *Elephant Man: A Study in Human Dignity.* New York, Outerbridge, 1972.

356. Freud, S.: *An Outline of Psychoanalysis.* New York, Norton, 1949.

357. Salzman, L.: Modern concepts of psychoanalysis. In Salzman, L., and Masserman, J. A. (Eds.): *Modern Concepts of Psychoanalysis.* New York, Citadel Press, 1962, pp. 5-20.
358. Gardner, L. J.: Deprivation dwarfism. *Sci Am, 227* (No. 1):76-82, 1972.
359. Genes and depression. *Time,* p. 33, Aug. 28, 1972.
360. The biochemistry of depression. *Science News, 102* (No. 3):33-48, 1972.
361. Up from depression. *Time,* p. 71, Oct. 30, 1972.
362. Emotional deprivation and dwarfism. *Psychology Today, 5* (No. 11): 114-115, 1972.
363. Archart, J. L.: Helping youngsters to grow. *Science News, 101* (No. 19): 289-304, 1972.
364. Maclay, G., and Knipe, H.: *The Dominant Man: The Pecking Order in Human Society.* New York, Delacorte, 1972.
365. Aronson, E.: *The Social Animal.* New York, Viking, 1972.
366. Morris, D.: *The Naked Ape: A Zoologist's Study of the Human Animal.* New York, McGraw-Hill, 1967.
367. Morris, D.: *The Human Zoo.* New York, McGraw-Hill, 1969.
368. Ardrey, R.: *African Genesis.* New York, Atheneum, 1961.
369. Ardrey, R.: *The Territorial Imperative: A Personal Inquiry into the Animal Origins of Property and Nations.* New York, Atheneum, 1966.
370. Ardrey, R.: *The Social Contract: A Personal Inquiry into the Evolutionary Sources of Order and Disorder.* New York, Atheneum, 1970.
371. Lewis, J., and Towers, B.: *Naked Ape or Homo Sapiens?* New York, Humanities Press, 1969.
372. Montagu, M. F. A.: *Man and Aggression.* New York, Oxford, 1968.
373. Masters, R. D.: Of nature and nurture. *Saturday Review,* p. 38, 52, Oct. 19, 1968. [Review of Montagu, A.: *Man and Aggression.*]
374. Alland, A., Jr.: *The Human Imperative.* New York, Columbia University Press, 1972.
375. Dollard, J., Miller, N. E., Doob, L. W., Mowrer, O. H., Sears, R. R., in collaboration with Ford, K. S., Hooland, C. I., and Sollenberger, R. T.: *Frustration and Aggression.* New Haven, Yale University Press for the Institute of Human Relations, 1939.
376. Storr, A.: *Human Aggression.* New York, Atheneum, 1968.
377. Zuckerman, S.: *The Social Life of Monkeys and Apes.* London, Kegan Paul, Trench, Trubner, 1932.
378. *Behavior Today, 2* (No. 9): 2, 1972.
379. Wade, N.: Anabolic steroids: doctors denounce them but athletes aren't listening. *Science, 176:*1399-1403, 1972.

380. Lawrence, C. W., and Haynes, J. R.: Epinephrine and norepinephrine effects on social dominance behavior. *Psychol Rep*, 27:195-198, 1970.
381. Forever female? *Newsweek*, p. 58, Oct. 9, 1972.
382. Cooper, W.: *Hair*. New York, Stein & Day, 1971.
383. Smith, J. J.: A medical approach to problem drinking. Preliminary report. *Q J Stud Alcohol*, 10:251-257, 1949.
384. Abraham, K.: The psychological relations between sexuality and alcoholism. *Int J Psychoanal*, 7:2-10, 1926.
385. Testosterone levels under stress. *Science News*, 101 (No. 21):331, May 20, 1972.
386. McGenty, D.: Alcoholism—hidden malady and anonymous recovery. National Council on Alcoholism, n.d. (reprint from *Sanctity and Success in Marriage*. Family Life Bureau, Nat. Cath. Wel. Conf., Washington, D.C.).
387. Maslow, A.: Dominance feeling, behavior and status. *Psychol Rev*, 44:404-429, 1937.
388. Wexberg, L. E.: Alcoholism as a sickness. *Q J Stud Alcohol*, 12:217-230, 1951.
389. Durkheim, E.: *Suicide: A Study of Sociology*. New York, The Free Press, 1951.
390. Riot your troubles away. *Human Behavior*, 1 (No. 3):32, 1972.
391. Sattler, J. M., and Pflugrath, J. F.: Future-time perspective in alcoholics and normals. *Q J Stud Alcohol*, 31:839-850, 1970.
392. Manson, M. P.: A psychometric differentiation of alcoholics from non-alcoholics. *Q J Stud Alcohol*, 9:175-206, 1948.
393. Janov, A.: *The Primal Scream: Primal Therapy: The Cure for Neurosis*. New York, Dell, 1970.
394. Gerard, D. L., Saenger, G., and Wile, R.: The abstinent alcoholic. *AMA Arch Gen Psychiat*, 6:83-95, 1962.
395. Bolman, W. M.: Abstinence versus permissiveness in the psychotherapy of alcoholism; a pilot study and review of some relevant literature. *AMA Arch Gen Psychiat*, 12:456-463, 1965.
396. Moore, R. A., and Ramseur, F.: Effects of psychotherapy in an open-ward hospital on patients with alcoholism. *Q J Stud Alcohol*, 21:233-252, 1960.
397. Wilby, W. E., and Jones, R. W.: Assessing patient response following treatment. *Q J Stud Alcohol*, 23:325, 1962.
398. Pfeffer, A. Z., and Berger, S.: A follow-up study of treated alcoholics. *Q J Stud Alcohol*, 18:624-648, 1957.
399. Flaherty, J. A., McGuire, H. T., and Gatski, R. L.: The psychodynamics of the 'dry drunk.' *Am J Psychiat*, 112:460-464, 1955.
400. Wellman, M.: Fatigue during the second six months of abstinence. *Can Med Assn J*, 72:338-342, 1955.

401. Assagioli, R.: *Psychosynthesis: A Manual of Principles and Techniques.* New York, Viking, 1971.
402. Maslow, A. H.: Peak experience as acute identity experiences. *Am J Psychoanal, 21*:254-260, 1961.
403. Maslow, A. H.: Lessons from peak experiences. *Journal of Humanistic Psychology, 2* (No. 1): 9-18, 1962.
404. Maslow, A. H.: *Religions, Values and Peak Experiences.* Columbus, Ohio State University Press, 1964.
405. Maslow, A. H.: *The Farther Reaches of Human Nature.* New York, Viking, 1971.
406. Williams, E. Y.: The anxiety syndrome in alcoholism. *Psychol Q, 24*:782-787, 1950.
407. Free, J. L.: *Just One More: Concerning the Problem Drinker.* 2nd ed. New York, Coward-McCann, 1957.
408. Weigert, E.: Sympathy, empathy and freedom in therapy. In Salzman, L., and Masserman, J. H. (Eds.): *Modern Concepts of Psychoanalysis.* New York, Citadel, 1962, pp. 143-159.
409. Alcoholism, problems of the elderly. *San Francisco Chronicle,* p. 34, Oct. 21, 1972.
410. Frankl, V. E.: *Man's Search for Meaning: An Introduction to Logotherapy.* New York, Pocket Books, 1963.
411. Frankl, V. E.: *Psychotherapy and Existentialism: Selected Papers on Logotherapy.* New York, Washington Square Press, 1967.
412. May, R.: *Power and Innocence: A Search for the Sources of Power.* New York, Norton, 1972.
413. Jellinek, E. M.: Cultural differences in the meaning of alcoholism. In Pittman, D. J. and Snyder, C. R. (Eds.): *Society, Culture and Drinking Patterns.* New York, Wiley, 1962, pp. 382-394.
414. Simenon, G.: *Maigret and the Headless Corpse.* New York, Avon Books, 1971.
415. Hamburger apostle brings Yank cuisine to Paris. *San Francisco Chronicle,* p. B-7, April 9, 1972.
416. Davis, V. E., and Walsh, M. J.: Diversion and dopamine metabolism to alkaloid formation by alcohol (EtOH) and acetaldehyde (CH_3CHO). *Fed Proc, 29*:649, 1970.
417. Davis, V. E., and Walsh, M. J.: Alcohol, amines, and alkaloids: a possible biochemical basis for alcohol addiction. *Science, 167*:1005-1006, 1970.
418. Cohen, G.: A biochemical basis for alcoholism as a disease. *Medical Counterpoint, 11*:28-36, 1971.
419. Trindade, F. H. G.: *Matt Talbot: Worker and Penitent.* Paterson, N.J., St. Anthony Guild Press, 1953.
420. Kessel, J.: *The Road Back.* New York, Knopf, 1962.
421. Barnouw, V.: *An Introduction to Anthropology.* Vol. 2: Ethnology. Homewood, Ill., The Dorsey Press, 1971.

422. de Tocqueville, A.: *Democracy in America.* Vol. II. New York, Knopf, 1954.
423. Bock, P. K.: *Modern Cultural Anthropology.* New York, Knopf, 1969.
424. Maxwell, M. A.: The Washingtonian movement. *Q J Stud Alcohol,* *11*:410-451, 1950.
425. Malinowski, B.: *Coral Gardens and Their Magic.* London, Allen & Unwin, 1935.
426. Malinowski, B.: *Magic, Science and Religion and Other Essays.* Boston, Beacon Press, 1948.
427. Malinowski, B.: *A Scientific Theory of Culture and Other Essays.* Chapel Hill, University of North Carolina Press, 1944.
428. Linton, R.: Nativistic movements. *American Anthropologist, 45*:230-240, 1943.
429. Wallace, A. C.: Revitalization movements. *American Anthropologist, 58*:264-281, 1956.
430. La Barre, W.: Materials for a history of studies of crisis cults: a bibliographic essay. *Current Anthropology, 12* (No. 1): 3-44, 1971.
431. Barber B.,: Acculturation and messianic movements. *Am Sociol Rev,* *6*:663-669, 1941.
432. Mooney, J.: The ghost dance religion and the Sioux outbreak of 1890. Washington, D.C.; *Bureau of American Ethnology, Annual Report, 14* (1892-1893), 1896.
433. Belshaw, C. S.: The significance of modern cults in Melanesian development. *Australian Outlook, 4*:116-125, 1950.
434. Worsley, P.: *The Trumpet Shall Sound: A Study of "Cargo" Cults in Melanesia.* London, Macgibbon & Kee, 1957.
435. Gellman, I. P.: *The Sober Alcoholic: An Organizational Analysis of Alcoholics Anonymous.* New Haven, College & University Press. 1964.
436. Anonymous: *Alcoholics Anonymous Comes of Age. A Brief History of A.A.* New York, Alcoholics Anonymous, 1957.
437. Benedict, R.: *The Concept of the Guardian Spirit in Native North America.* American Anthropological Association, Memoir No. 29, 1923.
438. Durkheim, E.: *The Elementary Forms of Religious Life.* New York, The Free Press, 1947.
439. Ruark, R.: *Uhuru.* New York, Fawcett, Crest, World, 1971.
440. Callahan, D.: Search for an ethic: living with the new biology. *Center Magazine, 5* (No. 4):4-12, 1972.
441. McCabe, C.: The fearless spectator. *San Francisco Chronicle,* p. 47, Oct. 12, 1972.
442. Eliade, M.: *Shamanism: Archaic Techniques of Ecstasy.* Princeton, Princeton University Press (Bollingen Series, Vol. 76), 1964.

443. Kiev, A.: *Curanderismo: Mexican-American Folk Psychiatry.* New York, The Free Press, 1972.
444. Kiev, A. (Ed.): *Magic, Faith and Healing: Studies in Primitive Psychiatry Today.* New York, The Free Press, 1964.
445. Ramos, S.: *Profile of Man and Culture in Mexico.* Austin, University of Texas Press, 1962.
446. Paz, O.: *The Labyrinth of Solitude: Life and Thought in Mexico.* New York, Grove Press, 1961.
447. Adler, A.: *The Neurotic Constitution.* New York, Moffat, 1917.
448. Van Gennep, A. L.: *Rites de Passage.* Paris, E. Nourry, 1909.
449. Augustine, Saint: *Confessions.* Inglewood Cliffs, N.J., Prentice-Hall, 1941.
450. Hume, D.: *An Inquiry Concerning Human Understanding.* New York, Bobbs-Merrill, 1955.
451. Meyer, L.: *Off the Sauce.* Garden City, N.Y., Doubleday, 1967.
452. Schaller, G.: *Mountain Gorilla: Ecology and Behavior.* Chicago, University of Chicago Press, 1963.
453. Sinclair, U.: *The Cup of Fury.* Great Neck, N.Y., Channel Press, 1956.
454. A.A. Grapevine: *A.A. Today.* (A special publication commemorating the 25th anniversary of Alcoholics Anonymous.) New York, The Cornwall Press, 1960.
455. Doe, J.: *Sobriety Without End.* Indianapolis, The SMT Guild, 1957.
456. Adams, C. C.: *The Cure. The Story of an Alcoholic.* New York, Exposition Press, 1950.
457. Westheimer, D.: *Days of Wine and Roses.* New York, Bantam Books, 1963.
458. W., W. G.: Alcoholics Anonymous. *NY State J Med,* 50:1708-1710, 1711-1712, 1716, 1950.
459. Nace, R. K.: Alcoholics Anonymous speaks to the church. *J Clin Pastoral Work,* 2:124-132, 1949.
460. Turner, I.: Ascetic Protestantism and alcoholism. *Psychiatry,* 16:167-176, 1953.
461. Dellinger, J. B.: Alcoholics Anonymous operating in a prison setting. 1953. [Mimeographed.]
462. Mann, M.: Alcoholics Anonymous: a new partner for hospitals. *Mod Hosp,* 66 (No. 1):77-78, 1946.
463. W., W.: Alcoholics Anonymous in a postwar emergency. *Q J Stud Alcohol,* 6:239-242, 1945.
464. Alstrup, K.: Gruppebehandlingen af alkoholikeri i foreningen "Ring i Ring," Dansk A.A. (Group treatment of alcoholics in the organization "Ring i Ring," the Danish AA) *Ugeskr Laeg, Kbh,* 112:807-812, 1950. (Abstract) *Q J Stud Alcohol,* 12:534, 1951.
465. Bales, R. F.: The therapeutic role of Alcoholics Anonymous as seen by a sociologist. *Q J Stud Alcohol,* 5:267-278, 1944.

466. Chamber, F. T., Jr.: Analysis and comparison of three treatment measures for alcoholism: Antabuse, the Alcoholics Anonymous approach, and psychotherapy. *Br J Addict, 50*:29-41, 1953. (Abstract) *Q J Stud Alcohol, 15*:132, 1954.
467. Schulman, A. J.: Group psychotherapy in the treatment of alcoholic addiction. *Bull Vancouver Med Assoc, 26*:274-277, 1950.
468. Vogel, S.: Psychiatric treatment of alcoholism. *Ann Am Acad Polit Soc Sci, 315*:99-107, 1958.
469. Holmes, R. M.: Alcoholics Anonymous as group logotherapy. *Pastoral Psychol, 21* (No. 202): 30-36, 1970.
470. Zusman, J.: "No-Therapy": a model of helping persons with problems. *Community Ment Health J, 5*:482-486, 1969.
471. Heersema, P. H.: Present role of "Alcoholics Anonymous" in the treatment of chronic alcoholism. *Minn Med, 25*:204-205, 1942.
472. Groves, D. H.: Charismatic leadership in Alcoholics Anonymous: a case study. *Q J Stud Alcohol, 33*:684-691, 1972.
473. Köhler, W.: *Gestalt Psychology.* New York, New American Library, n.d.

AUTHOR INDEX

SUBJECT INDEX

233

division and chaos in psychotherapy, 11
drinking as rite of social conformity, 43
drinking for power, 43
drinking in the hope of death, 43
drinking therapy in, 80
dysfunction in the endocrine system, 55
emotional factors in, 59
explanation of, 44, 55
  behaviorist, 44
  faulty metabolism as, 55
  in biological terms, 44
gamma alcoholism, 87, 110-132
  occurrence in America, 110
  subspecies of, 112
  (*see also* Alcoholic, primary)
  (*see also* Gamma alcoholism)
  (*see also* Alcoholic, secondary)
genesis of, 28
genetic factor in, 46
  behaviorist denial of, 46
  first formal study of, 45
  probability of, 45
genetic research, 53
  political implications of, 53
geographic cure of, 95
  futility of, 95
glandular malfunctions, 56
hereditary factor in, 46
hereditary predisposition to, 46
hooking mechanism of, 51
horror of death, 149
hypoadrenocorticism, 55
  treatment of, 56
hypoglycemia in, 50-51
  condition or product, 50-51
  frequency of, 50
hypothalamus, involvement of, 56
implication of term "disease," 20
in Western culture, 116
inappropriate response, 40-41
indication of alcoholic recovery, 24
incidence of, 106
  among deculturated Jews, 106
  among Italians, 106-107

among traditional Jews, 106
among traditional societies, 105-107
limitation by cultures, 108
regional differences in, 53-54
individual most prone to, 48
interpretation of, 17, 18, 93, 121
  by major social sciences, 17
  inability to communicate, 18
  nature of aggression, 121
  steps of, 93
Jellinek's classification of, 85-89
  alpha alcoholism, 86-87
  beta alcoholism, 87
  epsilon alcoholism, 87
  gamma and delta alcoholism, 87
lack of aggressiveness in, 42
lack of specific definition of, 20-21
library of, 15
male preponderance in, 57
malfunctions in, 63
mental illness, 30
metabolic variation between populations, 53
metronidazole, value of, 82-83
modification of terms, 90
  alcoholic and *symptomatic problem drinker,* 90
monocausality in, 16-17
multicausality in, 12, 15-16
nature—nurture approach, 18
nature-nurture conflict, 5-14
  environmental determinism, 6
  genetic determinism of the 18th century, 6
nutritional deficiencies in, 49
  correction of, 49
  use of vitamins, 49-50
nutritional theories, 49
occasional and *real* alcoholics, 14
"one drink—one drunk" hypothesis of, 65
  attempts to disprove, 67-68
  misinterpretation of, 68
oral correlation of, 38
orality of, 39
oral syndrome, 38
origin of, 28

in primitive cultures, 104-105
loss of, 140
  alcoholic progression, 140
reinforcement of social bonds,
    105-106
socially-proper, 105
Behavior, "irrational," 9
  as result of bad learning, 9
Benzedrine, use of, 81
  in alcoholism, 81
Beta alcoholism, 87
  inclusion within alcoholism, 87
"Biofeedback," basis of, 84
Blackout (*see* Alcoholic amnesia)
Body hair, association with power,
    129, 130
  growth and distribution, 55
  in male alcoholics, 129
Bottle feeding, human metabolism, 154
Breast feeding, human metabolism, 54

C

Calcium, administration of, 50
  in alcoholism, 50
  low levels of, 50
Calcium cynamide, use of, 82
  in alcoholism, 82
Calcium imbalance, behavioral
    abnormalities, 50
  "arctic hysteria," 50
Casper Milquetoast response, 133
Childhood deprivation, and alcoholism,
    116
  set for addiction, 119
Civilization, and folk society, 99
  ratio of "alternatives" and
    "universals," 99
Color blindness, and alcoholism, 47
Compartmentalization, 102
  segregation of value conflicts, 102
Craving, concept of, 65, 66, 67, 68, 69
  cyclic periods of, 70
Cultures, "Apollonian," 108-109
  "Dionysian," 108-109
  incidence of alcoholism, 106
  limitation of, 106

D

Delta alcoholic, group affiliation, 167
  intoxication in, 151
    absence of signs of, 151
Delta alcoholism, addictive
    alcoholism, 151
  biochemical factor in, 151
  metabolic aberration, 151-152
  occurrence of, 150-151
    in America, 151
    in countries with wine
      consumption, 150-151
  true alcoholism, 87
Dependency, a character defect in
    alcoholism, 40
  classification as pathological, 40
  factor in alcoholism, 39
Depression, biochemistry of, 118
  definitions of, 118
  epinephrine levels and supply of
    norepinephrine, 129
  location of gene associated with, 118
Deprivation dwarfism, 119
Dexedrine, use of, 81
  in alcoholism, 81
Diethanolamine-rutin, 83
  block to intoxicating effects of
    alcohol, 83
Dime therapy, in Alcoholics
    Anonymous, 171
Drinking, Dionysian goal, 109
Drinking history, secondary alcoholic,
    148-149
Drugs, as alcohol substitutes, 178
Drug addiction, role of amines, 59
Drug culture, quest of another reality,
    108
Drug reactions, genetic factors, 113
  involvement of, 113
Drunk, as an emotional purge, 135
  product of, 141
  setting for, 135
Drunks, high-bottom, 164
  alcoholic recovery of, 174
  facilitation of identification with
    A.A., 165

physical type and, 48
correlation of, 48
Pineal gland, control of epinephrine
levels, 64
extracts from, 63
origin of alcoholic syndrome, 64
role of, 63-64
normal and abnormal behavior,
63-64
Power hypothesis, in alcoholism, 42-43
Problem drinker, alpha alcoholic, 86
lack of addictive physiological
mechanism, 152-153
neurotic behavior of, 90
relief of physical or psychobiological
pain, 152
relief of tension or stress, 152
segregation from alcoholics, 93
subvarieties among, 152
Propranolol, action on biogenic amines,
83-84
anxiety-releasing property of, 83
block to intoxication, 83
block to symptoms of hypoglycemia,
84
decrease in lactate levels, 83
use in alcoholism, 83-84
Psychoanalysis, basic assumption
behind, 84
Psychology, and psychiatry, 14
dominance over alcoholic field, 14
Psychosis, alcohol-induced, 105
or spiritual attainment, 108
Psychotherapy, division in, 10-11
failure of, 10
denial of biological involvement in
mental illness, 10
inadequacy in treatment of mental
patients, 9-10

S

Schizophrenia, a biological problem, 11
and Klinefelter's syndrome, 12
approach to, 12
a psychobiological phenomenon, 12,
14

childhood deprivation, 11
genetic basis for, 11
genetic hypothesis, 12
identical twins, 11-12
lack of valid definition, 11
role of adrenochrome in, 60
treatment of, 50
Serotonin, drops in, 59
enhancement of aggression, 59
removal of need for alcohol, 58
effects on emotion and behavior, 59
Sex, and alcohol, 130-131, 173
Societies, civilized, 100
presence of stress, 100
primitive, 100
absence of stress, 100
stress-laden, 96
seed-bed for alcoholism, 96
traditional, 105-106
drunken behavior in, 105-106
Stress, alteration of homeostasis,
117-118
experience of, 100
psychological and physiological
symptomology, 61
Stress disease, definition of alcoholism
as, 62
Sugar consumption, *dry drunks,* 52
amelioration of anxiety of, 52
Sugar, hypoglycemic reaction, 52
production of, 52
Suicide, occurrence of, 141
among primary alcoholics, 141

T

Tension, an orally based neurosis, 37
nature and sources of, 37
reduction by alcohol, 32, 33, 36, 37
reduction by humor and laughter,
179
responsibility of sociocultural setting
for, 37
Terror, the morning after, 140-141
alcoholic progression, 140-141
Testosterone, administration of, 128
determinant of aggression, 128